Marketing Models
and
Econometric Research

Marketing Models
and
Econometric Research

Leonard J. Parsons
Claremont Graduate School

Randall L. Schultz
Purdue University

North-Holland
PUBLISHING COMPANY
NEW YORK · AMSTERDAM

AMERICAN ELSEVIER PUBLISHING COMPANY, INC.
52 Vanderbilt Avenue, New York, N.Y.   10017

ELSEVIER SCIENTIFIC PUBLISHING COMPANY
335 Jan Van Galenstraat, P.O. Box 211
Amsterdam, The Netherlands

Library of Congress Cataloging in Publication Data

Parsons, Leonard J
  Marketing models and econometric research.

  Bibliography: p.
  Includes index.
  1. Marketing—Mathematical models. 2. Marketing
research—Mathematical models. I. Schultz, Randall L.,
joint author. II. Title.
HF5415.P2494   658.8'007'2   76-476
ISBN 0-7204-8601-7

To Our Parents

CONTENTS

Part Three. ECONOMETRIC RESEARCH IN MARKETING

PREFACE

Marketing is a well-defined activity in any social system and its business function is particularly well developed. From this perspective, marketing research aims to improve our understanding of the marketing process and (ultimately) seeks to improve the process itself. This book is about the modeling of marketing systems using, principally, econometric methodology for the purpose of developing marketing decision models that can be implemented to improve marketing decision making. Thus, this research volume has a strong professional marketing orientation.

This book fits into marketing and marketing research in the following way: It analyzes the methodology and empirical evidence of sales response research and, at the same time, it discusses the development and implementation of marketing decision models. It should, therefore, be of interest to both marketing researchers and marketing practitioners. The book is designed and offered as a research contribution, though, and so some immediate payoffs have been supressed to make room for increased emphasis on investment in future research.

This book is organized into four major parts. Part One, Introduction, discusses marketing systems and models of marketing systems and develops the basic argument. Part Two, The Econometric Model-Building Approach, presents the main results of econometric theory by showing how specific techniques are special cases of a general model and offers a comprehensive scheme for evaluating (and testing) econometric models. Aggregation issues and data problems are also covered. Part Three, Econometric Research in Marketing, consists of chapters dealing with the specification of marketing models, sales response models, lagged response to marketing variables, and empirical decision models. Part Four, Policy and Research Implications, deals with three additionally important topics. First, the measurement of industry advertising effects is analyzed. Second, the problem of implementing empirical decision models is discussed using a new base of empirical research. And, third, the relation of sales response research to buyer behavior research is explored.

We will comment critically on the work of many authors, including our own work. Degradation of these efforts is not intended. Indeed, when placed in historical perspective, they are often landmarks. Rather our intent is to indicate what constitutes good practice today.

The book assumes an elementary knowledge of the calculus and matrix algebra, elementary mathematical statistics, and some prior knowledge of econometrics. In the latter respect, the book is self-contained but not complete. The serious reader and certainly the researcher would want to do advanced study in econometrics. To this end, we have adopted the notation of Henri Theil in his *Principles of Econometrics*.

Although this work reports on present research, it is just as much a blueprint for future research, or so we hope. As with any architectural endeavor, the building of a marketing science requires plans and materials, and this is the spirit in which the book was written.

Leonard J. Parsons
Claremont, California
Randall L. Schultz
West Lafayette, Indiana

ACKNOWLEDGMENTS

Since this book has been essentially in us since our graduate school days, we first express profound gratitude to our mentors: Frank Bass (Purdue) and Phil Kotler (Northwestern). We met as assistant professors at Indiana University and Ralph Day played no small role in our intellectual life. While writing the book, a number of individuals read parts of the manuscript including Neil Beckwith (Columbia), Pete Clarke (Harvard), Luis Dominguez (Indiana), Laurence Takeuchi (Claremont), and Dick Wittink (Stanford). Although he did not read the manuscript, Don Ebbeler (Claremont) was very helpful in answering some specific econometric questions that we had. To these people and to others who are unmentioned, we express thanks. The collaboration of Dennis Slevin (Pittsburgh) is implicit in the discussion of implementation and we have acknowledged Joe Dodson (Northwestern) and Dick Wittink for their contributions in the text. The manuscript was typed efficiently by Mrs. Maureen Bart at Purdue and Ms. Candy Moore at Claremont and we appreciate their assistance. As authors, this book is the first we began to write (although for each of us not the first to appear) and hence we have dedicated it to our ultimate source—our parents.

Part One. Introduction

Chapter 1

MARKETING SYSTEMS
AND ECONOMETRICS

In an advanced economy, marketing is the process by which
systems of consumption are developed and changed by individuals
and organizations. A modern marketing system consists of an
organization which provides goods and/or services to a market of
consumers, the flows of communciation between the organization
and the market, and the physical flows of exchange. Econometric
research in marketing is the process of building models of marketing
systems which delineate the relationships between organizations and
markets through flows of communication and exchange.

This broad conception of the role of econometric research in the
process of marketing model building is carried throughout this
chapter, where the emphasis is on marketing systems, levels of
aggregation, and the econometric approach. In Chap. 2, the focus
narrows to models of marketing systems that are designed as aids to
decision making, called marketing decision models. By examining the
necessary dependence of applied models on theories of marketing
behavior, the main point of the book can be established: Econometric research in marketing is a means to the end of developing useful
models, both to explain marketing behavior and to guide marketing
managers.

In economics, "econometrics" refers to the estimation and
testing of economic models. The source of the model is economic
theory and thus econometrics is mostly concerned with measurement
issues. In marketing, there is no well-developed theory from which to
derive models and so the scope of econometric research *as applied to
marketing* must be broadened to include the theory development as
well as measurement and testing processes. As it happens, this is not
unlike economic research where the building of an econometric
model may sharpen economic theory or even revise it. The use of
econometric methods in marketing, then, is not simply a technical
consideration of measurement. It is, rather, the creative essence of
the model building process. In a field where theory is elusive and

where methodology is usually thought of as an unorganized set of techniques, the econometric approach in marketing offers a rigorous alternative to casual research. It places in the hands of marketing researchers a careful and consistent way to study marketing systems.

Although the concept of a marketing system is broad enough to encompass many types of organizations, the discipline of marketing has traditionally focused on business firms and the profession of marketing is traditionally viewed as a group of individuals whose major concern is the business function of marketing.[1] Because the traditional setting of marketing is business, this book limits its scope to the analysis of marketing systems where the organization is a business firm and the market is made up of consumers (or potential consumers) of the firm's offering. These business marketing systems can be studied on several levels, including the firm level, industry level, or the level of a national economy. In addition, a number of microbehavioral processes can be analyzed within each level.

BASIC MARKETING SYSTEMS

As a point of departure, we will consider the simplest form of a marketing system where there is no competition so that the firm and industry are identical. An illustration of such a simple marketing system is given in Fig. 1.1. The system is made up of two primary

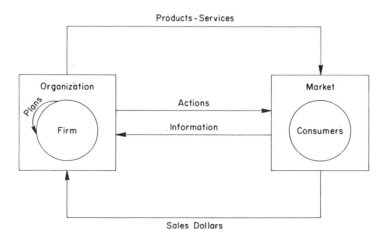

Fig. 1.1. A simple marketing system. Source: Adapted from Kotler (1966).

elements: the marketing organization or firm and the market or consumers. Linking these elements are three communication flows and two physical flows of exchange. The firm communicates to the market through various marketing actions, such as advertising its products or services, setting prices, and so forth. The consumers in the market respond to the firm's actions through sales (or the lack of sales) and this information is sought by the firm. In an internal flow of communication, the firm makes plans for future actions on the basis of current and past information. The physical flows are the movement of products-services to consumers and the simultaneous movement of sales dollars to the firm. The process of physical exchange is characteristic of all commercial trade. The process of communication flows is the distinguishing characteristic of modern marketing systems.

If a firm had only one marketing instrument (controllable variable) which was thought to influence demand, say advertising, a positive model of its market behavior might be the *sales response function*

$$Q_\alpha = f(A_\alpha, E_\alpha), \tag{1.1}$$

where

Q_α = firm's sales in units at time α,
A_α = firm's advertising expenditures at time α,
E_α = environmental factors at time α.

In this model, the market is considered to be well defined, for example, a standard metropolitan statistical area (SMSA), and the environmental factors are taken to include all uncontrollable factors affecting demand, for example, population and income.

If this firm had, in addition, a *decision rule* for setting its advertising budget at time α equal to some percentage of the prior period's sales revenue, this heuristic could be represented as

$$A_\alpha = f(P_{\alpha-1} \cdot Q_{\alpha-1}), \tag{1.2}$$

where

A_α = firm's advertising expenditures at time α,
$P_{\alpha-1}$ = price of the product at time $\alpha-1$,
$Q_{\alpha-1}$ = firm's sales in units at time $\alpha-1$.

This type of decision rule, or some variation of it in terms of current or expected sales, is a positive statement of executive behavior.

Ultimately, we may be interested in some expression for A^*, the optimal advertising budget, which would be a normative decision rule for managers to follow.

Functions (1.1) and (1.2) completely specify the marketing system model in this case. The system works in the following manner. We start with some *firm* offering a product at a specific price. Its marketing *action* at time α is advertising. In response to this action, the *market* responds in some manner. The *consumers* may become aware of the product, develop preferences for it, purchase it, or react negatively to it. This *information* on consumer behavior, including sales, is obtained by the firm either directly or through marketing research. If purchases have been made, physical exchange has taken place. On the basis of its sales in period α, the firm makes marketing *plans* for period $\alpha + 1$. In this case, the advertising budget is planned as a percentage of the prior period's sales. This *decision rule* yields a new level of advertising expenditure, which is the marketing action of the firm for period $\alpha + 1$. Thus, the process is continued for all α.

Despite the obvious simplifications involved, this model can be thought of as a representation of a marketing system. In econometric research, models of this kind (and more complex versions) can be formulated, tested, and estimated in order to discover the structure of marketing systems and explore the consequences of changes in them. For example, suppose a researcher wants to model the demand structure for an electric utility company. As a starting point, he adopts the model given above (or develops one like it) since he believes it captures the essential characteristics of the marketing situation. The firm offers a product, electricity, to a well-defined market, say a SMSA, at a regulated and hence (strictly) uncontrollable price. Since the product is homogenous and the price is fixed, advertising is seen as the only marketing decision variable. Although there are competitive sources of energy, the analyst concentrates on the demand for electricity and so there is no competition; industry and firm demand are identical in this monopoly situation. The analyst completes his model by specifying the environmental factors, say income and population, and the decision rule for advertising.

To simplify further, the analyst assumes the relationships in his model will be linear and stochastic. The linearity assumption may be one of convenience but the stochastic representation is necessitated

both by (possible) omitted variables and by truly random disturbances (even a percent-of-sales decision rule will be subject to
managerial discretion). He is now ready to write his model of the
electric company as an *econometric model* so that he can confront it
with empirical data. In this way, he seeks to *test* whether or not the
model is any good and also to *estimate* the parameters of marketing
action and reaction. The model to be tested is

$$Q_\alpha = \gamma A_\alpha + \beta_1 Y_\alpha + \beta_2 N_\alpha + \beta_3 + \epsilon_{\alpha 1}, \tag{1.3}$$

$$A_\alpha = \beta_4 S_{\alpha-1} + \epsilon_{\alpha 2}, \tag{1.4}$$

where, in addition to the variables defined above,

Y_α = disposable personal income plus corporate income
before tax for the SMSA at time α

N_α = population of the SMSA at time α

$S_{\alpha-1}$ = firm's sales revenue at time $\alpha - 1$, $S = P \cdot Q$

γ = parameter of an endogenous variable

β = parameter of a predetermined variable

ϵ_α = random disturbance.

This model includes two endogenous variables, Q_α and A_α, which
means that they are determined within the system at time α. The
predetermined variables include the purely exogenous variables, Y_α
and N_α, and the variable, $S_{\alpha-1}$, which is a lagged endogenous variable, but is exogenous at time α. The causal ordering of this econometric model is shown in Fig. 1.2.

   The theory of identification, estimation, and testing of econometric models is developed in Chap. 3 and so we can just hint at the
analyst's next steps. If the analyst can assume that the structural
disturbances, $\epsilon_{\alpha 1}$ and $\epsilon_{\alpha 2}$, are independent, his model is a special
kind of econometric model called a *recursive* model. In such a model,
the equations are identified and ordinary least squares estimates are
consistent and unbiased. This simplifies the statistical problem and if
a time series of sufficient length is available, these data can be used

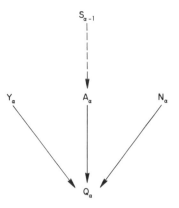

Fig. 1.2. Causal ordering of a simple econometric model. Causal link:————; Decision rule:- - - - - - -.

to test the model. With some luck, the analyst will end up with a model which describes the demand for electricity and yields estimates of advertising elasticity, income elasticity, and so forth. The model may have value in forecasting future sales and in designing better decision rules.

Another form for a model involving sales and advertising, where the advertising decision rule is based on current or expected sales, would be a simultaneous-equation system. Besides being different in a substantive sense, such a model requires special estimation techniques if consistent parameter estimates are to be obtained. Our preoccupation with the quality of estimates, especially the unbiasedness property, stems from the policy implications of the parameters, e.g., in their use in finding an optimal advertising budget. These issues of the form of models, parameter estimation, and model use unfold in subsequent chapters.

Most marketing systems are not as simple as this illustration. The effects of competition, more than one marketing decision variable, lagged advertising, and so forth make the task of modeling complex marketing systems a difficult one. Some of these complexities and possible ways of dealing with them are discussed next.

Complexities of Marketing Systems

The simple marketing system discussed above, like many economic models of competition, has a certain conceptual appeal, but its value in describing real world markets is limited. Since the purpose of marketing econometrics is to build models of markets that are representative of the real world, many real complexities of marketing systems must be explicitly embodied in the models. Some of the more important complexities which must be handled in the development of marketing system models include (1) organizational complexities, (2) multiple products-services, (3) market complexities, (4) complex actions, (5) complex information, (6) middlemen, (7) competitors, and (8) marketing dynamics.

1. *Organizational Complexities.* Decision making in a marketing organization is a behavioral process; thus, it involves complex relationships between individuals, groups, and the organization. Although econometric models are usually not concerned with this behavior *per se*, the researcher is often interested in the decision rules that an organization employs to set marketing budgets (such as the advertising decision rule described above). To the extent that behavioral processes mediate these decision rules, they are at least an implicit part of econometric models and their effects should be explored in some detail. They will also be seen to have a significant bearing on the implementation of marketing decision models.

2. *Multiple Products-Services.* Most modern marketing organizations offer more than one product or service and hence these product or service mixes become important in the measurement of sales response. Demand analysis usually proceeds by analyzing each product separately. For firms with multiple brands, each brand may be treated as a separate sales response function. If there are significant product or brand interactions on the demand side, it may not be appropriate to treat the products separately as if their sales were independent or merely uncorrelated.

3. *Market Complexities.* The market for a product or service is generally not homogeneous and this complexity has important implications in marketing research. For example, market segments can be defined as relatively homogeneous subsets of a heterogeneous market set. Market segments can be characterized by a number of dimensions, including geographic territories (say the suburban market for station wagons), socioeconomic groups (say the blue collar market for air conditioners), and so forth. The intersection of subsets provides another way of defining market segments (say the market for compact automobiles among suburban, blue-collar workers). Typically, econometric studies define the market geographically

rather than demographically, but the behavioral difference of different consumer reactions among segments is an important consideration.

4. *Complex Actions.* The firm has several variables which it can change in order to influence sales. Although competition and regulation often reduce the number of effective marketing instruments, many firms have marketing (variable) mixes involving some combination of price, advertising, distribution, sales force, product quality, etc. In these situations, the firms' actions or communications to the market are complex. The interaction of marketing mix variables is an important problem in econometric research.

5. *Complex Information.* A firm selling a product in a well-defined market segment using multiple marketing instruments (or even a single instrument) initiates complex patterns of consumer behavior. The firm seeks this information through marketing research or through an established marketing information system. In either case, the information from the market, reflecting complex behavior, is itself complex. Consumers see advertisements, learn prices, form attitudes, discuss products, develop preferences, seek information, make purchases, and so on. Any or all of this information can be useful to the firm.

6. *Middlemen.* The simple marketing system described in Fig. 1.1 does not include any middlemen. The product or service and communications flow directly from the producer to the consumer. In most marketing systems this is an inadequate description since it omits the important role of the middlemen such as retailers and wholesalers. Marketing channels of distribution impose definite structures on econometric models and thus the development of these models is influenced by the nature of middlemen and their relationships with the firm and market.

7. *Competitors.* One of the principal justifications of marketing econometrics is its concern with real marketing systems and hence competitive markets. The effects of competition on a firm's sales and marketing decisions are among the most challenging problems of marketing science. Within the broad range of market behavior between monopoly and perfect competition, the influence of competition is both varied and substantial. In most marketing situations, the firm's interaction with its market is an explicit function of its interaction with competition.

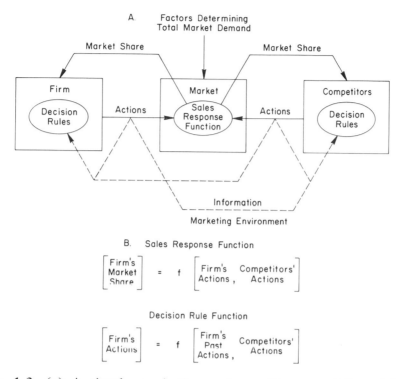

Fig. 1.3. (a) A simple marketing system with competition; (b) A simple marketing model with competition.

8. *Marketing Dynamics.* Marketing systems are dynamic. Even within the shortest time horizons, planning delays, execution delays, and lagged market responses occur. For example, the planning and execution of the advertising budget is a time-dependent process. After ads are scheduled, there is still a delay until they appear. The consumer response to advertising is also time dependent. The carryover effect (good will) of advertising is an important factor in modeling sales response. Econometric research provides a method for studying these kinds of complex market dynamics.

Thus, econometric models of marketing systems can become quite complex, raising important questions of model development and model implementation. Typically, however, some middle-ground representation of market complexities can be employed. A simple marketing system with competition is shown in Fig. 1.3(a). In this scheme, factors determining total market demand, say income and population, are separated from factors (actions) determining the firm's and its competitors' market shares. A simple marketing model with competition corresponding to this conceptualization is given in Fig. 1.3(b). Although the total market demand function is omitted, the dependence of a firm's market share and its own actions on the behavior of competition now defines this more complex marketing situation.

Approaches to the Study of Marketing Systems

There are two basic approaches to the study of marketing systems. The first approach focuses on processes within a marketing system. In this approach only part of the marketing system is studied or modeled explicitly. For example, studies of consumer decision processes seek to explain the behavior of individual consumers within a market, but` usually take the organization and communication flows as given. Even in larger, more general models of consumer behavior, the analysis is usually keyed to the dynamics of processes within the system rather than the dynamics of the system itself.

The second approach centers on the whole marketing system and is concerned with processes only to the extent that they are necessary to the understanding of system dynamics. Many econometric models of marketing systems, for example, seek to account for the behavior of total marketing systems by including parameters of the system but not necessarily parameters of processes within the system. As an illustration of this difference, the model specified in Eqs. (1.3) and (1.4) is a system model to the extent that it seeks to explain overall firm-market interaction in terms of system and not process parameters. In addition, this approach assumes that for certain purposes (such as forecasting or even planning), system models do not need to specify the microprocesses which may make up the system. Thus, while a complete process model, i.e., one that completely specifies the system by including all the relevant processes necessary to explain system dynamics, may be able to explain both process and system behavior, a system model can usually only explain system behavior.

Given these ideas, the choice between the process and system approaches must depend on the purpose of the investigation. If the purpose of a study is to explain how executives make advertising decisions, it may not be necessary to explicitly model consumer behavior. Rather, it may be sufficient to study how executives react to market behavior as an input to the executive decision process. Similarly, studies of consumer behavior, as noted above, may not require explicit modeling of firm-executive behavior. If, however, the purpose of a study is to account for firm-market interaction, then some parameters of both the firm and the market (and implicitly the flows between them) must be included, even if in a very aggregate way.

For the development of marketing theory, the process and system approaches are clearly complementary. The explanation of total marketing behavior through well-developed theories will rest on analyses of systems and their processes. The work of Amstutz (1967) seems to represent a beginning toward these *complete* models. For other purposes and for theory development at a more modest level (or if not more modest, more aggregate), the process and systems approaches are competitors. Suppose a company wants a model that will be useful in planning marketing actions and forecasting market response. The system parameters may be considered to be sales, price, advertising, and so forth. If a model can be developed at the system level which serves this purpose, then the modeling of micro-processes may not be relevant. On the other hand, process-level models could also be developed with such an aim in mind. The test in this competition would seem to be a cost-benefits one.

Econometric methods can be used to empirically determine theories of marketing systems or marketing processes. The difference is one of scope only. The method is general and thus has application in a variety of situations. In some special cases, it may be argued that econometrics is the most efficient method in terms of meeting the objective of the research, but this is usually an argument that rests on other grounds. The following section discusses the trend of marketing research and the issue of aggregation.

MARKETING RESEARCH AND AGGREGATION

Since the approach to the study of marketing systems depends upon the researcher's interest in marketing processes *per se* and hence the level of aggregation, it seems worthwhile to further discuss the nature of marketing processes and then the issue of aggregation. The simplest way to dichotomize marketing research is by methodology. The leading schools of marketing thought are characterized by their methods of research and so there is a *behavioral* school and a *quantitative* school. To the extent that a researcher's methodological predisposition shapes his view of the marketing world, it determines in large part his contribution to marketing theory. But this is a rather indefensible state of affairs since methodological rather than substan tive issues dictate the progress of marketing research. If these schools are the result of different interests, however, the situation is more tenable. In other words, if the behavioral school is defined by its interest in marketing processes and the quantitative school by its interest in marketing systems, the schools, like the approaches, are complementary. Still, a better division of interest would seem to be between consumer, executive, and system behavior. The following discussion develops this view.

Consumer Behavior

Consumer behavior is a set of processes within a marketing system. In Fig. 1.1, it is the microspecification of the market (the right-hand side of the diagram). Consumer behavior can be studied by using behavioral or quantitative methods, or both. It should not be defined by method, but rather by substance. This perspective allows the most efficient methods to be used in analyzing consumer behavior.

There is a large and growing body of research on consumer behavior although the number of generalized models is small. Only a few attempts have been made to test these general models.[2] Most consumer behavior research involves the testing of limited hypotheses about individual consumers. These studies include investigations of attitudes, risk-taking, preferences, dissonance, perception, innovation, and so forth. Robertson's compact book on consumer behavior is a fine introduction to the spirit of this research [Robertson (1970)]; his reader provides ample examples of the major studies [Kassarjian and Robertson (1973)] and other volumes provide theoretical perspective [Ward and Robertson, (1973); Sheth (1974)].

The general models of consumer behavior are attempts to explain consumer processes by an appropriate linkage of individual hypotheses. The Nicosia (1966), Howard and Sheth (1969), and Engel, Kollat, and Blackwell (1973) books report on major research models. Amstutz's computer model (1967) also embodies a general theory of consumer behavior. The validity of the general models is a serious question and one deserving a good deal more research. When tested, the general models can provide good descriptions of consumer behavior, although the larger problem of marketing system behavior would still be open. Consumer behavior research is an important part of marketing system research, although for certain purposes they can be pursued independently.[3]

Executive Behavior

Like consumer behavior, executive behavior is a set of processes within a marketing system. In Fig. 1.1, it is the microspecification of the organization (the left-hand side of the diagram). Marketing executive behavior is thus the process by which the organization changes its marketing plans in response to market information. This process can often be described by a set of decision rules, although human factors may make the process stochastic. An appropriate combination of behavioral and quantitative methods is necessary in the study of executive behavior.

Models of executive behavior in marketing are of two general kinds—normative and positive. There are many more normative than positive models. Normative models are designed to provide solutions to such marketing problems as new product introductions, sales force allocation, media selection, pricing, and others. Reviews of these model-building efforts have been made by Montgomery and Urban (1969) and Kotler (1971).

Every normative model for executive decision-making embodies some implicit theory of executive behavior. The building of positive models to make this behavior explicit has lagged far behind normative developments. There is good reason to believe that a better understanding of executive behavior will lead to better normative models. Howard argued for such new research over a decade ago [Howard (1963)]. His own contribution is one of the few models developed to date [Howard and Morgenroth (1968)].

Executive processes and consumer processes can both be modeled in rich detail, although the testing of these theories and the estimation of these microparameters is a formidable task. Some marketing systems may be modeled in a more aggregate way and then the focus of testing and estimation would be on the macroparameters of the system. In such a model describing system behavior, consumer and executive factors would be the forces motivating the system dynamics.

Levels of Aggregation

Marketing systems can be described on various levels of aggregation. The electric utility company model described above was modeled on the *economic* level of company demand (or industry demand in the case of a monopoly). This implies that the economic variables of interest are company sales and the determinants of company sales. The *behavioral* level modeled was that of company sales response as opposed to individual sales response. In other words, the purposes of the model were assumed to be served by concentrating on group response to marketing actions rather than the various responses of individual consumers. In this case, the "group" is defined as the customers of the firm. A knowledge of consumer behavior beyond this aggregate response is only incidental to the model.

Table 1.1

Levels of Aggregation

1. Economic Levels

   a. Firm or company demand
   b. Industry demand
   c. Economy or national demand
   d. World or international demand

2. Behavioral Levels for a Firm's Demand

   a. Individual sales response
   b. Market segment sales response
   c. Company sales response

3. Behavioral Levels of Individual Sales Response[a]

   a. Awareness
   b. Knowledge
   c. Liking
   d. Preference
   e. Conviction
   f. Purchase

[a]E.g., A "Hierarchy of Effects" Model.

If the knowledge of consumer behavior is paramount, then a model could be developed at an economic level of company demand and a behavioral level of individual sales response. This approach would permit the variance of individual sales to be investigated. An even more detailed study of consumer behavior could focus on levels of individual sales response or the behavioral steps that a consumer goes through from exposure to a marketing stimulus to a particular kind of response. Table 1.1 presents a conceptual ordering of various levels of aggregation. Only one of many alternative models of individual sales response has been used as an illustration. In addition, company demand may sometimes be regarded as the demand for a brand of the company and it is possible that several brands of the same company compete against each other.

Econometric models can be developed at any of these levels of aggregation. The generality of the approach and some applications in marketing and other areas are covered in the following section.

ECONOMETRIC MODELS: AN OVERVIEW

Econometric research in marketing has been described as the process of building models of marketing systems which delineate the relationships between organizations and markets through flows of communication and exchange. In this context, the econometric approach is a method for developing and testing, through empirical research, theories of market behavior. We have seen how the theories can be of systems or of processes and at various levels of aggregation. We next turn to a more exact statement of the econometric approach and show how it has been used in marketing and economics.

The Econometric Approach

Econometrics is a general method for securing explanations of the behavior of economic variables and making predictions about future behavior. The econometric approach in marketing is character-ized by the following.

1. Developing a theory of marketing behavior.
2. Expressing the theory as a set
    of mathematical relations—a model.
3. Designing a rigorous test of the model.

4. Choosing an appropriate set of statistical hypotheses.
5. Confronting the model with data.
6. Testing the conjunction
    of the model with the data.
7. Estimating the parameters of the model.
8. Evaluating the usefulness of the model.

Thus, there is a major reliance on the mathematical formulation of marketing theory and on the techniques of statistical inference. In addition, the empirical content of marketing theory depends upon the extent to which available observations are subjected to rigorous analysis.

The philosophical setting of the econometric approach in marketing most clearly resembles *logical positivism* in that assumptions of the model (both statistical and substantive) are maintained in the analysis whereas postulates based on the model are tested as hypotheses.[4] In this respect, marketing econometrics follows Basmann who argues that: "An econometric model is a chain of logical deductions beginning in a set of economic propositions (employed as postulates) and ending in a set of propositions (theorems) whose *terms* are probability distributions of sample statistics" [Basmann (1963b), 944]. Although the methods of testing and estimating them may differ, most econometric studies in marketing are in the logical positivist tradition.

Historically, in marketing as in economics, a good deal of research can be philosophically classified as *empiricist*. This approach features less reliance on testing theories and more on developing theories out of empirical facts. Since all marketing models must embody some theory, even if in an implicit way, the difference between positivist and empiricist approaches is one of degree, not kind. To a large extent, the state of prior information about markets and marketing determines the philosophical basis of the research. The state of prior information also determines the nature of model testing and the quality of estimation. These important and complex issues are more fully developed in the middle chapters of this book.

In our view, econometric models require some degree of *explicit* attention to the theory of marketing behavior which is to be tested. Many applications of regression analysis in marketing do not conform to this view because they either assume an underlying theory or expect one to be revealed in the analysis. These regression studies do not meet the eight "standards" we have set out above as characterizing econometric research in marketing. For this reason, we have limited our review of regression analysis studies in marketing to those that qualify as *econometric studies*.

Research Traditions Outside Marketing

Econometrics, as the name implies, originated with economists who wanted to develop methods for testing economic theories. Although the econometricians "borrowed" the methods from mathematical statistics, they have made important methodological contributions themselves.[5] Marketing researchers have employed the methods of econometrics to solve marketing problems and thus are concerned with both the theoretical and empirical development of econometrics. Since multivariate statistical applications are not unique to economics, there are important developments in other fields as well, notably psychology, where correlation analysis has long been a significant method of research.

Goldberger defines econometrics as "the social science in which the tools of economic theory, mathematics, and statistical inference are applied to the analysis of economic phenomena" [Goldberger (1964), 1]. He distinguishes between "econometric theory"—the development of appropriate techniques of statistical inference and "empirical econometrics"—actual statistical inference from economic data. The state of the art of econometric theory is best represented in one of many good texts on the subject. Some of the well-known works are those by Goldberger (1964), Christ (1966), and Johnston (1972). We have chosen Theil's *Principles of Econometrics* (1971) as a companion volume to this book and have adopted his notation to make the interplay more simple. For the reader with a limited background in mathematics, we could recommend the book by Walters (1970), which also contains an excellent review of empirical econometrics.

Actual statistical inference from economic data was initially focused on the elementary concepts of economic theory including demand functions and production functions. There are several approaches to the measurement of demand [Baumol (1965), 210-249]. One approach is to interview consumers to seek their willingness to purchase a product at alternative prices. Another approach is to experiment directly in the market. But both of these approaches are filled with cost and statistical problems. Interviews and especially experiments are expensive to the firm (the latter, in addition, involves considerable risk as customers lost at high prices may never be regained). Statistical problems resulting from small samples in interviewing and lack of experimental control make these methods less desirable.

The statistical approach is generally considered to be most attractive. This approach exploits the power of regression analysis to identify relationships among variables. It is a method of analyzing past data—time series—and/or data from different sectors of the market—cross section—to obtain estimates of parameters of sales response. Statistical demand analysis rests on the major assumptions and is subject to the major limitations of regression analysis. Although the researcher has open to him several options of model specification, such as single-equation multiple regression or simultaneous-equation structural models, he is bound by questions of the statistical and theoretical significance of his results.

Econometrics involves the application of regression analysis in economics to test theories and estimate relationships. The models can also be used for forecasting. In psychological research (and many other social science research fields), the primary tool for investigating relationships between dependent and explanatory variables is correlation analysis. Here the focus is usually on forecasting and regression coefficients often have no theoretical interpretation. For example, a study of the relationship between job satisfaction and individual performance would probably concentrate on the correlation between these two variables. The regression coefficients have little if any basis in theory and so their estimates may not be an important part of the investigation. This procedure contrasts sharply with research in economics, where coefficients almost always have an economic meaning, such as elasticities or multipliers.

The use of regression or correlation analysis in these fields rests on substantive and not statistical considerations. Kendall and Stuart note that "a statistical relationship, however strong and however suggestive, can never establish a causal connection; our ideas on causation must come from outside statistics, ultimately from some theory or other" [(1973), 291]. Economic applications of regression analysis almost always embody some economic theory which is subjected to rigorous testing procedures. If the theory is accepted (as a causal model), then the question of forecasting ability and thus degree of correlation may become relevant. In psychological research, the link between theory and forecasting is less useful because of the state of the art. Thus, predictor variables may be chosen on the grounds of high covariance with a criterion variable. One psychologist has stated that "ordinarily when we are interested in variables for purposes of forecasting we do not care whether the attribute being measured is of any particular interest in and of itself. . . . A predictor variable is one which is of value primarily because it has appreciable covariance with some other variable which may be important" [Horst (1966), 87]. Kendall and Stuart summarize this view by noting that ". . . there are large fields of application (the social sciences and psychology, for example) where patterns of causation are not yet sufficiently well understood for correlation analysis to be replaced by more specifically 'structural' statistical methods" [(1973), 291-292].

The research tradition of regression and correlation in marketing is more closely related to economic research than to psychological research. Most marketing studies aim at both *explaining* and *forecasting* market behavior, and so the standing of a model as a marketing theory receives prime consideration. The next section previews some of these marketing applications which are covered in more detail in Chaps. 7 and 10.

Marketing Applications

The rigorous study of sales response functions in marketing through econometric and other multivariate methods is of recent vintage. Most of the extant research can be classified according to the nature of the market being investigated; that is, by grouping studies into those dealing with individual demand of a firm or brand, industry demand, or aggregate (national) demand. This taxonomy provides a convenient way of assessing the breadth and depth of marketing knowledge on sales response behavior.

A review of the literature shows that most empirical findings relate to individual demand for a brand. Although some depth has been achieved with respect to such problems as carryover effects (usually of advertising), competitive effects, interactive effects (of marketing mix variables), and simultaneous relationships, the breadth of such studies has generally not extended beyond "frequently purchased branded goods" and thus broad knowledge of the demand structure for goods and services is severely restricted. (See Chaps. 7 and 8.)

At the level of industry demand, the general situation is probably worse. Only a few studies deal with industry sales-advertising relationships, and fewer still with industry sales-marketing relationships which deal with more complex formulations of demand by including more than one marketing variable, e.g., price and advertising. (See Chap. 10.)

The question of marketing's influence on aggregate (national) demand has been explored by a number of researchers. These studies focus on the economic impact of advertising in the economy. While this is also an area of minimal knowledge, the lack of appropriate data makes further investigation very difficult [cf. Parsons and Schultz, (1973)].

Another way of classifying econometric sales response studies would be by the type of regression model used. The two major categories are single-equation regression models and multiple-equation regression models. Since the regression model must be appropriate to the theory being tested, this distinction is a theoretical one as well as methodological. The first marketing sales response studies were based on single-equation formulations of demand or market share. These studies usually neglected the possibility of simultaneous relationships, such as between sales and advertising, but, where identification could be assumed, they often provided useful findings for practical decision making and future research.

The growing recognition of the significance of simultaneous or joint relationships in marketing, however, has recently led to a new branch of sales response research—multiple-equation models. These models deal explicitly with identification problems involving sales response functions and marketing decision rules and show considerable promise as means for developing theories of market behavior. Marketing systems have been modeled as seemingly unrelated equations, recursive systems, and simultaneous (structural) systems. The distinction between these approaches is more than a technical one; it reflects the observed differences in real markets.

In successive chapters, we develop approaches to econometric model-building, discuss problems encountered in building such models, show important marketing applications, and raise questions about scientific and practical implications of the research. Marketing systems are seen as eminently appropriate settings for new and better work along these lines.

FOOTNOTES

[1] Recent attempts to broaden the concept of marketing have been made by Kotler and Levy (1969), Kotler and Zaltman (1971), Kotler (1975), and others. A growing number of research studies are directed at the marketing aspects of nonbusiness organizations.

[2] The most notable attempt was an econometric test of a general model by Farley and Ring (1970). Although this work was more estimation than test, it is interesting to note that econometrics plays a central role in the estimation-testing process of behavioral models, a point developed in Chapter 12.

[3] An example would be a forecasting model which requires only simple relations among system parts; in this case, details on individual consumer behavior would not be relevant.

[4] In terms of the philosophy of science, the econometric approach is just a statistical application of the *hypothetico-deductive method*, but one that can take into consideration both *plausibility* (discovery) arguments and *falsifiability* (confirmation) criteria [cf. Salmon (1967)].

[5] The contributions are too numerous to mention, but see the journal *Econometrica* and the classic volume by Hood and Koopmans (1953) for a view of this important work.

Chapter 2

MODELS OF
MARKETING SYSTEMS

In the previous chapter a rather general background for the use of econometric methods in marketing was presented. Econometric research in marketing was defined as "the process of building models of marketing systems." Econometrics was described as a rigorous technique that can aid in the development of marketing theory in a variety of settings and at various levels of aggregation. The purpose of the present chapter is twofold: first, to shift the focus of our concern from basic research on the nature of marketing systems to more applied work on the development and implementation of marketing decision models; and, second, to discuss in specific terms the idea of marketing decision models and their research requirements. To a considerable extent, this chapter motivates the remainder of the book. This is true because marketing econometrics plays a major role in providing the empirical content both of marketing theories and of marketing decision models.

The relationship between what we call "marketing theories" and "marketing decision models" is one of dependence of the latter on the former. Every marketing decision model must incorporate some representation of the market, a sales response function, and this representation is, in effect, a hypothesis about market behavior. Thus, theories of market behavior must be developed *and tested* before the sales response function component of a marketing decision model achieves technical validity. The development of practical decision aids places major reliance on the theoretical specification of marketing relationships and this interplay between scientific and managerial considerations determines the structure of the research approach. The theoretical basis of marketing decision models is explored in Chap. 6. A discussion of the practical aspects of model implementation is given in Chap. 11. For now, we turn to an argument for the development of marketing decision models that is managerial in orientation.

AN OUTLINE OF THE BASIC ARGUMENT

Although the importance of technology to the advancement of organizations and markets is well understood, the significance of a special form of technology, *decision-making* technology, is not well appreciated. This situation illustrates more than anything else the gap between successful model building and successful implementation. This circumstance itself has motivated considerable research on the process of implementing decision models in all areas of management [Schultz and Slevin (1975)]. Special difficulties arise in marketing as attempts are made to close this gap because of the complexities of consumer and executive behavior (cf. Chap. 1). Nevertheless, progress is being made in understanding market processes and in converting this knowledge into marketing actions. This milieu, of research and decision making, provides the organizational context in which we examine marketing decision models.

Our basic argument can be succinctly stated in the following points, all of which are elaborated in this chapter or in succeeding ones.

1. Premise—the development and implementation of decision-making technology known as *marketing decision models* will result in better marketing decisions.

2. A marketing decision model is a formal method designed to make or support recurring marketing decisions.

3. The decision model incorporates a representation of the market, a sales response function, and a representation of the firm's goals, an objective function.

4. It can be contrasted with informal methods of making decisions such as ad hoc procedures and decision heuristics.

5. The model is formal. Since it is a mathematical one; both analytical and simulation approaches are possible.

6. The sales response function component of the model can be empirically based; both stochastic and econometric approaches are possible.

7. An ideal sales response function includes explicit consideration of marketing mix interaction effects, carryover effects, competitive effects, and simultaneous relationships; in addition, consideration of the dimensions of marketing decision variables is possible.

8. When conjoined with a method of information processing

(data collection and parameter estimation), the model becomes part of a *marketing decision system.*

9. The system can be designed to be adaptive so that changes in the environment are reflected by changes in the model.

10. The validity of a marketing decision system depends upon the fit of the sales response function with actual market behavior, upon the adequacy of the technical solution, and upon the compatibility of the model with the user organization.

11. Implementation of the system, then, depends upon the expected net benefits of the system and upon the technical and organizational validities of the system.

12. Prototypes of marketing decision models and systems include

- Parsons and Bass (1971)
- SIMAREX [Lambin (1972a)]
- BRANDAID II [Little (1975)]
- AIRPLAN [Schultz (1971)]

Before proceeding with our exposition of this argument, some consideration will be given to the general process of model building. Here we are concerned with how models are discovered rather than how they are subsequently justified in the literature. The framework for this discussion can be found in Morris (1970).

THE PROCESS OF MODEL BUILDING

The process of model building involves sequential development of a model from a rudimentary one to a more complex one. The process begins with a statement of the deductive objective of the model. For instance, the purpose of the model[1] might be to recommend the sequence of advertising expenditures which generate the maximum profits. Thus, the firm's objective function must be known. The statement provides one criterion for judging the viability of the model at each stage of its development. If the current version of the model can be "solved" to achieve the deductive objective, then the next version can be made more complex. Otherwise, it should be simplified. Similarly, each successive version should be confronted by new data in order to test whether it is a reasonable representation of the underlying market mechanism. The test results may suggest appropriate modifications.

The aspects of the model which lend themselves to enrichment or simplification are usually obvious. Morris [(1969), 91] states that a model can be simplified by making variables into constants, by eliminating variables, by using linear relations, by adding stronger assumptions and restrictions, and by suppressing randomness. A model can be enriched by taking the opposite actions. An important characteristic of a model is the degree to which it can be modified along each of these lines.

The first version of a model is constructed taking into account those properties required by current marketing theory and previous empirical evidence. Our focus is on models of market mechanisms which represent causal processes, that is, we are only concerned with what Nicosia and Rosenberg (1972) call substantive mathematical models. In addition, we share their concern that the elements of a model, in particular, its parameters, have some intrinsic meaning. Imposition of this seemingly minor requirement forestalls some of the difficulty managers encounter in interpreting and confirming models. The formulation of marketing mix models so that the response coefficients are elasticities is one example. The role of *a priori* information about parameters in predictive testing is discussed in Chap. 5.

Since the research traditions in most areas of marketing are incomplete, there will be wide latitude in formulating a model. Thus, analogies with known logical structures are often sought. However, it is important to start with a logical structure that will permit evolutionary development of the model.

Solutions to each version will be suboptimal. By increasing the level of model detail, the confidence that the solution is approaching the global optimum increases. Confidence in the model is also affected by the degree to which the model relates to previously known results, by its intuitive plausibility, and by its sensitivity to changes in assumptions.

Some advantages of an evolutionary approach have been pointed out by Urban and Karash [(1971), 66]. These include: (1) increased managerial understanding and acceptance; (2) orderly development of data base and data analysis capability; (3) opportunity to make a marginal cost-benefit analysis; (4) reduction of project risk by the availability of abort opportunities at marginal analysis points; (5) learning by model builders about the level of detail for the model and about managers; (6) availability of short-term benefits. The relation of this approach to the more general approach of behavioral model building is discussed in Chap. 11.

DECISION MODELS

Decision models are aids to management judgment. They are sometimes referred to as "normative models" or "prescriptive models" since they give an indication to managers of what ought to be done under certain conditions. The "optimization models" of operations research are decision models because their output can be considered to be a recommendation to management on how to make the best choice from a number of decision alternatives. Some decision models are designed to generate alternatives or to suggest actions which lead to better decisions. In all of these cases the common element of such models is the provision of some aid to management judgment built around variables over which the manager has some control.

In Wagner's apt terms, the "managerial cutting edge" of operations research can produce four kinds of practical benefits: (1) better decisions, (2) better coordination, (3) better control, and (4) better systems [Wagner, (1969), 25-26]. The result, in other words, of management science activity can be *increased organizational effectiveness.* Marketing organizations offer an especially rich environment in which to develop and implement decision models. There are a number of well-defined variables under management's control such as price, advertising, personal selling, and so forth, and a reasonably well-defined set of decision criteria including sales, market share, profit, and others facilitating the development of models. The challenge to model builders in marketing comes from the many behavioral factors that mediate market response. Marketing models, like marketing organizations and processes, must reflect quite a bit of the complexity of the real world. This makes the process of developing, validating, and implementing marketing decision models a very difficult but important one.

As we have noted above, a marketing decision model is a formal method designed to make or support recurring marketing decisions. The idea that models will be used to *make* decisions may seem somewhat remote, although some precedents exist in other fields, e.g., production scheduling models. The use of marketing decision models will more likely be *supportive* only. This view is reinforced by the difficulty in obtaining "complete" models of market behavior so that the manager's inputs will undoubtedly continue to have considerable weight. Still, the balance may shift from subjective to empirical analysis or from manager to model as management science in marketing advances.

We have defined a marketing decision variable in terms of *recurring* marketing decisions because this includes most of the tasks of marketing management. It includes, for example, marketing mix decisions, new product decisions (the products are new but the decisions are the same), product phase-out decisions, and even corporate strategy decisions. For nonrecurring marketing decisions, we suggest that models have a limited role, if any, and that recourse be made to both executive judgment and the extant models of ongoing processes.

A marketing decision model has two major components—a sales response function which provides a representation of the market and an objective function which provides a representation of the firm's goals. The sales response function component of the model supplies the mechanism by which controllable inputs plus other noncontrollable factors are converted into outputs in the market. Capturing this behavioral process in a model becomes the primary task of the model builder and thus it should be no surprise that we devote much of our space to this pivotal enterprise.

The sales response function can be subjective, empirical, or some combination of judgment and data. Empirical versions can be developed using stochastic or econometric paradigms, or both. Thus, there is a great deal of flexibility in how the model builder approaches this problem. We can consider the goal of this work to be the·creation of an *ideal* sales response function which would include explicit consideration of marketing mix interaction effects, carry over effects, competitive effects, and simultaneous relationships. In addition, some consideration of the dimensions of marketing decision models (such as total expenditure, media selection, and message and copy dimensions of advertising) is possible and desirable. The objective function of a marketing decision model can also take a variety of forms, and approaches ranging from analytical to simulation are available.

A *marketing decision system* is a broader concept than a marketing decision model, akin to the "decision-information" system expounded by Montgomery and Urban (1969). In our view, when conjoined with a method of information processing, including data collection and parameter estimation, the decision model becomes part of a decision system. The system itself can be designed to be adaptive so that changes in the environment are reflected by changes in the model. In other words, the system concept provides for linking the decision model with a means of supplying it with data, of finding structural parameters, and of regenerating it as the world changes. A decision system may seem to be rather grandiose, but it is surely worth considering.

The validity of a marketing decision system (including the decision model) depends upon the fit of the sales response function with actual market behavior, upon the adequacy of the technical solution to the model (also upon the adequacy of the solution to the problem which may not be coincident with the model!), and upon the compatibility of the model with the user organization. We will argue elsewhere that these technical and organizational "fits" of the model are important determinants of its validity and ultimately its utility (see Chap. 11). Implementation of the system, then, depends upon the expected net benefits of the system and upon the technical and organizational validities of the system. Prototypes of marketing decision models and systems include: Parsons and Bass' (1971) empirical decision model for advertising appropriations; SIMAREX, Lambin's (1972a) decision model for marketing mix policies for gasoline; BRANDAID II, Little's (1975) decision model for marketing mix policies for brand managers; and AIRPLAN, Schultz's (1971) decision model for advertising and scheduling of airlines. Other models are reported by Montgomery and Urban (1969), Kotler (1971), and in Montgomery (1971).

Decision Calculus

John Little defines a decision model, or in his terms a *decision calculus*, as "a model-based set of procedures for processing data and judgments to assist a manager in his decision making" [Little (1970), 470]. He views the process of operations research/management science as one of first building simple but complete models to solve practical problems, then getting managers to actually use them, and finally working with managers on more complex and presumably more useful versions of the models. This strategy shows in several model-building efforts by Little (1966, 1969, 1970, 1975) and in the work of Lodish (1971), Urban (1970, 1971, 1975), and others.

According to Little, the relationship between the model and the manager can be explained as an "analysis-education-decision process built around man-model-machine interaction in which the man does not lose responsibility or control and instead of understanding less understands more" [Little (1970), 469]. Models designed to assist managers must meet certain requirements *if they are to be used.* More specifically, Little [(1970), 466] has postulated that:

> A model that is to be used by a manager should be simple, robust, easy to control, adaptive, as complete as possible, and easy to communicate with. By simple is meant easy to understand; by robust, hard to get absurd answers from, by easy to control, that the user knows what input data would be required to produce desired output answers; adaptive means that the model can be adjusted as new information is acquired; completeness implies that important phenomena will be included even if they require judgmental estimates of their effect; and, finally, easy to communicate with means that the manager can quickly and easily change inputs and obtain and understand the outputs.

These characteristics of models can serve as guidelines for the model development and implementation process itself. They fall within a broad perspective of management science called *behavioral model building* which is discussed more fully in Chap. 11. A key issue in the decision calculus approach is the conflict between the model requirements of completeness and simplicity. Little argues that, "An important aid to completeness is the incorporation of subjective judgments. People have a way of making better decisions than their data seem to warrant" [(1970), 470]. The implication here (and the author discusses this notion) is that subjective models may be both more simple and more complete than empirical models. The simplicity stems from the direct utilization of subjective judgments about model structure, parameter values, and other factors without the necessity of bringing more complex measurement and hence modeling techniques into play. The completeness apparently arises because the manager's experience is embodied in the model through his subjective input and thus the "model" becomes more complex and realistic with such human content. This argument recognizes the power of empirical measurement, but also its practical limitations. As Little notes ". . . at any given point in time, subjective estimates will be valuable for quantities that are currently difficult to measure or which cannot be measured in the time available before a decision must be made" [(1970), 470].

Up to this point, we are basically in agreement with the tenets of decision calculus. The possible superiority of managerial judgment over empirical measurement has been discussed by Schultz (1973) in the context of predicting competitive behavior and by Schultz and Slevin (1972) in the context of implementing marketing decision models. In both cases, the subjective assessment of certain aspects of marketing behavior is shown to be an important practical consideration. We do, however, see an increasingly important role for empirically-based decision models as the measurement technology of sales response analysis grows. Thus, we would extend the idea of decision calculus by imposing another requirement on models, namely that they be evaluated in terms of the *representativeness* of the mechanism describing market behavior.[2] This additional requirement guarantees that at least the sales response function component of the decision model faces a rigorous test of its validity as a theory of market response. We would argue that a test of a theory is its validity while the test of a model is its utility and so it is possible for a model to be useful even though it is based on an inadequate theory of sales response. But it is better to have both a valid *and* useful model.

In this extended view, empirical decision models are preferred to subjective decision models, at least in terms of the sales response function. This does not preclude decision models from using subjective inputs, particularly where these are more expedient. It does, however, assert that *where possible* measurement should be employed to modify or reinforce judgment. The manager is still "in control" of his model, but he now finds himself in a position to bring as much of the real world into the model (hence explicit consideration) as possible. The techniques of econometric model building described in this volume are well suited to bringing this kind of empirical relevance to marketing decision models.

Subjective Vs. Empirical Models

To what extent should marketing decision models be empirical? What are the benefits of empirically-based decision models *vis à vis* their cost? How can subjective judgments be incorporated into decision models? How can decision models be welded to data? These questions require answers, but there are no definite ones as of yet. A number of factors can be identified, however, which relate to the questions and provide a point of departure for future research.

One of the most straightforward factors is purpose: Models are designed to explain or to forecast, or both. Since we have argued that every decision model must contain some sales response function which represents a theory of market behavior, we conclude that this requires a certain reference to empirical data. Models that embody theory must be confronted with data to test the validity of the theory. Of course, some models may have forecasting abilities without being able to explain the marketing processes in question, but we prefer to argue that this "special case" involves substantial risk to the decision maker precisely because of his inadequate understanding of market dynamics. On the other hand, the goal of decision models is to aid in making better decisions and the utility of a model may be enhanced by careful use of judgmental inputs. This may especially be true where theories (whether of sales response, competitive behavior, or whatever) can only be validated with considerable effort and/or uncertainty. We will have more to say about the *research questions* involved in this issue later in the book.

The two major uses of decision models are for planning and forecasting and the appropriateness of subjective inputs depends to some extent on the model's intended function. It is well known, for example, that good forecasts can emanate from good managers or from good forecasting models, neither of which may be capable of providing good explanations of underlying processes. Most decision models as well as managers deal in some fashion with *plans* and *anticipations*. Plans are statements referring to the manager's own actions in the future. Plans involve the setting of policy variables under the manager's control. Anticipations are statements about events which are likely to happen, but without the intervention of the managers. Anticipations may concern the actions of competitors, the state of the economy, and so forth. Now, plans can either be the subjective inputs of managers or the "objective" outputs of optimization models. Similarly, anticipations can be handled through direct managerial judgment or through a forecasting model. Despite the potential of models to help managers organize their judgments and perhaps exceed their own insight, the cost of securing adequate models of plans or anticipations may exceed their practical benefits.

How does subjectivity enter into decision models? Consider some of the dimensions of decision models and their relationship to subjective judgment. First, variables must be defined and assembled in a logical way to reflect the basic processes under consideration. In a sales response function, for example, sales may be posited to be a function of relative price and advertising plus per capita disposable personal income. This simple relation includes control, competitive, and environmental variables. The fact that the model has *any* form is the result of someone's judgment (the researcher or model builder hopefully in cooperation with the manager and in concert with the data). Given the model, subjective inputs may occur when the manager sets control variables, estimates competitive variables, or predicts environmental variables. In each case, the manager's function *could* be taken over by an empirical model. Whether this can or should be done is an important question for further work.

The second aspect of decision models that raises the subjective vs. empirical question is the estimation of parameter values. Should management's judgment be directly utilized or should reliance be placed on empirical data? The situation sometimes provides an answer to this question. In the most notorious case, data may not be available and so recourse must be to management opinion. As we discuss below, combinations of subjective and empirical estimation of model parameters are possible and probably desirable.

Third, changes in the world require changes in the model. Thus, the model itself may become obsolete or, for that matter, so may the manager! The model must be updated formally or informally and this process is another important avenue for bringing management's judgment directly to bear on the shape and use of the decision model. Other aspects of models and their use could also be identified. For example, should model- or manager-generated alternatives be used? Model or manager sensitivity analysis? Again, answers can only be supplied through further research.

Some Tangible Results

There are some more concrete results and opinions available on the issue of subjective vs. empirical decision models. Kotler (1971), for example, has written on collecting primary data through subjective estimation, say, market size from salesmen, competitive reactions from brand managers, or advertising copy effectiveness from marketing researchers. He comments that, "In all of these cases, the numbers do not exist anywhere in objective form but there are experts who are expected to produce better than average estimates. The expert bases his estimate on existing objective data plus personal insights that come from experience. The distinguishing characteristic of judgmental data is that it is produced by a data transformation model that is usually not made explicit by the data producer" [(1971), 583].

In some cases there is no past history to support an empirical model or there are poor inadequate data and so subjective estimates cannot be avoided (this is especially true in new product situations). In all cases, some element of judgment is involved even if, at the extreme, it is whether or not to completely rely on a model. Kotler goes on to discuss the "quantification of judgment" including problems of obtaining estimates from single managers and pooling estimates. He shows how estimates of sales response functions can be obtained and how to assess subjective probability distributions. Of course, the entire field of Bayesian decision theory relates to this latter task. Kotler concludes that "judgmental data allows the use of many interesting decision models that could not otherwise be used because of lack of objective data" [Kotler (1971), 584]. An interesting alternative approach to obtaining judgmental estimates of sales response functions is given in Little (1975).

As indicated above, a few prototype decision models illustrate the various approaches to the utilization of judgmental and empirical data. We sketch here their main features in this regard.

1. **Little (1975), BRANDAID II.** This model, designed to aid brand managers in making marketing mix decisions, is mostly subjective but tempered empirically. A five-step "calibration" process is suggested to obtain parameter values; it includes (a) judgment, (b) historical analysis, (c) tracking, (d) field experiments, and (e) adaptive control. Little argues that "Sometimes

historical analysis leads to useful response estimates, sometimes it does not. One of the reasons for starting with judgmental numbers is to prevent people from overinterpreting historical analysis . . . Statistical results sometimes take on too great an air of authority because of their seeming objectivity" [(1975), 661-2].

2. **Lambin (1972a) SIMAREX.** This model is also a marketing mix one, but combines empirical and subjective estimation in the reverse order of BRANDAID II. It is empirical since an econometric sales response function is used and subjective in treating regression coefficients as *a priori* estimates to be modified by judgment (informally) and in using management to generate alternatives, estimate competitive behavior, and evaluate model outcomes. Lambin argues that ". . . here empirical estimates come first in updating input parameters. Thus the decision maker at least has objective measurements to start which summarize the brand's past history . . . It seems very unrealistic, indeed, to expect judgmental estimates of the different response coefficients from the decision maker, even if he is very well informed, without giving him some *organized* prior information or reference values" [(1972a), 126].

3. **Parsons and Bass (1971).** In this model, parameter values are obtained via simultaneous-equation regression analysis and then employed in a multiperiod optimization procedure to obtain optimal advertising expenditure strategies. The model is essentially "all empirical" and judgment enters only in a "what should managers do with the output?" way. The authors conclude that "There is reason to believe . . . that it is possible, in at least some circumstances, to develop useful explanatory models of sales and advertising systems. Simultaneous-equation regression procedures appear to offer substantial promise both in dealing with theoretical issues of simultaneous dependencies and in providing a basis for forecasting the profit consequences of alternative strategies" [(1971), 830].

4. **Schultz (1971, 1973), AIRPLAN.** This model, also designed as a marketing mix planning tool, is mostly empirical but has a key role for the subjective assessment of competition. The parameter values are obtained through econometric procedures and then the sales response function is embedded in a decision model. The

decision model requires judgmental inputs for competitive reactions and other exogenous variables. Refinement of this procedure was later shown to be possible by first specifying possible competitive decision rules and then simulating possible outcomes [Schultz and Dodson (1974)]. Even in this case, management judgment is required to give probability distributions for the various possible competitive strategies. A more recent version that deals with these probabilities is Schultz and Little (1975).

Each of the models discussed above adopts a different view of the optimal balance between subjective and empirical inputs in marketing decision models. Little and Lambin appear to take quite opposite positions on the starting point for such analyses. Parsons and Bass do not discuss the role of subjective parameter estimates, nor does Schultz. In AIRPLAN, however, Schultz discusses the place of subjective assessment of competitive behavior. Still, there seems to be basic agreement on the objective of such model building and on various features of the decision models. As theoretical work progresses and as implementation considerations are brought into play, there will undoubtedly be a convergence in both views and models.

SALES RESPONSE MODELS

The notion of sales response to marketing variables is the core of the theory and practice of marketing management. In making decisions, marketing managers must have some idea about how their actions will influence sales and profits. Usually these ideas concerning the link between apparent causes (marketing decision variables, the actions of competitors, and certain environmental factors) and measurable market responses such as sales or market share are based on experience—a "feel" for the implications of a firm's marketing decisions. These casual interpretations of market response may be expedient, serving managers as guides to marketing planning, but they are severely limited in their ability to provide managers with more objective evidence on how to improve the quality of their decisions. Sales response models are formal ways of describing the complex relationship between a firm and its market. They are designed to overcome as much of the uncertainty as possible regarding the nature of sales response, and, in addition, to provide the behavioral mechanism in a decision model which allows management to explore optimal policies.

As discussed in the previous chapter, sales response models can be developed at various levels of aggregation, ranging from brand sales to industry sales. For that matter, response functions can be designed to relate any number of *intermediate-level* responses to each other or to marketing factors (cf. "hierarchy of effects" models in Chap. 1), such as models relating advertising to attitudes, or attitudes to preferences, or preferences to choice, and so forth. While the explication of these intermediate-level responses undoubtedly contributes to a more thorough understanding of consumer behavior, especially at the individual consumer level (since most of this microbehavioral research deals with single consumer units, individuals or households, for example), the purposes of marketing management can usually be served by more aggregate knowledge (and modeling) with focus on marketing policy variables and standard measures of marketing success. For this reason, and not because we don't value research on individual consumer behavior, we choose to deal with the relationships between variables that are of the most immediate concern to managers.

It is worth noting that the apparent chasm between management science and consumer behavior researchers, reflecting the orientations noted above, must be regarded as more of a "state-of-the-art" problem than anything else. As sales response models become more sophisticated, they will accomodate intermediate-level responses, and thus become more complete explanations of market behavior. As consumer behavior research advances, it will allow marketing policy variables to be brought into the analysis. Consumers can then be collected into managerially-useful market segments (which we nevertheless argue must be greater than size one) and decision models constructed in this more inclusive way. Thus, the approach that we have taken in this book reflects both a managerial perspective and an assessment of the state of marketing science.[3]

At the chosen level of aggregation, a sales response model should be as good a representation of the process generating sales as possible. For technical and substantive reasons, an ideal sales response function should include the following elements:

1.   **Marketing mix interaction effects.**   A sales response function should take into account all of the relevant marketing decision variables, such as price, advertising, personal selling, distribution outlets, and so forth. Beyond this, the interaction of these variables with each other should be considered.

2.   **Carryover effects.**   The impact of some marketing decision variables, notably advertising, is spread over a period of time and these lagged responses should be part of a sales response function. These effects represent notions like good will and brand loyalty that are too important to neglect.

3.   **Competitive effects.**   A sales response function should include the effect of competitive actions on sales. This is especially important since it is usually the relative setting of marketing decision variables, not their absolute value, that determines sales.

4.   **Simultaneous relationships.**   An ideal sales response function should recognize that a sales equation is often part of a system of equations that are simultaneous in nature. This may be due to the presence of decision rules that set policy variables on the basis of sales or to the existence of competitor's sales or market share equations which imply a joint behavioral process.

5.   **Dimensions of decisions.**   Marketing decision variables are not homogenous and their various dimensions should be part of an ideal sales response function. Advertising, for example, is made up of expenditures, media, message and copy; personal selling, of number of salesmen, number of calls, territory design, etc. To be "complete," a sales response function should model these richer effects.

An ideal sales response function would, of course, also include relevant environmental variables such as consumer income and wealth and important technical variables such as trends and seasonality. Given this list of requirements, it is not surprising that progress toward such "ideal models" has been slow. In the next two sections, we discuss the major methodological approaches to the identification and measurement of sales response functions. A discussion of many of the creative aspects of their design appears in Chap. 6.

Stochastic Vs. Econometric Models

There are two basic approaches to building a sales response model, each reflecting a different world view.[4] These are stochastic and econometric approaches.

At the present time, stochastic and econometric models of sales response embody different perspectives on how sales are produced. The stochastic model presumes that sales determination is a probabilistic process and thus can be represented by some probability distribution. The econometric model presumes that sales are generated by a process that is part stochastic and part deterministic. The stochastic model builder is pleased when he achieves a good fit between his (purely) stochastic model and empirical data. The econometric model builder, on the other hand, seeks to maximize the deterministic explanation of sales behavior at the expense of stochastic residuals. Since the world, or at least all we are likely to know of it, is part stochastic and part deterministic, both approaches can make contributions to marketing science although the econometric model seems to us to be a more reasonable gestalt. On the criterion of an ideal sales response function, however, the difference is a practical one: Econometric models have a comparative advantage in representing marketing mix, carryover, competitive and simultaneous effects, and the dimensions of marketing decisions.

There is quite a large amount of literature on the stochastic modeling of sales response, the key sources being Massy, Montgomery and Morrison (1970) and Haines (1969) with contributions by Aaker (1971, 1973), Herniter (1971), Bernhardt and Mackenzie (1972), and others. In discussing these models, Montgomery and Urban [(1969, 53-54] suggest the spirit of this research approach.

Stochastic models allow for a multitude of the factors that affect consumer behavior by means of response uncertainty. That is, market responses are regarded as outcomes of some probabilistic process. The impact of all factors not explicitly considered in the model is accounted for in the stochastic nature of the response. In a given model these exogenous factors might include the firm's marketing mix, competitive activity, and customer characteristics. Thus the problem of describing and predicting customer response is reduced to the problem of specifying and estimating a probability law for the response of interest. This procedure is parsimonious in that consumer behavior may often be described by relatively simple stochastic models, whereas the adoption of a deterministic approach would require exceedingly complex models.

An argument for parsimony is always appealing but sometimes without merit if crucial factors are consequently omitted. Let us consider the balance sheet of stochastic models. On the asset side, stochastic models are relatively easy to build (given some mathematical sophistication on the part of the model builder), can utilize typically available data (such as panel data), can often be solved analytically, and are, of course, relatively parsimonious. Most make statements about individual behavior (brand choice, loyalty, and learning models), although others deal with more aggregate processes (diffusion models). To achieve the level of aggregation that we have argued is necessary for marketing planning, most stochastic models must add together their individual behavior outputs. This technique has been used by Massy (1969) and may not be too severe a limitation (although it is not parsimonious!). In this same paper, Massy makes an interesting argument for the use of a stochastic, disaggregative approach to forecasting new product demand and the comparative disadvantage of econometric models in this special case.[5]

On the liability side of stochastic modeling of sales response functions, we find two major factors, one substantive and one methodological. In terms of substance, most extant stochastic models are incapable of incorporating marketing decision variables. Now clearly, this is a major limitation since it does not provide the mechanism that represents the core of a marketing decision model. A stochastic model can trace out paths of individual consumer behavior, treating them as a probabilistic process, but the behavior is not influenced, at least explicitly, by marketing factors. Some attempts have been made to deal with this problem, including Telser (1962a), Haines (1964), and more recently MacLachlan (1972). At this time, however, stochastic models cannot be used without modification as sales response functions in decision models.

The methodological limitation revolves around the procedures for validating stochastic models and is, in essence, the argument against using goodness of fit as a test of a theory [cf. Bass (1969b)]. The fact that a variety of stochastic (or any) models may fit the data equally well shows that this criterion does not provide a meaningful basis for discriminating among the models as theories of market response. Models with high R^2's may, of course, be useful for forecasting purposes and in this regard stochastic models can be an important management tool. As we have noted above, this forecasting role for stochastic models is especially significant in new product situations where no stable market process has (by definition) yet developed. The model testing issue also applies to econometric models of sales response, but there is often other information available to evaluate the model as a theory. In particular, the relationships between marketing variables and sales and even their coefficients of response can be specified *a priori*. This "prior knowledge," then, can be employed in testing the model. These arguments are explained in more detail in Chap. 5. For stochastic models, this approach is more tenuous since there is no strong reason why a certain probabilistic process should obtain.[6]

Now at this point we are not prepared to declare econometric models to be the final answer to these model building and testing questions. This book itself illustrates the many problems which remain to be overcome. Still, there are several important features of econometric models which make them appropriate vehicles for representing sales response behavior. They should be regarded not so much as comparative advantages over stochastic models, but as factors conducive to this whole line of research.

First, econometric models of sales response embody a world view that recognizes both the deterministic and stochastic nature of the process of sales determination. Sales are not purely a probabilistic outcome, but rather the result of certain determining factors (such as relative price and advertising, consumer incomes, etc.) plus a random component. The random part can be regarded as a proxy for variables that we are unable to observe, to measure or even to discover, the implication being that omniscience would drive the randomness to zero. On the other hand, the random component may be thought to represent a true behavioral phenomenon in the sense that human behavior always has some positive randomness that can be summarized (described) by a probability model, or random disturbance term in this case, but not necessarily explained. The appropriate interpretation of the random component may be a function of the level of aggregation. Certainly, in models of individual behavior, we subscribe to the second view.

Second, econometric models, because of their world view, can accomodate those elements that define an ideal sales response function. Although it is by no means an easy task, the various complexities of marketing processes, including important marketing policy variables, can be handled within the econometric framework. In some cases, recourse may be necessary to non-traditional techniques for estimating model parameters (search techniques) or to other methods such as simulation (see below) for operationalizing the model, but the basic econometric approach will hold. Econometrics can thus provide an explicit methodology for dealing with systematic factors of market response that are relevant to both scientists and managers.

Third, appropriate procedures are available for testing the theory represented by an econometric model. A well-ordered set of tests, ranging from predictive tests on model parameters to tests of dynamic stability (and including the assessment of goodness of fit), provide a rigorous evaluation of the theoretical basis for the model. Beyond this scientific trait, econometric models have a good deal of "face validity" for managers and, given our pragmatic goal, this is no small advantage. An econometric sales response function has this property precisely because it represents those factors that managers and researchers believe influence sales. As a codification of their experience and judgment, an econometric sales response model has practical as well as theoretical significance.

Simulation Models

Simulation complements the econometric and stochastic approaches to building sales response models by providing a methodology that can incorporate them in a more complex model or can augment them in a more complex model. Simulation has been defined as "the use of a process to model a process" [Schultz and Sullivan (1972)] and this flexible technique seems quite appropriate to the representation of sales response processes. There are many applications of simulation in marketing [cf. Kotler and Schultz (1970)], but the ones of concern here are those simulations that are models of some sales response process. This includes the work of Balderston and Hoggatt (1962), Preston and Collins (1966), Kuehn and Weiss (1965), Herniter and Cook (1970), and the extensive work of Amstutz (1967).

One use of simulation in modeling sales response functions is to provide a vehicle for incorporating econometric or stochastic models in a more complex version of the sales response mechanism. For example, most simulations embody stochastic processes and require some (usually econometric) technique for estimating the parameters of the model. Thus, simulation is not independent from these other modeling techniques. In cases where simple econometric or stochastic models do not adequately represent the process generating sales, a more complex model may be required and this often leads to simulation as a way of handling the integration of the (otherwise separate) approaches. When a stochastic model is used to trace out time paths of market behavior, it can be interpreted as simulation of a dynamic market process; similarly, when the dynamics of an econometric model are explored numerically, this process can be thought of as a simulation of market behavior.[7] Examples of such stochastic and econometric simulations are given in Massy (1969) and Schultz and Dodson (1974b).

Another use of simulation in sales response research is in the construction of more complete models of marketing behavior. Models that include various aspects of individual consumer behavior, the structure of distribution systems, marketing-production-finance interfaces, governmental relationships, and so forth, necessarily exceed the power of purely stochastic and econometric approaches. In this case, where the model builder seeks to put sales response functions into a broader marketing context, simulation becomes a logical way of dealing with the increased scope of the investigation. The additional flexibility and capability of simulation is not obtained without increased costs. The model development, data collection, parameter estimation, model solving, and implementation costs associated with the simulation approach can be substantial and must, of course, be weighed against the expected benefits of more complete modeling.

RECAPITULATION

In this chapter we have been concerned with the development and implementation of marketing decision models and with means of research and modeling to that end. Because of the applied orientation of such work, we have attempted to constrain our scientific bent with the practical requirements of marketing decision making. This line of thinking has resulted in the following conclusions.

First, there is a good deal of promise in the idea of decision models and, in particular, in *empirical* decision models. Second, sales response functions are the foundation of empirical decision models and, as such, must be developed with certain ideals in mind. Third, of the two major approaches to obtaining sales response models, econometric techniques offer a number of advantageous features, including the implied world view, the ability to handle marketing decision variables, and an appropriate testing procedure, that make them viable research tools. Fourth, simulation offers a complementary approach to modeling sales response functions that can be useful in obtaining more complete and perhaps more relevant decision models. Finally, considerable research must be undertaken before the promise of empirical decision models will become a reality.

These conclusions, especially the last, motivate this chapter and in the following chapters we provide discussions of the major techniques incident to and primary issues surrounding the development and implementation of such marketing decision technology. In Part Two, we present the econometric model-building approach. In Part Three, we discuss econometric research in marketing. And, in Part Four, we analyze policy and research implications of the work.

FOOTNOTES

[1] We will sometimes refer to "the" model. Our meaning is that this model is the one under consideration or discussion, not that it is the only true representation.

[2] Another aspect of the representativeness of a decision model is its compatibility with the user organization. This notion is pursued in Chap. 11.

[3] Two further points are relevant here. First, even with more complete behavioral knowledge, the aggregate models may be preferred on a cost-benefits basis. Second, for studying the structure of marketing systems, competitive behavior, marketing-production-finance interfaces, etc., aggregate models are the natural constructs for scientific investigation.

[4] A third approach would be one that asserts that the world is deterministic. In some respects, the work of Ehrenberg (1972) uses this perspective, although his major contribution, NBD theory, is stochastic. Models focused on individual stochastic behavior, such as Herniter (1973) and Bass (1974), are excluded from this discussion.

[5] Massy's points, that disaggregative data allow more detailed modeling (e.g., depth of trial stratification) but also lead to complex, nonlinear functions, support stochastic vs. econometric methods. In new product situations, however, the stochastic approach may be more appropriate simply because of lack of data.

[6] Additional problems with the stochastic approach are discussed in Montgomery and Urban [(1969), 85-93]. An analysis of stochastic model testing issues appears in Massy, Montgomery and Morrison [(1970), Chap. 2].

[7] We are referring here to exploring the dynamic implications of stochastic and econmetric models numerically rather than analytically. Analytical procedures are also available, but they are not "simulations."

Part Two.   The Econometric Model-Building Approach

Chapter 3

LINEAR ECONOMETRIC MODELS

Most marketing theories are not very detailed. At best, we usually only know the signs of relationships among variables. Consequently, model builders tend to begin with simple linear models which subsequently can be elaborated if necessary. Moreover, even nonlinear market mechanisms freqently are linear over the range of observations available. In addition, many marketing variables are measured with considerable error. The relationship among observed variables is apt to be more linear than the relationship among the true variables. All in all, linear models are very robust.[1]

Econometrics covers a number of techniques for estimating the parameters of a model. The choice of the appropriate technique depends on the nature of the model and its assumptions. We will impose a set of strong assumptions so that our discussion may be self-contained. Even with these assumptions, the choice of an appropriate technique is somewhat indeterminant. For some procedures our knowledge of the properties of the estimators is limited to asymptotic results. Knowledge of exact finite results are required in order to make the correct choice when the sample size is small.

We will begin with the required assumptions and associated terminology, will turn to how to choose the appropriate technique, and will end with a discussion of each of the major "least-squares" techniques.[2] We will restrict ourselves to linear models. See Goldfeld and Quandt (1972) for an introduction to nonlinear methods.

THE SIMULTANEOUS LINEAR
STRUCTURAL EQUATION MODEL

Classification of Variables

Within a dynamic simultaneous equation model, it is possible to make several distinctions among the variables. The first dichotomy is between whether the variables pertain to the present time period or to previous time periods. The former are called current variables, the latter, lagged variables. For simplicity, we will consider only one period lags. The second dichotomy is between whether the values of the variables are determined in a way that is independent of the operation of mechanism of the model or are determined by the model. The former are called exogenous variables, the latter, endogenous variables. The third dichotomy is between whether or not the variable is stochastically independent[3] of all current and future disturbances in the model. The former are called predetermined, the latter, current endogenous. The predetermined variables include lagged endogenous variables as well as both current and lagged exogenous variables. The fourth dichotomy is between whether or not within a given equation the variable is to be explained. The former is called a dependent variable, the latter are called explanatory variables. When an equation contains only one current endogenous variable, it is the dependent variable. The explanatory variables are predetermined variables. When an equation contains more than one current endogenous variable, one must be the dependent variable while the others are classified as explanatory variables along with the predetermined variables. These concepts will be illustrated in the example in the next section. First, the concept of a dummy variable will be introduced.

A qualitative variable such as sex may be represented by dummy variables. There is one dummy variable for each characteristic such as male or female. If an intercept is present, it must represent one of the characteristics. When the characteristic is present, the value of the dummy variable is one; if it is absent, its value is zero. The dummy variable usually captures a shift in the intercept, but it can be used to capture a shift in a slope parameter (see Chap. 4).

Palda (1964) represented changes in the quality of Lydia Pinkham's advertising copy over the period from 1908 to 1960 by three dummy variables. The first dummy was assigned the value of one from 1908 to 1914 and of zero thereafter. The second dummy was assigned the value of zero from 1908 to 1914, the value of one from 1915 to 1925, and the value of zero thereafter. The third dummy was assigned the value of zero from 1908 to 1925, the value of one from 1926 to 1940, and the value of zero thereafter. The copy effect in the period 1941 to 1960 was reflected in the intercept. Stobaugh and Townsend (1975) represented the degree of product standardization of petrochemicals by a dummy variable. The dummy variable was assigned a value of one for petrochemicals sold as a specific chemical and of zero for petrochemicals sold primarily on the basis of performance.

The Structural Form

The existence of a theory which predicts a relationship among the variables within an equation causes an equation to be structural. This theory provides the *a priori* information necessary to perceive the structure to be estimated, that is, to distinguish it from the other structures capable of generating the observed data. This is the identification problem.

Suppose that the market mechanism for a frequently purchased grocery product can be described by three linear equations. The first relationship specifies that the current sales of the product are explained by the current retail availability, the current advertising expenditure, the sales in the previous period, and the current price. The second relationship specifies that current retail availability is explained by current advertising expenditures and sales in the previous period. The third relationship specifies that current advertising expenditures are explained by current sales, advertising in the previous period, and the current price. This set of three relationships comprise the structural equations.

$$Q_\alpha = \gamma_{21}D_\alpha + \gamma_{31}A_\alpha + \beta_{11}Q_{\alpha-1} + (0)A_{\alpha-1} + \beta_{31}P_\alpha + \beta_{41}(1) - \epsilon_{\alpha 1}, \quad (3.1)$$

$$D_\alpha = (0)Q_\alpha + \gamma_{32}A_\alpha + \beta_{12}Q_{\alpha-1} + (0)A_{\alpha-1} + (0)P_\alpha + \beta_{42}(1) - \epsilon_{\alpha 2}, \quad (3.2)$$

$$A_\alpha = \gamma_{13}Q_\alpha + (0)D_\alpha + (0)Q_{\alpha-1} + \beta_{23}A_{\alpha-1} + \beta_{33}P_\alpha + \beta_{43}(1) - \epsilon_{\alpha 3}, \quad (3.3)$$

where

Q = unit sales
D = retail availability
A = advertising expenditures

P = price
1 = constant for the intercept
ϵ = random disturbances

There are three current endogenous variables ($Q_\alpha, D_\alpha, A_\alpha$). The predetermined variables include two lagged endogenous variables

$(Q_{\alpha-1}, A_{\alpha-1})$ and two current exogenous variables $(P_\alpha, 1)$. Sales is the dependent variable in the first equation. The explanatory variables include two other current edogenous variables (D_α, A_α), one lagged endogenous variable $(Q_{\alpha-1})$, and two exogenous variables $(P_\alpha, 1)$. Variables in the next two equations in the model also could be similarly classified. If there are n observations, the model can be expressed in matrix notation as:

$$
\begin{bmatrix} Q_1 & D_1 & A_1 \\ Q_2 & D_2 & A_2 \\ \cdot & \cdot & \cdot \\ \cdot & \cdot & \cdot \\ \cdot & \cdot & \cdot \\ Q_n & D_n & A_n \end{bmatrix}
\begin{bmatrix} -1 & 0 & \gamma_{13} \\ \gamma_{21} & -1 & 0 \\ \gamma_{31} & \gamma_{32} & -1 \end{bmatrix}
+
\begin{bmatrix} Q_0 & A_0 & P_1 & 1 \\ Q_1 & A_1 & P_2 & 1 \\ \cdot & \cdot & \cdot & \cdot \\ \cdot & \cdot & \cdot & \cdot \\ \cdot & \cdot & \cdot & \cdot \\ Q_{n-1} & A_{n-1} & P_n & 1 \end{bmatrix}
\begin{bmatrix} \beta_{11} & \beta_{12} & 0 \\ 0 & 0 & \beta_{23} \\ \beta_{31} & 0 & \beta_{33} \\ \beta_{41} & \beta_{42} & \beta_{43} \end{bmatrix}
$$

$$
=
\begin{bmatrix} \epsilon_{11} & \epsilon_{12} & \epsilon_{13} \\ \epsilon_{21} & \epsilon_{22} & \epsilon_{23} \\ \cdot & \cdot & \cdot \\ \cdot & \cdot & \cdot \\ \cdot & \cdot & \cdot \\ \epsilon_{n1} & \epsilon_{n2} & \epsilon_{n3} \end{bmatrix}
\tag{3.4}
$$

or more compactly as

$$
\mathbf{Y\Gamma} + \mathbf{XB} = \mathbf{E}. \tag{3.5}
$$

Equation (3.5) can also represent a more general model.

    We will consider only models containing as many equations as current endogenous variables. When this condition is met, the system is said to be complete. Suppose there arc n observations on a system of L equations. Then the data on the current endogenous variables are placed in the matrix $\mathbf{Y}$. Since the system is complete, the matrix $\mathbf{\Gamma}$, which contains the coefficients of the current endogenous variables in each equation, is square. Furthermore, the matrix $\mathbf{\Gamma}$ is assumed to be nonsingular.

$$
\mathbf{Y} = \begin{bmatrix} y_{11} & y_{12} & \cdots & y_{1L} \\ y_{21} & y_{22} & \cdots & y_{2L} \\ \cdot & \cdot & & \cdot \\ \cdot & \cdot & & \cdot \\ \cdot & \cdot & & \cdot \\ y_{n1} & y_{n2} & \cdots & y_{nL} \end{bmatrix}
\qquad
\Gamma = \begin{bmatrix} -1 & \gamma_{12} & \cdots & \gamma_{1L} \\ \gamma_{21} & -1 & \cdots & \gamma_{2L} \\ \cdot & \cdot & & \cdot \\ \cdot & \cdot & & \cdot \\ \cdot & \cdot & & \cdot \\ \gamma_{L1} & \gamma_{L2} & \cdots & -1 \end{bmatrix}
\qquad (3.6)
$$

The equations have been arranged so that the ith variable in the ith equation is that equation's dependent variable.

The observations on the predetermined variables, either exogenous or lagged endogenous or both, are found in the matrix $\mathbf{X}$. The intercept constant is represented by a variable whose values always equal one. The coefficients of the predetermined variables in each equation are contained in the matrix $\mathbf{B}$.

$$
\mathbf{X} = \begin{bmatrix} x_{11} & x_{12} & \cdots & x_{1k} \\ x_{21} & x_{22} & \cdots & x_{2k} \\ \cdot & \cdot & & \cdot \\ \cdot & \cdot & & \cdot \\ \cdot & \cdot & & \cdot \\ x_{n1} & x_{n2} & \cdots & x_{nk} \end{bmatrix}
\qquad
\mathbf{B} = \begin{bmatrix} \beta_{11} & \beta_{12} & \cdots & \beta_{1L} \\ \beta_{21} & \beta_{22} & \cdots & \beta_{2L} \\ \cdot & \cdot & & \cdot \\ \cdot & \cdot & & \cdot \\ \cdot & \cdot & & \cdot \\ \beta_{k1} & \beta_{k2} & \cdots & \beta_{kL} \end{bmatrix}
\qquad (3.7)
$$

It is assumed that there are no linear dependencies among the predetermined variables. Violation of this assumption is called multicollinearity. We will require that the moment matrix of the exogenous variables converge to a nonstochastic limit as the sample size goes toward infinity.

Finally, the disturbances are contained in the matrix E.

$$
\mathbf{E} = \begin{bmatrix} \epsilon_{11} & \epsilon_{12} & \cdots & \epsilon_{1L} \\ \epsilon_{21} & \epsilon_{22} & \cdots & \epsilon_{2L} \\ \cdot & \cdot & & \cdot \\ \cdot & \cdot & & \cdot \\ \cdot & \cdot & & \cdot \\ \epsilon_{n1} & \epsilon_{n2} & \cdots & \epsilon_{nL} \end{bmatrix} .
\qquad (3.8)
$$

An identity (or definitional equation) is an equation which has no unknown parameters and whose disturbance is always zero. Obviously, the presence of an identity would result in its column in matrix **E** containing only zeros. The absence of definitional equations from the model will be assumed. This assumption is made to simplify our exposition.

In order that the estimates of the unknown parameters in matrices Γ and **B** have certain desirable statistical properties, assumptions are made about the disturbances. The rows of the disturbance matrix are assumed to be stochastically independent and identically distributed with zero mean vector and an unknown but finite covariance matrix Σ. The matrix Σ, the contemporaneous convariance matrix of disturbances in different equations, is the same for all periods. The problem of heteroscedasticity arises when the variances are not constant.

$$\Sigma = \begin{bmatrix} \sigma_{11} & \sigma_{12} & \cdots & \sigma_{1L} \\ \sigma_{21} & \sigma_{22} & \cdots & \sigma_{2L} \\ \cdot & \cdot & & \cdot \\ \cdot & \cdot & & \cdot \\ \cdot & \cdot & & \cdot \\ \sigma_{L1} & \sigma_{L2} & \cdots & \sigma_{LL} \end{bmatrix} . \qquad (3.9)$$

More specifically, this assumption states that the mean value for the disturbances in a particular equation is zero. Furthermore, it implies that all lagged covariances between disturbances in the same or different equations are zero. The former restriction can be written as

$$E(\epsilon_l \epsilon_l') = \sigma_{ll} I \qquad l = 1, \ldots, L. \qquad (3.10)$$

Lastly, it permits the lagged endogenous variables to be considered predetermined variables. These predetermined variables are assumed to be independent of the disturbances. The contemporaneous covariance matrix is assumed to be positive definite (assuming that the system contains no identities). The rows of the disturbance matrix are assumed to be normally distributed.

Reduced Form and Final Form

The structural equation system can be transformed into a logically equivalent system of equations in which each member equation contains only one endogenous variable:

$$\mathbf{Y} = - \mathbf{XB\Gamma}^{-1} + \mathbf{E\Gamma}^{-1} \equiv \mathbf{X\Pi} + \mathbf{U} . \tag{3.11}$$

This new system is called the reduced form. Each reduced-form equation contains all the predetermined variables in the equation system. The contemporaneous covariance matrix of the reduced-form disturbances is

$$\Omega = (\mathbf{\Gamma'})^{-1} \, \Sigma \mathbf{\Gamma}^{-1} . \tag{3.12}$$

The reduced form can be transformed further so that each current endogenous variable is described solely in terms of current and lagged exogenous variables and disturbances. The resultant system is called the final form. Recall that we have restricted our lagged variables so that they consist only of one period lags. The reduced form can be partitioned and rearranged so that

$$\mathbf{y}_\alpha = \mathbf{d}_0 + \mathbf{D}_1 \mathbf{y}_{\alpha-1} + \mathbf{D}_2 \mathbf{x}_\alpha + \mathbf{D}_3 \mathbf{x}_{\alpha-1} + \epsilon_\alpha^* , \tag{3.13}$$

where

$\mathbf{y}_\alpha$ = vector of endogenous variables in period α.

$\mathbf{x}_\alpha$ = vector of exogenous variables (excluding the constant variable)

ϵ_α^* = vector of reduced-form disturbances.

By lagging Eq. (3.13) one period and substituting back and repeating this procedure s times and then letting s go to infinity, the final form is obtained:

$$\mathbf{y}_\alpha = (\mathbf{I} - \mathbf{D}_1)^{-1} \mathbf{d}_0 + \mathbf{D}_2 \mathbf{x}_\alpha + \sum_{t=1}^{\infty} \mathbf{D}_1^{t-1} (\mathbf{D}_1 \mathbf{D}_2 + \mathbf{D}_3) \mathbf{x}_{\alpha-t} + \sum_{t=0}^{\infty} \mathbf{D}_1^t \epsilon_{\alpha-t}^* . \tag{3.14}$$

The system is stable if the roots of $\mathbf{D}_1$ are all less than one in absolute value.

Another perspective on stability comes when we rewrite the structural model (3.5) as

$$Y\Gamma + X_0 B_0 + Y_{-1} B_1 = E, \qquad\qquad (3.15)$$

where

Y_{-1} = matrix of endogenous variables lagged one period
X_0 = matrix of exogenous variables.

Then, we will require that all roots of the determinantal equation $|z\Gamma + B_1| = 0$ have absolute values less than one. Each solution of z is a latent root of the reduced form matrix $-B_1 \Gamma^{-1}$ of the lagged endogenous variables.

Even with the numerous assumptions made thus far, we are still not ready for estimation. We must address ourselves to the identification problem. A summary of our assumptions is provided in Table 3.1.

Table 3.1

List of Assumptions

A1	Model is linear
A2	Maximum lag equals one period
A3	Model is complete
A4	Matrix Γ is nonsingular
A5	Predetermined variables are linearly independent
A6	Moment matrix of exogenous variables converges
A7	Model contains no identities
A8	Rows of disturbance matrix are assumed to be stochastically independent
A9	Disturbances are identically distributed with zero mean and an unknown but finite covariance matrix Σ
A10	Matrix Σ is positive definite
A11	Model is stable
A12	Disturbances are normally distributed
A13	Equations are identified

IDENTIFICATION

The ability to express the structural parameters as explicit functions of the reduced-form parameters is unfortunately not automatic and, indeed, is sometimes impossible. Determination of whether there is a one-to-one correspondence between the structural parameters and the reduced-form parameters is called the identification problem. Identification is logically prior to estimation.[4]

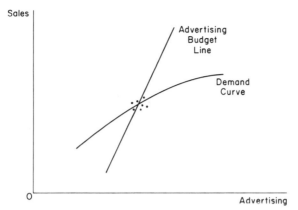

Fig. 3.1. Neither curve shifts.

The identification problem may be easier to understand if we return to our example of the electric company.[5] Our primary interest is in statistically estimating the demand curve, not the advertising budget line. These two hypothetical relationships are drawn in Fig. 3.1, along with the observations available to the market researcher. If the two curves do not shift over time, but maintain their present positions and if other external marketing factors have minimal effect, then our observed data collected over time will be densely clustered around the intersection of the two curves. This scatter of points does not provide any information about the shape of either curve and so we say that neither curve is identified.

A more frequent case occurs when the demand curve shifts while the firm's advertising budgeting practices remain rigid. In such situations, there will be a series of different intersection points, but they will merely trace out the advertising budget line (Fig. 3.2). One danger lies in mistaking the advertising budget line for the demand curve. In this example, the advertising budget line is identified, whereas the demand curve is not.

Both curves can be identified only when both curves shift over time. The observations available from such a process may bear no resemblance to either curve (Fig. 3.3). The fact that the plot of the observations reveals a long and narrow dispersion is not in itself sufficient to ensure that the observed dependence expresses one of the relationships. Both curves could shift simultaneously resulting in the observations lying along the path of their point of intersection.

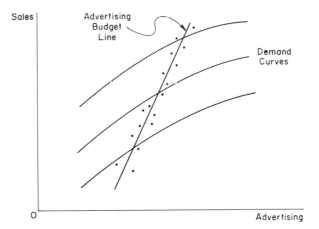

Fig. 3.2. Demand curve shifts.

How may we, in principle, test whether the relationships we are seeking are identifiable? A sufficient condition for identification of the two relationships is that some distinguishable factors influencing advertising may leave demand unchanged and some distinguishable factors affecting demand may not influence advertising.

To evaluate whether an equation is sufficiently distinctive from the others in its system, we examine the *a priori* information available. There are several types of *a priori* information. Two structural parameters may be known (or assumed) to be equal, to sum to a known constant, or to have a known ratio. The covariance

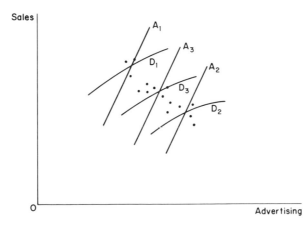

Fig. 3.3. Both curves shift.

between two structural disturbances might be known to be zero. We will focus on the most important of these *a priori* restrictions, the one that tells us which variables are absent in a particular equation. Let us return to the example of the frequently purchased grocery product. In Eq. (3.1) we have the *a priori* restriction that lagged advertising does not enter the equation; that is, its coefficient (β_{21}) is zero.

We may use the following rule, called the order condition for identifiability, to assist us. For an equation in a model consisting of L linear equations to be identified, the equation must exclude at least $L-1$ of the variables contained in that model (i.e., their coefficients are zero). The key to this rule is the realization that by excluding a variable we are also omitting an unknown parameter. While logically an equation may satisfy this rule, yet remain unidentified, pragmatically when we restrict ourselves to the omitted variables case any equation fulfilling this rule may be considered identified. In our system (3.1)-(3.3) we have three equations so the $L = 3$. Thus, a minimum of $L-1 = 2$ coefficients are required to be zero in order to achieve identification. In our first equation, only one coefficient (β_{21}) is zero. We therefore say our first equation is not identified. Three coefficients ($\gamma_{12}, \beta_{22}, \beta_{32}$) are zero in the second equation and we say that this equation is overidentified. In the last equation exactly two coefficients (γ_{23}, β_{13}) are missing so we say that it is just identified.

Bass (1969) proposed the following four equation model of sales and advertising of cigarettes:

$$-1Q_{\alpha 1} + (0)Q_{\alpha 2} + \gamma_{31}A_{\alpha 1} + \gamma_{41}A_{\alpha 2}$$
$$+ \beta_{11}X_{\alpha 1} + \beta_{21}P_{\alpha 2} + \beta_{31}(1) + \epsilon_{\alpha 1} = 0, \qquad (3.16)$$

$$(0)Q_{\alpha 1} - 1Q_{\alpha 2} + \gamma_{32}A_{\alpha 1} + \gamma_{42}A_{\alpha 2}$$
$$+ \beta_{12}X_{\alpha 1} + \beta_{22}P_{\alpha 2} + \beta_{32}(1) + \epsilon_{\alpha 2} = 0, \qquad (3.17)$$

$$-1Q_{\alpha 1} + \gamma_{23}Q_{\alpha 2} + \gamma_{33}A_{\alpha 1} + (0)A_{\alpha 2}$$
$$+ (0)X_{\alpha 1} + (0)P_{\alpha 2} + \beta_{33}(1) + \epsilon_{\alpha 3} = 0, \qquad (3.18)$$

$$\gamma_{14}Q_{\alpha 1} - 1Q_{\alpha 2} + (0)A_{\alpha 1} + \gamma_{44}A_{\alpha 2}$$
$$+ (0)X_{\alpha 1} + (0)P_{\alpha 2} + \beta_{34}(1) + \epsilon_{\alpha 4} = 0, \qquad (3.19)$$

where the variables are all in logarithmic form. These variables include per capita sales of filter and nonfilter cigarettes, Q_1 and Q_2, respectively, per capita real advertising expenditures of filter and nonfilter cigarettes, A_1 and A_2, respectively, per capita real income, X_1, and the real price of nonfilter cigarettes, P_2.

Dominguez and Page (1971) pointed out that the key sales response equations, (3.16) and (3.17), are not identified. The order condition requires that at least $(4-1) = 3$ coefficients in each equation be zero. Only one coefficient in each of these two equations is zero. Bass (1971) responded that his concern was testing which is prior to estimation. However, we do not consider it meaningful to "test" an unidentified relation.

A more rigorous rule is called the rank condition for identifiability. Let us begin by defining the matrix of structural parameters as

$$A = [\Gamma' \quad B']. \tag{3.20}$$

Next, for each equation construct a matrix ϕ such that it contains a column for each *a priori* excluded variable. Each column will contain $L + K$ elements only one of which is nonzero. The position of the excluded variable will be indicated by a one. Then the rank condition requires for identification that

$$r(A\phi) = L - 1, \tag{3.21}$$

where $r(\ )$ stands for "rank of". Continuing with our example, we find that the matrix A is

$$A = \begin{bmatrix} -1 & \gamma_{21} & \gamma_{31} & \vdots & \beta_{11} & 0 & \beta_{31} & \beta_{41} \\ 0 & -1 & \gamma_{32} & \vdots & \beta_{12} & 0 & 0 & \beta_{42} \\ \gamma_{13} & 0 & -1 & \vdots & 0 & \beta_{23} & \beta_{33} & \beta_{43} \end{bmatrix} \tag{3.22}$$

Now let's examine the identifiability of each equation. The matrix ϕ will be a vector for the first equation since there is only one unknown:

$$\phi' = [0 \ 0 \ 0 \ 0 \ 1 \ 0 \ 0], \tag{3.23}$$

and

$$A\phi = \begin{bmatrix} 0 \\ 0 \\ \beta_{23} \end{bmatrix} . \tag{3.24}$$

The rank of $A\phi$ equals one if $\beta_{23} \neq 0$. This equation is not identified. For the second equation we find that

$$\phi' = \begin{bmatrix} 1 & 0 & 0 & 0 & 0 & 0 & 0 \\ 0 & 0 & 0 & 0 & 1 & 0 & 0 \\ 0 & 0 & 0 & 0 & 0 & 1 & 0 \end{bmatrix} , \tag{3.25}$$

and

$$A\phi = \begin{bmatrix} -1 & 0 & \beta_{31} \\ 0 & 0 & 0 \\ \gamma_{13} & \beta_{23} & \beta_{33} \end{bmatrix} . \tag{3.26}$$

The rank of $A\phi$ equals two if $-\beta_{23} \neq 0$ or $-\beta_{33} - \gamma_{13}\beta_{31} \neq 0$ or $-\beta_{23}\beta_{31} \neq 0$. Now turning to the third equation, we have

$$\phi = \begin{bmatrix} 0 & 1 & 0 & 0 & 0 & 0 & 0 \\ 0 & 0 & 0 & 1 & 0 & 0 & 0 \end{bmatrix} . \tag{3.27}$$

and

$$A\phi = \begin{bmatrix} \gamma_{21} & \beta_{11} \\ -1 & \beta_{12} \\ 0 & 0 \end{bmatrix} . \tag{3.28}$$

The rank of $A\phi$ is two if $\gamma_{21}\beta_{12} + \beta_{11} \neq 0$. The equation is identified. Since the true values of the structural parameters are unknown, estimates of the structural parameters may be used to test the hypothesis that the relevant determinant is zero. The prospect of failing the rank condition increases if there is an *a priori* mathematical relationship between the parameters.

The **A** matrix for Farley and Ring's operational version of the Howard-Sheth model of buyer behavior (see Chap. 12)[6] is

$$(3.29)$$

Inspection of the **A** matrix reveals that the order condition seems to be met. This is only an illusion as we will show in Chap. 12. However, our concern now is with the rank conditions. Lutz and Resek (1972) noted that a number of the equations failed to meet the rank condition. For instance, the **A**ϕ matrix for the first equation in the Farley-Ring is

$$
A\phi =
\begin{bmatrix}
0 & 0 & 0 & 0 & 0 & 0 & 0 & 0 & 0 & 0 & \cdots & 0 \\
-1 & \gamma_{23} & & & & & & & & & & \\
& -1 & & & & & & & & & & \\
\gamma_{42} & \gamma_{43} & & & & & & & & \beta_{4,5} & \cdots & \beta_{4,17} \\
0 & 0 & 0 & 0 & 0 & 0 & 0 & 0 & 0 & 0 & \cdots & 0 \\
\gamma_{62} & & -1 & & \gamma_{68} & & & & & \beta_{6,5} & \cdots & \beta_{6,17} \\
\gamma_{72} & & \gamma_{76} & -1 & & \gamma_{79} & & & & \beta_{7,5} & \cdots & \beta_{7,17} \\
\gamma_{82} & & & -1 & & & \gamma_{8,11} & & & & & \\
& & & \gamma_{98} & -1 & & & & & & & \\
& & \gamma_{10,6} & & & -1 & & \beta_{10,4} & & & & \\
& & & & \gamma_{11,10} & & & & & & &
\end{bmatrix}
$$

$$(3.30)$$

The rank of **A**ϕ is 9 or less. Minimally, the first equation can not be distinguished from the fifth equation and so it is not identified.

If the identifiability condition is met, the researcher may then proceed to estimate the parameters in his model. There are alternative techniques for this estimation. These include ordinary least squares, generalized least squares, seemingly unrelated equations estimation, indirect least squares, two-stage least squares, and three-stage least squares. We must decide which technique to use.

CHOOSING AN ESTIMATION METHOD

The choice among the alternatives will be made primarily on the basis of the nature of the matrix of coefficients of the current endogenous variables Γ and the contemporaneous covariance matrix Σ. Lack of knowledge of the exact finite sample properties of the estimators means that we cannot be sure that we have made the correct choice in situations involving small samples.

The first step is to examine the matrix Γ. If the matrix Γ is diagonal, the matrix Σ is examined. If the matrix Σ is diagonal, determine whether $E(\epsilon\epsilon') = \sigma^2 I$ or not. If it does, use ordinary least squares; if not, use generalized least squares. If the matrix Σ is not diagonal, use seemingly unrelated equations estimation methods. If the matrix Γ is triangular and the matrix Σ diagonal, apply ordinary least squares directly to the recursive model. For the remaining categories involving the matrix Γ, if the matrix Σ is not diagonal and some equations are overidentified while none are not identified, use three-stage least squares. If these conditions are not met, use indirect least squares or two-stage least squares depending on whether an equation is just identified or overidentified. Figure 3.4

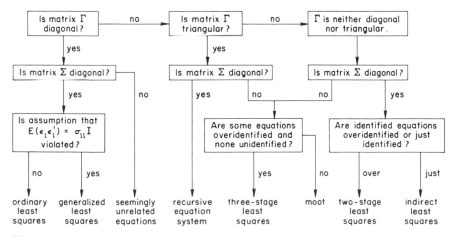

Fig. 3.4. Selection of an estimation method.

presents a diagram of this selection process. The exposition for each estimation method will center around the model, the estimating procedure, and the properties of the estimators.

The Model

We adopt Christ's definition that a structure is a set of autonomous relationships sufficient to determine uniquely the conditional probability distributions of the endogenous variables, given the value of the exogenous variables. A stochastic structure will also specify the form and parameters of the distribution of any disturbances. In addition, the structure specifies the numerical values of the structural coefficients. Since we do not yet know these numerical values, we will focus on the corresponding set of structures known as a model: We adopt the assumptions in Table 3.1 (relaxing them where noted) as part of our model. We will distinguish among classes of models on the basis of *a priori* information about the structural coefficients. With each of these broad classes of models will be associated a particular method for estimating the coefficients.

The Estimating Procedure

General methods for obtaining point estimators for the un-known parameters of a model include: (1) the maximum likelihood method, (2) the least-squares method, (3) the method of moments, and (4) the Bayesian method. The method of moments and the Bayesian method are not covered. The maximum likelihood method involves finding the value of a parameter that makes the probability of obtaining the observed sample outcome as high as possible. The method of least squares involves finding the values of the parameters that make the sum of squares of the deviations of the function as low as possible. The method of least squares is the method which will be used in our estimating procedure. However, this method does not permit hypothesis testing. So when possible, the results from the maximum likelihood method will be invoked. Whenever appropriate, references will be given to marketing articles that apply the estimating procedure under consideration. Full discussion of the marketing implications of these articles is left for subsequent chapters.

Properties of the Estimators

We are interested in the qualities that estimators possess. A brief review of these properties might be helpful. An estimator is *unbiased* if its expected value equals the population parameter being estimated. An estimator is *best unbiased* or *efficient* if among all the unbiased estimators, it possesses the minimum variance. Asymptotic properties appear only in the limit as the sample size tends to infinity. An estimator is *consistent* if it converges in probability to the value of the population parameter. An estimator is *asymptotically normally distributed* if it has a limiting distribution and that distribution is normal. An estimator is *asymptotically efficient* if its asymptotic variance is smaller than that of any other consistent and asymptotically normal estimator.

ORDINARY LEAST SQUARES

The Model

Each equation is independent of all other equations when the endogenous parameter matrix and the contemporaneous covariance matrix are both diagonal:

$$\mathbf{Y} = \begin{bmatrix} -1 & 0 & \cdots & 0 \\ 0 & -1 & \cdots & 0 \\ \cdot & \cdot & & \cdot \\ \cdot & \cdot & & \cdot \\ \cdot & \cdot & & \cdot \\ 0 & 0 & \cdots & -1 \end{bmatrix} + \mathbf{XB} = \mathbf{E}, \qquad (3.31)$$

and

$$\mathbf{\Sigma} = \begin{bmatrix} \sigma_{11} & 0 & \cdots & 0 \\ 0 & \sigma_{22} & \cdots & 0 \\ \cdot & \cdot & & \cdot \\ \cdot & \cdot & & \cdot \\ \cdot & \cdot & & \cdot \\ 0 & 0 & \cdots & \sigma_{LL} \end{bmatrix} \qquad (3.32)$$

The assumptions listed in Table 3.1 hold.

The Estimation Procedure

Given the above structure, each equation can be estimated separately. An individual equation can be written as

$$y = X\beta + \epsilon, \tag{3.33}$$

where ϵ is the disturbance vector. The corresponding equation of estimator is

$$y = X\hat{\beta} + e,$$

where e is the residual vector with elements $e_1, \ldots, e_n$. The principle of least squares is that the estimates of the parameters be chosen so as to make the sum of squared residuals as small as possible. The sum of squared residuals is written as

$$\sum e^2 = e'e = (y - X\hat{\beta})' \, (y - X\hat{\beta}) = y'y - 2y'X\hat{\beta} + \hat{\beta}'X'X\hat{\beta}. \tag{3.34}$$

The minimum sum of squared residuals is found by differentiating $e'e$ with respect to $\hat{\beta}$ and equating to zero.

$$\frac{\partial}{\partial\hat{\beta}} (e'e) = -2X'y + 2X'X\hat{\beta} \equiv 0. \tag{3.35}$$

The estimated coefficients are thus

$$\hat{\beta} = (X'X)^{-1}X'y. \tag{3.36}$$

By making use of the assumption that $E(\epsilon\epsilon') = V(\epsilon) = \sigma^2 I$, the covariance matrix of $\hat{\beta}$ can be derived:

$$V(\hat{\beta}) = \sigma^2 (X'X)^{-1}. \tag{3.37}$$

An unbiased estimator for the variance σ^2 can be shown to be

$$s^2 = \frac{e'e}{n - K}. \tag{3.38}$$

Least-squares estimation does not permit statistical inference. The results necessary for hypothesis testing are found by maximum likelihood estimation which makes use of the assumption that the disturbances are normally distributed. Although the maximum likelihood derivation is omitted, the results will be used.

Properties of the Estimators

The ordinary least-squares (OLS) estimator $\hat{\beta}$ is the best linear unbiased, that is, within the class of linear unbiased estimators the OLS estimator is the one with the smallest variance. The OLS estimator s^2 is an unbiased estimator for the variance σ^2. If we assume that the distribution of y is n-variate normal, then the OLS estimator $\hat{\beta}$ is normally distributed with mean vector β and covariance matrix $\sigma^2 (\mathbf{X'X})^{-1}$, and $(n - K) s^2 / \sigma^2$ is distributed as $\chi^2 (n - K)$.

Coefficient of Determination

A measure of the amount of variation in the dependent variable explained by predetermined variables is called the coefficient of determination or more commonly R^2. The fraction of the variation explained in the standard linear model is

$$R^2 \equiv 1 - \frac{\mathbf{e'e}}{\mathbf{y'Ay}} , \tag{3.39}$$

where $\mathbf{A} = \mathbf{I} - (1/n)\iota\iota'$ and ι is a vector containing n unit elements. This formulation does not count the contribution of the constant term. Extension of the coefficient of determination to distributed lag models and simultaneous equation models encounters serious difficulties in interpretation.

GENERALIZED LEAST SQUARES

The Model

The structure for generalized least squares (GLS) is the same as that for ordinary least squares with one exception. The assumption that $E(\epsilon\epsilon') = \sigma^2 \mathbf{I}$ is relaxed to the extent that it allows for heteroscedasticity and autocorrelation. The new assumption is that

$$E(\epsilon_l \epsilon_l') = \sigma_{ll}^2 \mathbf{V} \qquad l = 1, \ldots, L , \tag{3.40}$$

where σ^2 is an unknown finite positive parameter and $\mathbf{V}$ is a *known* symmetric positive definite matrix whose trace is equal to n.

The Estimation Procedure

The generalized least-squares estimator can be found by first transforming the data matrix so that the covariance matrix $\sigma^2 \mathbf{V}$ becomes $\sigma^2 \mathbf{I}$ and then applying ordinary least squares. There exists a transformation matrix $\mathbf{P}$ such that $\mathbf{P}'\mathbf{P} = \mathbf{V}^{-1}$. Then Eq. (3.33) can be written as

$$\mathbf{P}y = \mathbf{P}\mathbf{X}\beta + \mathbf{P}\epsilon, \tag{3.41}$$

with covariance matrix

$$\text{Var }(\mathbf{P}\epsilon) = \mathbf{P}E(\epsilon\epsilon')\mathbf{P}' = \sigma^2 \mathbf{P}\mathbf{V}\mathbf{P}' = \sigma^2 \mathbf{P}(\mathbf{P}'\mathbf{P})^{-1}\mathbf{P}' = \sigma^2 \mathbf{I}. \tag{3.42}$$

Replacing the original data matrices by the transformed data matrices in equation (3.36), GLS estimator is found to be

$$\hat{\beta} = [(\mathbf{P}\mathbf{X})'(\mathbf{P}\mathbf{X})]^{-1}(\mathbf{P}\mathbf{X})'(\mathbf{P}y) = [\mathbf{X}'\mathbf{P}'\mathbf{P}\mathbf{X}]^{-1}\mathbf{X}'\mathbf{P}'y \tag{3.43}$$

$$\hat{\beta} = (\mathbf{X}'\mathbf{V}^{-1}\mathbf{X})^{-1}\mathbf{X}'\mathbf{V}^{-1}y. \tag{3.44}$$

Sawyer (1973) used a special case of GLS called weighted least squares in his study of the effects of repetition of advertising appeals. His purpose was to correct for possible inequalities in the variance of observations due to differences in sample size.

The problem is that the matrix $\mathbf{V}$ is seldom known. The solution is a two-step procedure in which a consistent estimate $\hat{\mathbf{V}}$ of $\mathbf{V}$ is obtained and then an estimate $\hat{\beta}$ based on this $\hat{\mathbf{V}}$ is obtained. In the presence of lagged dependent variables and autocorrelated residuals, this two-step procedure must be repeated. If this iterative procedure converges, a solution is achieved [Maddala (1971a)].

Properties of the Estimators

When the matrix $\mathbf{V}$ is known, the properties of GLS estimators are the same as those for OLS as would be anticipated. The GLS estimator is best linear unbiased. Similarly $\hat{\sigma}^2$ is an unbiased estimator of σ^2. When $\mathbf{V}$ is unknown but a consistent estimate of it is available, GLS estimators are consistent.

SEEMINGLY UNRELATED EQUATIONS

The Model

Sometimes equations are seemingly unrelated because each equation contains only one dependent variable when, in fact, they are disturbance related. The contemporaneous covariance matrix is not a diagonal matrix:

$$\mathbf{Y} = \begin{bmatrix} -1 & 0 & \cdots & 0 \\ 0 & -1 & \cdots & 0 \\ \cdot & \cdot & & \cdot \\ \cdot & \cdot & & \cdot \\ \cdot & \cdot & & \cdot \\ 0 & 0 & \cdots & -1 \end{bmatrix} + \mathbf{XB} = \mathbf{E}. \tag{3.45}$$

and

$$\Sigma = \begin{bmatrix} \sigma_{11} & \sigma_{12} & \cdots & \sigma_{1L} \\ \sigma_{21} & \sigma_{22} & \cdots & \sigma_{2L} \\ \cdot & \cdot & & \cdot \\ \cdot & \cdot & & \cdot \\ \cdot & \cdot & & \cdot \\ \sigma_{L1} & \sigma_{L2} & \cdots & \sigma_{LL} \end{bmatrix}. \tag{3.46}$$

The assumptions in Table 3.1 hold.

Estimation Procedure

In the last section, generalized least squares was the method used when the disturbance covariances within a single equation were not zero. The goal is to reformulate the model so that generalized least squares may again be used. First recall that an individual equation can be written as

$$\mathbf{y}_j = \mathbf{X}_j \beta_j + \epsilon_j \qquad j = 1, \ldots, L . \tag{3.47}$$

Next, combining these equations and making the appropriate definitions

$$
\begin{bmatrix} y_1 \\ y_2 \\ \cdot \\ \cdot \\ \cdot \\ y_L \end{bmatrix} = \begin{bmatrix} X_1 & 0 & \cdots & 0 \\ 0 & X_2 & \cdots & 0 \\ \cdot & \cdot & & \cdot \\ \cdot & \cdot & & \cdot \\ \cdot & \cdot & & \cdot \\ 0 & 0 & \cdots & X_L \end{bmatrix} \begin{bmatrix} \beta_1 \\ \beta_2 \\ \cdot \\ \cdot \\ \cdot \\ \beta_L \end{bmatrix} + \begin{bmatrix} \epsilon_1 \\ \epsilon_2 \\ \cdot \\ \cdot \\ \cdot \\ \epsilon_L \end{bmatrix} \tag{3.48}
$$

the standard form, $y = X\beta + \epsilon$, results. The covariance matrix is now

$$
V(\epsilon) = \begin{bmatrix} \sigma_{11}I & \sigma_{12}I & \cdots & \sigma_{1L}I \\ \sigma_{21}I & \sigma_{22}I & \cdots & \sigma_{2L}I \\ \cdot & \cdot & & \cdot \\ \cdot & \cdot & & \cdot \\ \cdot & \cdot & & \cdot \\ \sigma_{L1}I & \sigma_{L2}I & \cdots & \sigma_{LL}I \end{bmatrix} = \Sigma \otimes I, \tag{3.49}
$$

where $\otimes$ denotes Kronecker multiplication. In Kronecker multiplication, every element in the first matrix is multiplied by the second matrix. All that is required to find the GLS estimator of β is the inverse of the covariance matrix, which is $\Sigma^{-1} \otimes I$. The estimator is

$$
\beta = [X'(\Sigma^{-1} \otimes I)X]^{-1} X'(\Sigma^{-1} \otimes I)y, \tag{3.50}
$$

which has the covariance matrix

$$
V(\hat{\beta}) = [X'(\Sigma^{-1} \otimes I)X]^{-1} \tag{3.51}
$$

Since Σ is usually unknown, it must be replaced by an estimate. A consistent estimator is the moment matrix of residuals from OLS. Similarly the moment matrix of GLS residuals could be used to reestimate Σ, and so on *iteratively* until convergence [Zellner (1962)]. Beckwith (1972), Wildt (1974), and Houston and Weiss (1974) used this procedure to analyze the response of competing brands to advertising expenditures. The procedure can be extended to take into account autocorrelated disturbances [Parks (1967)]. Clarke (1973) used an iterative version of Parks' method in his investigation of sales-advertising cross-elasticities.

RECURSIVE EQUATION SYSTEMS

The Model

Our attention now turns to equation systems in which a dependent variable is explained by not only predetermined variables but also endogenous variables. A special case is called a recursive equation system. A system which is not recursive is said to be interdependent. In a recursive system, the first equation contains only one of the current endogenous variables. The second equation contains a second current endogenous variable in addition to the dependent variable appearing in the first equation. The third equation adds a third endogenous variable to the two endogenous variables in the second equation. This pattern continues until the Lth equation contains all L current endogenous variables. The second feature of recursive systems is that the L disturbances at a given observation are stochastically independent. A recursive system can be written as

$$\mathbf{Y} = \begin{bmatrix} -1 & 0 & \cdots & 0 \\ \gamma_{21} & -1 & \cdots & 0 \\ \cdot & \cdot & & \cdot \\ \cdot & \cdot & & \cdot \\ \cdot & \cdot & & \cdot \\ \gamma_{L1} & \gamma_{L2} & \cdots & -1 \end{bmatrix} + \mathbf{XB} = \mathbf{E}. \tag{3.52}$$

and

$$\Sigma = \begin{bmatrix} \sigma_{11} & 0 & \cdots & 0 \\ 0 & \sigma_{22} & \cdots & 0 \\ \cdot & \cdot & & \cdot \\ \cdot & \cdot & & \cdot \\ \cdot & \cdot & & \cdot \\ 0 & 0 & \cdots & \sigma_{LL} \end{bmatrix}. \tag{3.53}$$

Due to the inadequate state of the marketing theory, extreme caution should be exercised when assuming that Σ is diagonal.

Identification

The triangularity of the matrix Γ is sufficient for the identification only of the first equation. The assumption that the matrix Σ is diagonal is necessary and sufficient for identification of the remaining $L-1$ equations. The rank condition can be modified to cover this case. An equation is identified if

$$r[A\phi \quad \Sigma] = L - 1. \qquad (3.54)$$

The Estimating Procedure

Because of its special structure in which the endogenous variables in any equation are "predetermined" by the preceding equations, ordinary least squares estimation may be used. Aaker and Day (1971) estimated the parameters of a recursive model of the communication process.

INDIRECT LEAST SQUARES

The parameters of any exactly identified structural equation can be found by indirect least squares. This method involves estimating the reduced form parameters, then deriving the structural parameters. Two-stage least squares is usually used instead of indirect least squares because it provides equivalent results and is computationally more convenient.

TWO-STAGE LEAST SQUARES

The Model

Two-stage least squares was developed to handle overidentified equations. The structural equations are written as

$$\mathbf{Y} = \begin{bmatrix} -1 & \gamma_{12} & \cdots & \gamma_{1L} \\ \gamma_{21} & -1 & \cdots & \gamma_{2L} \\ \cdot & \cdot & & \cdot \\ \cdot & \cdot & & \cdot \\ \cdot & \cdot & & \cdot \\ \gamma_{L1} & \gamma_{L2} & \cdots & -1 \end{bmatrix} + \mathbf{XB} = \mathbf{E}. \qquad (3.55)$$

with a diagonal contemporaneous covariance matrix

$$\Sigma = \begin{bmatrix} \sigma_{11} & 0 & \cdots & 0 \\ 0 & \sigma_{22} & \cdots & 0 \\ \cdot & \cdot & & \cdot \\ \cdot & \cdot & & \cdot \\ \cdot & \cdot & & \cdot \\ 0 & 0 & \cdots & \sigma_{LL} \end{bmatrix}. \tag{3.56}$$

The Estimating Procedure

Each equation can be written in terms of an explanatory matrix partitioned between endogenous and predetermined variables:

$$\mathbf{y}_j = [\mathbf{Y}_j \ \ \mathbf{X}_j] \begin{bmatrix} \gamma_j \\ \beta_j \end{bmatrix} + \epsilon_j. \tag{3.57}$$

The first stage consists of OLS applied to the reduced form

$$\mathbf{Y} = -\mathbf{XB}\Gamma^{-1} + \mathbf{E}\Gamma^{-1} \tag{3.11}$$

to obtain

$$\mathbf{Y} = \hat{\mathbf{Y}} + \mathbf{U}, \tag{3.58}$$

where

$$\hat{\mathbf{Y}} = \mathbf{X}(\mathbf{X'X})^{-1}\mathbf{X'Y}, \tag{3.59}$$

and $\mathbf{U}$ is the matrix of reduced-form OLS residuals.
Equation (3.57) can now be replaced by

$$\mathbf{y}_j = [\mathbf{Y}_j - \mathbf{U}_j \ \ \mathbf{X}_j] \begin{bmatrix} \gamma_j \\ \beta_j \end{bmatrix} + \epsilon_j + \mathbf{U}_j \gamma_j \tag{3.60}$$

Now the observation matrix contains only nonstochastic elements. The second stage consists of OLS applied to Eq. (3.60). The estimators are found by solving the normal equations:

$$\begin{bmatrix} (\mathbf{Y}_j - \mathbf{U}_j)'\mathbf{y}_j \\ \mathbf{X}_j'\mathbf{y}_j \end{bmatrix} = \begin{bmatrix} \mathbf{Y}_j'\mathbf{Y}_j - \mathbf{U}_j'\mathbf{U}_j & \mathbf{Y}_j\mathbf{X}_j \\ \mathbf{X}_j'\mathbf{Y}_j & \mathbf{X}_j'\mathbf{X}_j \end{bmatrix} \begin{bmatrix} \gamma_j \\ \beta_j \end{bmatrix} \tag{3.61}$$

The method of two-stage least squares (2SLS) is the most popular of the simultaneous equation estimating procedures. This method has been applied by Farley and Leavitt (1968) to a model of the distribution of branded personal products in Jamaica; by Bass (1969) and Rao (1971) to models of the sales-advertising relationship of cigarettes; by Bass and Parsons (1969) to an analysis of sales and advertising of a frequently purchased grocery product[7]; by Dalrymple and Haines (1969) in an investigation of market period demand-supply relations for a firm selling fashion products; by Farley and Ring (1970) to an evaluation of the Howard-Seth model of buyer behavior; by Samuels (1970) to the advertising and sales of household cleansers; and by Cowling (1972) to the advertising and sales of various products.

Properties of the Estimators

The 2SLS estimators of the parameter vector are consistent and asymptotically normally distributed.

THREE-STAGE LEAST SQUARES

The Model

The most general method to be discussed is three-stage least squares (3SLS). In addition to the assumptions in Table 3.1 we will require that all of the equations be identified, with at least some being over-identified.[8]

$$
\mathbf{Y} = \begin{bmatrix} -1 & \gamma_{12} & \cdots & \gamma_{1L} \\ \gamma_{21} & -1 & \cdots & \gamma_{2L} \\ \cdot & \cdot & & \cdot \\ \cdot & \cdot & & \cdot \\ \cdot & \cdot & & \cdot \\ \gamma_{L1} & \gamma_{L2} & \cdots & -1 \end{bmatrix} + \mathbf{XB} = \mathbf{E} \tag{3.62}
$$

with contemporaneous covariance matrix

$$\Sigma = \begin{bmatrix} \sigma_{11} & \sigma_{12} & \cdots & \sigma_{1L} \\ \sigma_{21} & \sigma_{22} & \cdots & \sigma_{2L} \\ \cdot & \cdot & & \cdot \\ \cdot & \cdot & & \cdot \\ \cdot & \cdot & & \cdot \\ \sigma_{L1} & \sigma_{L2} & \cdots & \sigma_{LL} \end{bmatrix} . \tag{3.63}$$

The Estimating Procedure

The L-structural equations for all n observations combined can be written as $y = Z\delta + \epsilon$.

$$\begin{bmatrix} y_1 \\ y_2 \\ \cdot \\ \cdot \\ \cdot \\ y_L \end{bmatrix} = \begin{bmatrix} Z_1 & 0 & \cdots & 0 \\ 0 & Z_2 & \cdots & 0 \\ \cdot & \cdot & & \cdot \\ \cdot & \cdot & & \cdot \\ \cdot & \cdot & & \cdot \\ 0 & 0 & \cdots & Z_L \end{bmatrix} \begin{bmatrix} \delta_1 \\ \delta_2 \\ \cdot \\ \cdot \\ \cdot \\ \delta_L \end{bmatrix} + \begin{bmatrix} \epsilon_1 \\ \epsilon_2 \\ \cdot \\ \cdot \\ \cdot \\ \epsilon_L \end{bmatrix} . \tag{3.64}$$

where Z is the matrix of explanatory variables. The matrix Z contains the random matrices $Y_1, \ldots, Y_L$ which are not independent of the disturbance vector ϵ. Instead of using Eq. (3.64) directly, transform it by multiplying through by the transpose of the following Kronecker product:

$$(I \otimes X) = \begin{bmatrix} X & 0 & \cdots & 0 \\ 0 & X & \cdots & 0 \\ \cdot & \cdot & & \cdot \\ \cdot & \cdot & & \cdot \\ \cdot & \cdot & & \cdot \\ 0 & 0 & \cdots & X \end{bmatrix} , \tag{3.65}$$

which gives

$$(I \otimes X')y = (I \otimes X')Z\delta + (I \otimes X')\epsilon \tag{3.66}$$

with covariance matrix

$$\text{Cov } [(I \otimes X')] = \Sigma \otimes X'X. \tag{3.67}$$

Applying generalized least squares to (3.66), the estimator of δ is found to be

$$\delta = (Z'[\Sigma^{-1} \otimes X(X'X)^{-1}X']Z)^{-1} Z'[\Sigma^{-1} \otimes X(X'X)^{-1}X']y. \tag{3.68}$$

In practice, S, the product moment matrix of 2SLS residuals replaces the unknown Σ matrix.

Let us summarize the three-stage least-squares procedure in more conventional terms. In the first stage the OLS estimates of the values of all the endogenous variables are found through the reduced-form equations where each dependent variable is regressed on all of the K predetermined variables. In the second stage, the first stages estimates replace the actual values of the endogenous variables in the set of explanatory variables. Then OLS is applied to each structural equation. In the third stage, the product moment matrix of residuals found in the second stage is used to derive the 3SLS coefficients of the structural equations as shown in Eq. (3.68). The only application of 3SLS in marketing is the airline study by Schultz (1971).

Properties of the Estimators

The 3SLS procedure is *asymptotically* superior to the 2SLS procedure when the contemporaneous covariance matrix is not diagonal *and* at least some of the equations are over-identified. Otherwise, these two estimators are identical.

FOOTNOTES

[1] The fact that a linear model is robust does not mean that it is the correct model. Unfortunately it does mean that our ability to discriminate between it and the correct model is severely hampered.

[2] The maximum likelihood method provides a set of alternative techniques. See Bass and Parsons (1974) for an introduction to these techniques.

[3] The random variables $x_1, x_2, \ldots, x_n$ are said to be mutually stochastically independent if and only if their joint probability density function is equal to the product of the marginal density functions.

[4] The major reference on identification is Fisher (1966).

[5] This section follows Baumol (1965).

[6] The model deviates from Theil's notation in that it is written as $\Gamma Y + BX = E$.

[7] The Bass and Parsons model should have been estimated by three-stage least squares because they postulated that the contemporaneous covariance matrix was not diagonal. Insufficient computer capacity prevented use of 3SLS.

[8] When some of the equations are not identified, the practice has been to apply 3SLS to the identified equations, omitting those not identified. Kadiyala (1975) has proposed using the concept of a generalized inverse of a matrix to extend the 3SLS estimation procedure to cover systems which contain unidentified equations.

Chapter 4

LIMITATIONS OF
MARKETING DATA

An econometric study in marketing begins with data. In the broadest sense, data are the source of ideas on problem definition and model specification. This is equivalent to saying that observation of the real world predetermines the nature of our problems and the structure of our models. The specific use of data to test theories and estimate parameters of models comes later in the research process.[1] Still, the extent and form of data will shape the model development activity.

Beyond this "idea generation" function of data, the purpose of data is to give empirical content to marketing theory. Thus, given a model as a representation of marketing theory, the use of data will be to check the validity of the model, i.e., the correctness of the theory and the closeness of the model to the real world. In this way, data are used to verify the "representativeness" of models. A number of data considerations and issues are raised here because they bear on both model building and model testing processes. They are problems that the marketing researcher must deal with one way or another.

UNOBSERVABLE VARIABLES

The basic issue in data quality is how accurately the nature and effect of a variable can be measured. In an econometric model, parameters and random disturbances are presumed to be unobservable. If they were observable, there would be no problem of statistical inference, but only a problem of measurement. Explanatory variables in an econometric model, however, are presumed to be observable. This implies that they can be defined and measured. Marketing studies often contain observations on quantity of goods sold, dollar expenditures on advertising, prices, and so on. These kind of variables have well-defined meanings and measurements. Other marketing variables are unobservable, at least in a direct way, such as

81

attitudes about products, intentions to purchase, feelings of cognitive dissonance, and others. For these "psychological" variables we seek observable correlates of behavior through instruments of measurement.

There are two fundamental solutions to the problem of unobservable variables. First, they can be omitted from the analysis. A study of the relationship between advertising and sales, for example, could omit the intermediate and unobservable levels of the "hierarchy of effects" and focus simply on the observable variables sales and advertising. The second solution would be to devise instruments to measure the unobservable variables, either directly or as a function of observable variables. New advances in psychological measurement and multidimensional scaling, which are beyond the scope of our present discussion, seem to indicate that this second approach is a viable way to develop microanalytic econometric models.[2] The choice between the two approaches should, of course, be dictated by the purpose of the research.

Errors in Variables

Errors in variables means what it seems—that a variable is measured with error. The error may simply be a result of inaccurate measurement.[3] When aggregate data are used, as is often the case in sales response studies, the problem of *random* errors in variables in relatively less important than the other specification errors that we will discuss in the next chapter. However, when we use data on the individual consumer in buyer behavior models such as those in Chap. 12, the problem is a very central one. Moreover, in such models, the error may also encompass departures of the operational definitions of variables from their theoretical counterparts.

As almost anyone who has worked with marketing data knows, our variables are often measured with considerable uncertainty. We can consider three kinds of measurement problems: (1) problems of definition, (2) problems of operationalization, and (3) errors of measurement.

Definitional problems arise whenever theory or observation suggests a concept for research. For example, in a study of sales response to advertising, what is the concept "sales" and what is the concept "advertising"? Advertising can imply a broad spectrum of activities from public relations to point-of-purchase, the definition usually centering on media expenditures. And yet advertising *impact* comes closer to representing the factor that we seek to relate to sales. Is impact advertising expenditures, impressions, or what? Clearly having defined advertising leads to problems of operationalization. Suppose we operationalize the concept-definition of advertising as mass media expenditures on advertising in a certain time and space frame. Then we are still faced with problems of measurement. Each company knows its own media expenditures for brands but for all other companies the researcher must usually rely on some method for *estimating* advertising. The most common form of such estimation is the so-called media-counting technique which, as the name suggests, is a method of counting advertisements and adding up their (presumed) market value. We could add mere errors of transcription and other researcher mistakes to this list, but in any event it should be apparent that the assumption of error-free variables in marketing research is a strong one indeed.

The standard linear model assumes that the exogenous variables have been measured without error. The only error represented in the standard linear model [Eq. (3.26)] is that caused by the omission of some explanatory variables from the model and is captured by the disturbances

$$y = X^*\beta + \epsilon, \qquad (4.1)$$

where X^* denotes the matrix of true values of the exogenous variables. However, what happens if the exogenous variables are subject to measurement error? The matrix containing the observed values of the exogenous variables can be written as

$$X = X^* + \Psi, \qquad (4.2)$$

where Ψ denotes a matrix of measurement errors. This relationship can be substituted into the *a priori* model (4.1) to yield

$$y = X\beta + (\epsilon - \Psi\beta). \qquad (4.3)$$

The ordinary least-squares estimates of Eq. (4.3) will be biased and inconsistent [Theil (1971), 607-609].

This is a serious problem encountered in our attempts to obtain sales response functions. However, when our focus is on management decision rules, there may be no difficulty. The marketing decision makers quite likely react to measured data. In such a situation, measurement error is irrelevant and we can use ordinary least-squares procedures. Otherwise, we must use either the maximum-likelihood method or the method of instrumental variables [Theil (1971), 609-610]. Each of these methods has practical drawbacks which hinder implementation. The common "solution" seems to be to ignore the errors-in-variables problem.

One other possible solution is to adjust the data. A prerequisite for the use of this method should be a knowledge of the sources of observational error. If the sources are known, then it may be possible to adjust the data to "correct" the errors. In the advertising example given above, only a partial list of media may be surveyed in order to estimate total advertising expenditures. This procedure could thus lead to a systematic underestimate of advertising dollars. By adjusting the data, a more accurate figure may emerge than the strictly observed amounts.

Measurement error in a simultaneous equation model creates identification problems as well as estimation problems. Griliches (1974) and Goldberger (1974) survey these and other issues raised by unobservable variables. Moreover, in a single equation model, measurement errors in the dependent variable can be absorbed into the disturbances errors. This procedure can be followed in simultaneous equation models as well. However, these measurement errors will be correlated across equations and must be explicitly accounted for in the contemporaneous covariance matrix, and consequently in the estimation procedure.

Staelin and Winer (1975) assessed the effect of an advertising campaign on consumer behavior by means of an unobservable variable approach. The desired endogenous variables were the *predispositions* of households to buy various brands of a frequently purchased consumer nondurable. However, the consumer panel diaries provided observations only on the actual purchase quantity in a given time period. These purchases could vary from period to period because the household may stock up on a brand in one period in response to a favorable deal and then draw upon the stock in subsequent periods. Thus, the measurement of purchase quantities does not provide an accurate measure of consumer preferences.

Staelin and Winer developed a model to take this discrepancy into account. Their results showed that the time lag between the advertising input and its initial effect is about 4 months, and its peak effect about 7 months. These lags should be evaluated in light of an average interpurchase time of about 1 month.

Adjustments to the Data

Apart from errors of observation, another kind of measurement error can influence the quality of data and hence the quality of statistical results. These are qualitative effects. For example, even if advertising dollars were observed perfectly, the effect of advertising on sales may be mis-stated because the quality of advertising dollars is not considered. Adjustments for this and other effects including trend, seasonality, price change, and population change, are discussed below.

1. *Qualitative Adjustments.* Suppose that a model is being considered where

$$Q_\alpha = \beta_0 + \beta_1 A_\alpha + \epsilon_\alpha, \tag{4.4}$$

where Q = sales defined in units and A = advertising defined in dollar terms. The question arises as to whether advertising dollars represent, adequately enough, the concept of advertising impact. For the model builder usually wants to relate "impact" to sales and so "dollars" are just a proxy variable. If data were available on advertising effectiveness—say survey data on awareness or attitude—and if these data corresponded to the time series for advertising dollars, then it would be possible to define a qualitative-adjustment factor, θ_α, such that

$$[\text{advertising impact}]_\alpha = \theta_\alpha A_\alpha,$$

with θ_α scaled so that an average value would be equal to 1. Thus, θ_α adjusts A_α for the qualitative aspect of advertising dollars. The model would then be

$$Q_\alpha = \beta_0 + \beta_1 (\theta_\alpha A_\alpha) + \epsilon_\alpha, \tag{4.5}$$

and the testing and estimation would proceed as usual. Some purists might object to introducing such behavioral data into econometric work, but considering the quality of the dollar figures themselves, this may not amount to much subjectivity.

    2. *Trend.*   If a variable, say sales, is highly correlated with time, then this situation is called trend. For example, suppose the following model is under consideration

$$Q_\alpha = \beta_0 + \beta_1 A_\alpha + \epsilon_\alpha, \tag{4.6}$$

and suppose that we know that Q_α is highly correlated with α. Thus, even if A_α is shown to be significantly related to Q_α, there is an omitted factor—trend—to be accounted for. One way that this may reveal itself (besides in simply looking at the data and observing a trend) is in the correlation of the residuals, i.e., the correlation of ϵ_α with $\epsilon_{\alpha-1}$, for all α. This serial or autocorrelation, tested via several techniques such as Durbin-Watson, Durbin h, etc. (see Chap. 5), often suggests an omitted factor. But is the factor trend or time or some explanatory variable that is highly correlated with time? If the analyst has no basis for including an explanatory variable, linear trend can be added as a simple variable α, where $\alpha = 1, \ldots, n$. In this case the model would be

$$Q_\alpha = \beta_0 + \beta_1 A_\alpha + \beta_2 \alpha + \epsilon_\alpha. \tag{4.7}$$

This solution may serve forecasting quite well, but if the model has as explanatory purpose as well, the analyst would be advised to search further for the "cause" of the trend. The treatment of nonlinear trends and cycles involves classical time series analysis.

    3. *Seasonality.*   If a variable is highly correlated with certain regular subsets of the time unit of aggregation, then this situation is called seasonality. Of course the leading case is with yearly data and the subsets of quarters (seasons) or months. Two basic approaches to this problem are available. First, the data can be *seasonally adjusted*, i.e., the effects of the seasonality can be removed from the data, primarily by employing some type of moving average [cf. Chou (1969)]. Second, dummy variables can be used to represent the seasons. For example, the model

$$
\begin{aligned}
Q_\alpha = \beta_0 &+ \beta_1 D_2 + \beta_2 D_3 + \beta_3 D_4 + \beta_4 A_\alpha + \beta_5 [D_2 A_\alpha] \\
&+ \beta_6 [D_3 A_\alpha] + \beta_7 [D_4 A_\alpha] + \epsilon_\alpha,
\end{aligned} \tag{4.8}
$$

where the D_i are dummy variables, can be used to account for quarterly variation in the data. A dummy variable D_1 is not needed since all shifts are measured from a first quarter base. The coefficients β_1, β_2, β_3 capture shifts of the intercept β_0 and the coefficients β_5, β_6, β_7 capture shifts of the slope β_4. The estimation of models such as (4.8) may be difficult because of the likelihood of a high degree of multicollinearity among the exogenous variables.[4] These and related topics are discussed in the context of sales response functions by Beckwith (1972b) and Wildt (1975).

4. *Price Change.* One of the more painful aspects of contemporary economic reality is inflation and hence the changing real value of the dollar (or unit of currency). Price changes must be accounted for in econometric studies of time series data by adjusting current dollar figures to real dollar figures using some deflator or price index. Suppose the following model, similar to those above but with price $= P$ as an additional variable, is under consideration

$$Q_\alpha = \beta_0 + \beta_1 A_\alpha + \beta_2 P_\alpha. \tag{4.9}$$

Since both advertising and price are measured in dollars, and study covering a long period of time (i.e., one in which there has been substantial price change) should adjust A_α and P_α to real terms. P_α could be deflated by the Consumer Price Index since this series is, by definition, designed to reflect price changes in a "market basket" of goods and services. Ideally, we would also want a price index for advertising to adjust current advertising dollars to real terms. The point of these adjustments is to assure that the influence on sales being measured is due to true changes in advertising and price and not to artificial ones due to the change of prices in general.

5. *Population Change.* This final adjustment to the data is straightforward. Just as prices change, so does population and so sales in all of the above models may be more appropriately measured by *per capita* sales. It will turn out in applied work that per capita adjustments are often required for both dependent and explanatory variables, for example in the case where sales is a function of income as well as price and advertising.

AGGREGATION IN MARKETING

Closely related to the question of the form of the model and the variables to be used is the issue of the level of aggregation at which analysis should take place. In practice model building efforts appear to exclude considerations about the level of aggregation, probably because of the constraints surrounding availability of data.

Various kinds of aggregation are possible in marketing— aggregation can take place over entities, time or space. Aggregation over entities can be of two types corresponding to the two basic types of entities in a marketing system. The first type is aggregation over consumers, and the second type is aggregation over product levels. Consumer aggregation takes place when individual brands are added to obtain larger product categories or to obtain total sales of a firm (i.e., over all its products and brands). Temporal aggregation refers to the collection of shorter observation periods into longer observation periods. Spatial aggregation means the gathering of smaller geographic areas into larger geographic areas. The intersection of the various levels of aggregation for each of these dimensions defines the *aggregation space* of a sales response study. For example, the aggregation space of a study may be bimonthly data for states by households for consumption of the product category beer. It should be clear that the specification of the levels of aggregation has an important bearing on the nature of the relationships that can be discovered.

In this section,[5] some basic ideas about the theory of transformation of microrelations into macrorelations will be developed, the concept of aggregation bias will be defined, and some practical considerations related to the specification of aggregation levels in studies of sales response will be discussed.

The theory of linear aggregation in econometrics has been advanced by Theil (1954, 1971). Besides papers in econometrics on aggregation, two monographs by Green (1964) and Fisher (1969) are of interest. The point of departure is the fact that microrelations are the fundamental mechanisms of economic and marketing behavior. Microrelations such as the economic behavior of an individual with respect to a specific good are fundamental mechanisms because they represent the elementary processes of economic life.[6] The question is what happens to such relations when they are aggregated into larger entities.

The essential task is to show that certain conditions must hold before microrelations such as

$$y_i = X_i\beta_i + \epsilon_i \qquad i = 1, \ldots, N \qquad (4.10)$$

can be summarized into a macrorelation

$$\frac{1}{N}\sum_{i=1}^{N} y_i = \frac{1}{N}\sum_{i=1}^{N} X_i\beta_i + \frac{1}{N}\sum_{i=1}^{N} \epsilon_i \tag{4.11}$$

without committing a specification error (i.e., aggregation bias). It turns out that the model

$$\overline{y} = \overline{X}\beta + \overline{\epsilon} \tag{4.12}$$

can only be employed meaningfully if the parameter vectors $\beta_1, \ldots, \beta_N$ are all equal (to β, say) or under limited conditions [Theil (1971), 561].

Entity Aggregation

Consider studies of the aggregate effect of total industry advertising on total industry sales. A simple equation model of the process, some results of which are reported in Chap. 10, would be

$$Q = f(A), \tag{4.13}$$

where

Q = industry sales in units
A = industry advertising expenditures.

To examine the aggregation bias which would result from unequal and fixed parameter vectors for the microequations, we will use equations with one other exogenous variable (Z) in addition to the advertising variable. Following Zellner (1969), two equations representing two brands operating in the same industry are postulated.

$$Q_1 = \beta_{11}A_1 + \beta_{12}Z_1 + \epsilon_1, \tag{4.14}$$

$$Q_2 = \beta_{21}A_2 + \beta_{22}Z_2 + \epsilon_2, \tag{4.15}$$

where Q_i, A_i, and Z_i, for $i = 1,2$ are vectors of time series observations on respectively sales in units, advertising expenditures and some other variable representing the two brands. By aggregating (4.14) and (4.15) we obtain

$$Q = \beta_1 A + \beta_2 Z + \epsilon, \tag{4.16}$$

where

$$Q = \sum_{i=1}^{2} Q_i, \qquad A = \sum_{i=1}^{2} A_i, \qquad Z = \sum_{i=1}^{2} Z_i, \quad \text{and} \quad \epsilon = \sum_{i=1}^{2} \epsilon_i.$$

Using OLS to estimate the parameters in Eq. (4.16) we obtain

$$\begin{bmatrix} \hat{\beta}_1 \\ \hat{\beta}_2 \end{bmatrix} = \begin{bmatrix} A'A & A'Z \\ Z'A & Z'Z \end{bmatrix}^{-1} \begin{bmatrix} A'Q \\ Z'Q \end{bmatrix}$$

$$= \begin{bmatrix} E & -EA'Z(Z'Z)^{-1} \\ -(Z'Z)^{-1}Z'AE & (Z'Z)^{-1} + (Z'Z)^{-1}Z'AEA'Z(Z'Z)^{-1} \end{bmatrix} \begin{bmatrix} A'Q \\ Z'Q \end{bmatrix},$$

$$\tag{4.17}$$

where

$$E = (A'MA)^{-1},$$
$$M = I - Z(Z'Z)^{-1}Z'.$$

Concentrating on $\hat{\beta}_1$, the estimate of the parameter associated with total industry advertising, we have

$$\hat{\beta}_1 = EA'Q - EA'Z(Z'Z)^{-1}Z'Q. \tag{4.18}$$

Using the fact that $Q = \sum_{i=1}^{2} Q_i$ and substituting (4.14) and (4.15) into (4.18), the expression becomes

$$\hat{\beta}_1 = EA'M(\sum_{i=1}^{2} \beta_{i1}A_i + \sum_{i=1}^{2} \beta_{i2}Z_i + \sum_{i=1}^{2} \epsilon_i). \tag{4.19}$$

The expected value of $\hat{\beta}_1$, if the usual assumptions about the disturbance terms apply, is

$$E\hat{\beta}_1 = \beta_{11}EA'MA_1 + \beta_{21}EA'MA_2 + \beta_{12}EA'MZ_1 + \beta_{22}EA'MZ_2. \tag{4.20}$$

It is evident from (4.20) that expected value of $\hat{\beta}_1$ is dependent not only on the corresponding micro-parameters β_{11} and β_{21}, but also on the noncorresponding micro-parameters β_{12} and β_{22}. If **A** is orthogonal to **Z**, or $\beta_{12} = \beta_{22}$, the parameter associated with total industry advertising is a weighted average.[7] This can be observed by using the fact that $A_2 = A - A_1$ and $Z_2 = Z - Z_1$, such that

$$E\hat{\beta}_1 = \beta_{21} + (\beta_{11} - \beta_{21})\,\mathbf{EA'MA_1} + (\beta_{12} - \beta_{22})\,\mathbf{EA'MZ_1}.$$

(4.21)

Temporal Aggregation

Research regarding the relationship between economic or marketing variables can be carried out on, for example, monthly, bimonthly, quarterly or annual data. To some extent aggregation over time is unavoidable. In fact, the length of the time period that forms the basis for analysis is often not determined by the researcher. He simply uses the data made available to him. However, even if a researcher is constrained in this respect, he is not devoid of responsibility in considering the effect of temporal aggregation on the outcome of the analysis. The need for using the smallest possible time period involves the desirability of investigating the reasons for changes in the market position of a brand. If the average time between purchases for a given product is approximately a month, then it is important to have, as a minimum, monthly data. Each time period would then reflect, on the average, one purchase occasion per consumer. Using annual data for such a product instead would have the effect of smoothing the data, thereby not allowing the researcher to determine the reasons for the changes on a month-to-month basis.

The choice of the time period is particularly relevant for the purpose of interpreting the coefficient associated with a lagged dependent variable. Suppose the structural model postulated by a researcher is

$$MS_\alpha = \beta_1 MS_{\alpha-1} + \beta_0 (1 - MS_{\alpha-1}),$$

(4.22)

where

MS_α = market share of the brand in period α
β_1 = conditional repeat purchase probability
β_0 = conditional transfer purchase probability.

Equation (4.22) can also be expressed as

$$MS_\alpha = \beta_0 + (\beta_1 - \beta_0) MS_{\alpha-1}. \tag{4.23}$$

From (4.23) it is evident that the parameter associated with lagged market share can be interpreted as the difference between the "repeat" and "transfer" purchase probabilities. It is then possible to let these probabilities be a function of the marketing decision variables such that the model to be analyzed is of the form

$$MS_\alpha = f(MS_{\alpha-1}, AS_\alpha, RP_\alpha, \ldots), \tag{4.24}$$

where

AS_α = advertising share of the brand in period α
RP_α = relative price of the brand in period α.

Bass, Jeuland, and Wright (1975) have examined the relationship between the conditional purchase probabilities and market share. They suggest the following relationship

$$\begin{aligned} \beta_0 &= \rho + (1 - \rho) MS_\alpha, \\ \beta_1 &= (1 - \rho) MS_\alpha. \end{aligned} \tag{4.25}$$

Using (4.25), the difference between β_0 and β_1 equals ρ. Hence, the parameter associated with the lagged dependent variable equals ρ, which is called the "product class brand loyalty factor."

If (4.24) is the result of postulating a partial adjustment model, then the interpretation of this coefficient is quite similar. The presence of the lagged dependent variable is then caused by less than full (immediate) adjustment of the market to changes in the marketing decision variables. Full (optimal) adjustment takes place if the parameter associated with the lagged dependent variable equals zero. Reasons for the presence of a lag (and hence only partial adjustment) are ignorance, inertia, etc. [Johnston (1971), 300]. Meaningful interpretation of the magnitude of the coefficient for the lag can take place only if the time period of analysis reflects the average purchase interval. Aggregation over time resulting in a time period greater than the average purchase interval would tend to increase the coefficient of the lag implying slower adjustment or higher brand loyalty than is actually the case.

Spatial Aggregation

Data describing the behavior of the marketing variables over time are available in increasingly more detailed forms. This allows for separate analyses to be carried out for each of the geographic areas or sales territories in which a firm is competing. Analysis at the national level will certainly not reveal information about the differences in the relationship between such territories. Moreover such an aggregate analysis is likely to be invalid if the relationship between the marketing variables is not the same for all the areas. There are several reasons why this relationship may differ across sales territories. At least in some industries, the structure of the market is not homogeneous across territories, that is, some brands are available in some areas and not in other areas. The market position of a selected brand may differ substantially across territories, partly as a result of differences in market structure. Furthermore the characteristics of consumers may vary substantially across territories. If the relationship of interest depends on some of these characteristics and/or the presence and extent of competition provided by competing brands, then a certain amount of variation in the effectiveness of marketing decision variables can be expected.

COMBINING CROSS-SECTION AND TIME-SERIES DATA

Marketing data can be collected for the same entity over a period of time or for different entities at the same time, or both. The former results in a time series of marketing data and the latter, in a cross-section. It is also possible to measure over entities and over time and this produces a set of *combined* time-series and cross-section observations. For example, suppose we are interested in investigating the relationship between retail advertising and sales of department stores. We could do a time series study which would concentrate on one store (i.e., one entity) over a period of time, perhaps by relating advertising expenditures to sales for a number of quarters. If we had monthly data for two years, the length of the time series or the number of observations would equal 24. On the other hand, we could do a cross-section study covering a number of stores during the same time period. In this case, the observations are advertising expenditures and sales for each store and not time periods. If we had data for ten stores, we would have ten observations. Another research strategy would be to study the relationship by combining the time series and cross-section. This would result in 240 observations in this illustration, clearly a large sample (but, of course, subject to the pooling issues discussed above).

The choice between the three types of studies should depend upon the purpose of the research. The dynamic character of advertising can only be investigated with a time series. The generality of advertising-sales relationships may require a cross-section. The researcher is too often bound by the limitations of his data, so that the choice is, in a sense out of his control. This is especially true in marketing where good time series data may not be systematically recorded by firms, or perhaps recorded annually when the research question requires quarterly or monthly data. Cross-section studies in marketing are often limited by competitive considerations so that one researcher cannot obtain data for all firms in an industry. Assuming that the researcher can obtain appropriate data, he still faces a number of important issues regarding the use of that data.

A time series model of sales and advertising (single equation) could be written as

$$Q_\alpha = \beta_0 + \beta_1 A_\alpha + \epsilon_\alpha \qquad \alpha = 1, \ldots, T. \tag{4.26}$$

This model assumes that the parameters β_0, β_1 do not change as α changes from $1, \ldots, T$. In many marketing situations, this sort of assumption may be unsatisfactory since products move through life cycles, competitors enter and exit markets, and so forth. An alternative formulation of the model allows for systematic changes in β_0 and β_1 which are specified in the model. For example, the time series model could be rewritten as

$$Q_\alpha = \beta_0' + \beta_0'' \alpha + (\beta_1' + \beta_1'' \alpha) A_\alpha + \epsilon_\alpha' \qquad \alpha = 1, \ldots, T. \tag{4.27}$$

In this specification, both β_0 and β_1 are linear functions of time and so they can change although β_0', β_0'', β_1', and β_1'' do not. Such a formulation might be particularly relevant for capturing systematic variation in advertising elasticity over the product life cycle. One difficulty with this formulation is its susceptibility during estimation to multicollinearity.

A cross-section model of sales and advertising (single equation) could be written as

$$Q_i = \beta_0 + \beta_1 A_i + \epsilon_i \qquad i = 1, \ldots, N. \qquad (4.28)$$

In this model we have replaced the time subscript α with an entity subscript i for expositive purposes, although it makes no real difference what we call each observation. This model assumes that the parameters β_0 and β_1 do not change as i changes from $1, \ldots, N$. In other words, the parameters of different entities are taken to be constant. For real markets this may be an unrealistic assumption since it implies that each firm or brand has a constant advertising elasticity. An argument parallel to the one above permits the incorporation of systematic changes in β_0 and β_1. For example, suppose that the entities differed by size only and that size was introduced as a new variable. Then, the model could be rewritten to allow elasticities to vary with size. (This reformulation is not shown.)

A combined time-series and cross-section model of sales and advertising (single equation) could be written as

$$Q_{\alpha i} = \beta_0 + \beta_1 A_{\alpha i} + \epsilon_{\alpha i} \qquad i = 1, \ldots, N; \alpha = 1, \ldots, T. \qquad (4.29)$$

This model assumes constant parameters for $N \times T$ observations. Buzzell (1964) used this approach. A more common assumption is to allow for individual differences by introducing separate dummy variables for each cross-sectional entity:

$$Q_{\alpha i} = \beta_0 + \beta_1 A_{\alpha i} + \beta_2 D_2 + \ldots + \beta_N D_N + \epsilon_{\alpha i}$$

$$i = 1, \ldots, N; \alpha = 1, \ldots, T. \qquad (4.30)$$

In a similar manner, we could represent differences over time. The parameters in Eq. (4.30) can be estimated by ordinary least-squares regression.

Individual differences and temporal differences could each be represented by dummy variables in the same equation. This results in a substantial loss of degrees of freedom. Moreover, interpretation of the dummy variables may be difficult. In addition, these dummy variables are likely to account for a large share of the explanatory power of the model. Consequently, a *variance components* model is often used instead of the dummy variable technique. This model is

$$Q_{\alpha i} = \beta_0 + \beta_1 A_{\alpha i} + \mu_i + \tau_\alpha + \nu_{\alpha i}$$

$$i = 1, \ldots, N; \alpha = 1, \ldots, T. \qquad (4.31)$$

where the disturbance term $\epsilon_{\alpha i}$ has been partitioned into three components. The components are the individual or cross-sectional effect, μ_i, the time effect, τ_α, and the remaining effects which vary over both individuals and time periods, $\nu_{\alpha i}$. Estimation of this model is discussed in Maddala (1971) and Nerlove (1971).[8] Parsons (1974) and Moriarty (1975) used variants of the variance components formulation.

Parsons investigated the market mechanism for new product introductions. The individual entities were different brands. This model is discussed in somewhat more detail in Chap. 7. Moriarty was interested in the allocation of advertising funds to sales districts so that these were the individual entities. His model postulated that market share was a function of relative price, advertising per capita in the previous period, and market share in the previous period. There was a data problem in that sales volume was reported only in terms of shipments. The more appropriate retail sales figures were unavailable. Unhappily for his stated purpose, Moriarty's results failed to reveal any regional effect of advertising.

The models discussed have assumed that the individual and time effects manifest themselves in differences in the intercept. The impact of these effects on slope coefficients are captured by means of random coefficients models of the form

$$Q_{\alpha i} = (\bar{\beta}_1 + \xi_{1\alpha i}) A_{\alpha i} + (\bar{\beta}_0 + \xi_{0\alpha i})$$

$$i = 1, \ldots, N; \alpha = 1, \ldots, T, \qquad (4.32)$$

where $\bar{\beta}_k$ is the unknown mean of coefficient k and $\xi_{k\alpha i}$ is the additive random element of the same coefficient. Discussion of estimation of the random coefficient model can be found in Swamy (1974). The most complicated pooling model, the convergent parameter model, will be discussed in Chap. 7. McCann (1974), Bass and Wittink (1975), and Johansson (1975) present surveys of the various pooling methods.

One other consideration of time-series and cross-section models deserves mention here. In a pure time series, the observations are in natural (temporal) order, while in pure cross-sections, the observations typically have no natural order. Thus, we can speak of lagged values of time series variables with a definite time-delay meaning. There is no such simple and unambiguous analogy with cross-sections.[9] Models which include lagged endogenous variables raise estimation as well as interpretation difficulties.

OBSERVATIONAL EQUIVALENCE

Discrimination among alternative models is impossible if they are *observationally equivalent*. This occurs when two or more theories yield exactly the same implications about observable phenomena in all situations. Under such conditions no sample, no matter how large it is, can resolve the issue. Goldberger [(1964), 307-310] discusses observationally equivalent structures in the context of the identification problem inherent in systems of simultaneous relationships. Basmann (1965b) discusses the circum stances in which an explicit causal chain model can not be tested against an interdependent model because of the observational equivalence.

We will also use the term observational equivalence loosely to cover any observed space in which the models under consideration are not observationally distinguishable. We know that the interval between data collection points is often chosen for administrative convenience rather than its appropriateness for working with a particular model. Moreover, measurement at any fixed interval may be inappropriate in models of individual buyer behavior where interpurchase time is not only random but heterogeneous across the population. Even when we are able to set the values of variables for best discrimination among models, we should be aware that these values will not in general be those that give the best parameter estimation for the correct model.

Observational equivalence is an inherent problem with the hypothetico-deductive method of science. We can conclusively reject theories, but can not have the same confidence about their acceptance. The fact that a model can not be rejected does not imply that it is correct in the sense that any other model describing a sales response function is incorrect. This issue as it relates to the testing of theories is discussed in Chap. 6.

FOOTNOTES

[1] The successive steps of theory generation, testing, and estimation require independent sets of data.

[2] For examples of microanalytic econometric models, see Farley and Ring (1970) and Dominguez (1971). For overviews of modern methods of measurement and scaling in marketing, see Green and Tull (1975) and Green and Rao (1972). For an early attempt at integrating econometric and MDS techniques, see Houston, Weiss, and Westermeyer (1974).

[3] These errors arise from many diverse sources. For instance, see Carman (1974) and Hulbert and Lehmann (1975).

[4] Multicollinearity will be discussed in Chap. 5.

[5] Most of this section was prepared by Dick R. Wittink.

[6] An even more elementary level would be individual transactions, but we choose to define the elementary process as consumer choice behavior toward a specific good.

[7] This is a very strong assumption.

[8] The variance component model, along with the random coefficient model discussed next, also involves specific assumptions about how the errors are distributed.

[9] Christ offers a slightly extended discussion of this issue [Christ (1966), 209-210].

Chapter 5

EVALUATING
ECONOMETRIC MODELS

A broad set of tests can and should be applied to a model during its development and implementation. The evaluation of a model begins with the testing of the statistical assumptions of a model. The model must be examined for problems such as multicollinearity, autocorrelation, heteroscedasticity, simultaneity, and nonnormality. This portion of the evaluation is called specification error analysis. If no violations of the assumptions are found, the regression results can be tested. This involves tests of significance concerning each individual model and subsequently discrimination among alternative models. First, however, we will consider some tests of significance which assume that there is no specification error.

TESTS OF SIGNIFICANCE

When the disturbances in the standard linear model are assumed to be normally distributed, then we can conduct separate tests of hypotheses about each of the parameters of the model as well as a joint test on the significance of the entire linear relationship. The distribution of the least squares coefficient estimator $\mathbf{b}$ is normal with mean vector β and covariance matrix $\sigma^2 (\mathbf{X'X})^{-1}$ while that of $(n - K) s^2/\sigma^2$ is $\chi^2 (n - K)$. Hence the ratio

$$\frac{\mathbf{w'b} - \beta_0}{\sigma \sqrt{\mathbf{w'(X'X)w}}} ,$$

(5.1)

where $\mathbf{w}$ is a known vector and β_0 is a known scalar, is distributed as the standardized normal $N(0,1)$. The problem is that σ is unknown. Fortunately, $\mathbf{b}$ and s^2 are distributed independently. Consequently from the definition of the t-distribution, the ratio

$$t = \frac{\mathbf{w'b} - \beta_0}{s \sqrt{\mathbf{w'(X'X)w}}}$$

(5.2)

follows the t-distribution with $n - K$ degrees of freedom. This formulation permits the testing of any linear combination of coefficients. Usually we will want to test the null hypothesis $H_0 : \beta_i = 0$ against the alternative hypothesis $H_A : \beta \neq 0$. In this case, there will be a separate test for each coefficient i with $w_i = 1$ and $w_j = 0$ for $j \neq i$.

The joint test involves the null hypothesis, $H_0 : \beta = \beta_0$, where β_0 is a numerically specified $K - 1$ element vector. Remembering that if $K - 1$ independent random variables have standard normal distributions, then the sum of the squared variables is $\chi^2(K - 1)$, the quantity

$$F = \frac{(b - \beta_0)'X'X(b - \beta_0)}{(K - 1)s^2} \tag{5.3}$$

is thus distributed as $F(K - 1, n - K)$. The hypothesis that $\beta_0 = 0$ provides a test of the overall relation which assesses whether the independent variables have any influence upon the dependent variables. An equivalent formulation of the test statistic under this null hypothesis is

$$F = \frac{(n - K)R^2}{(K - 1)(1 - R^2)} \quad . \tag{5.4}$$

These tests of significance apply only to single equation models. Except in a few special cases, the small sample properties of various simultaneous equation estimators are unknown. We next turn to an examination of the maintained hypothesis which underlies the single equation tests of significance.

SPECIFICATION ERROR ANALYSIS

A true model is one that describes the distributional characteristics of a population. Specification error occurs when other than the true model is used.[1] We view the distribution of the disturbance term as an integral part of the model. Consequently, when an assumption about the error structure of a model is violated, the question is not merely one of not being able to obtain optimal properties for the estimators of the parameters of the model. Rather the violation poses a fundamental challenge to the model. This section will focus on specification error tests constructed primarily for the single-equation standard linear model.

The common types of specification error are: (a) omitted variables, (b) incorrect functional form, (c) simultaneous equation problems, (d) heteroscedasticity, (e) nonnormality of the disturbance term, (f) autocorrelation, and (g) errors in variables. Tests for these errors can either be general or specific. A general test is one against a broad group of alternatives. A specific test is one against a limited alternative. For instance, we could use a general test against nonlinearity or we might test against a specific alternative such as a quadratic relationship:

$$y_\alpha = \beta_0 + \beta_1 x_\alpha + \beta_2 x_\alpha^2 + \epsilon_\alpha. \tag{5.5}$$

The specific test would be the t-test for the null hypothesis $\beta_2 = 0$. In subsequent sections we will discuss general tests for specification error.

Residual Vectors

Specification error tests involve examination of the regression residuals. The least-squares residual vector

$$e = y - Xb = [I - X(X'X)^{-1}X']y \equiv My \tag{5.6}$$

provides one approximation to the disturbance vector. Unfortunately, even though the disturbances are stochastically independent and homoscedastic, the least-squares residuals are usually not. This causes problems in testing the distribution of the disturbance vector.

Consequently, a residual vector is required that has a scalar covariance matrix when the disturbance vector does. The BLUS residual vector is such a vector. BLUS stands for Best Linear Unbiased Scalar covariance matrix. Theil [(1971), 202-213] defines the BLUS residual vector and describes its properties. The BLUS residual vector is

$$\hat{\epsilon} = Cy, \tag{5.7}$$

where C is of order $(n - K) \times K$. The matrix C must satisfy

$$CX = 0, \tag{5.8}$$

which ensures that the residual vector is unbiased and

$$CC' = I, \tag{5.9}$$

which guarantees that the residual vector has a scalar covariance matrix $\sigma^2 I$. One property of the BLUS residual vector is that the maximum number of independent residuals which can be obtained is $n - K$. Thus, one must choose which subset of residuals to use. Theil [(1971), 217-218] discusses this selection procedure.

The Impact of Specification Error

One approach to specification error analysis [Ramsey (1969, 1974)] is to consider the impact of the various types of error. The null hypothesis is that a particular single-equation linear model is the true model. Under the usual assumptions, the BLUS residuals are normally distributed with mean zero and covariance matrix $\sigma^2 I_{n-K}$. If an alternative model is true, use of this given model will result in specification error. Alternative models which would give rise to omitted variables, incorrect function form, or simultaneous equation problems lead to the BLUS residuals being normally distributed with a nonzero mean and covariance matrix Ω. Thus, if the estimator was unbiased, the error creates bias or if the estimator was biased, but consistent, this error brings about a different bias and inconsistency.

The recognition of the presence of at least one of these errors is accomplished by regressing the BLUS residuals against a polynomial (usually of degree two or three) in transformed[2] least-squares estimates of the dependent variable:

$$\hat{e} = \alpha_0 + \alpha_1(C\hat{y}) + \alpha_2(C\hat{y}^2) + \ldots. \tag{5.10}$$

Under the null hypothesis of no specification error, the α's should all be zero. Unfortunately, if the null hypothesis is rejected, we do not know which of the three types of error caused this shift in the central tendency of the estimator.

Alternative models which would give rise to heteroscedasticity result in the BLUS residuals being normally distributed with mean zero and a diagonal covariance matrix with unequal nonzero elements. If the alternative hypothesis is that the BLUS residuals are distributed as $\sigma^2 \chi^2$, then Bartlett's M-test can be used. This involves the maximum likelihood ratio test statistic

$$\lambda^* = \frac{\sum\limits_{i=1}^{k} \left[\frac{1}{\nu_i} \sum\limits_{j=1}^{\nu_i} \epsilon_j^2 \right]^{\nu_i/2}}{\frac{1}{\nu} \sum\limits_{j=1}^{n-K} \hat{\epsilon}_j^2} \quad , \tag{5.11}$$

where k is the number of subgroups of squared residuals and each ν_i is integer $[(n-K)/k]$.[3] The value of k is typically set equal to three. This reflects a trade-off between the need for more subgroups and the need for large samples within each subgroup. The test statistic is $M = -2 \ln \lambda^*$, which is asymptotically distributed as central chi-square with $(k-1)$ degrees of freedom.

Semlow (1959) studied the linkage between potential in a territory and sales results as a first step in determining the optimal number of salesmen. Semlow plotted the relationship between sales potential per territory, P_i and sales volume per one percent of potential, S_i/P_i, for 25 territories of one firm. Examination of this graph revealed that the data displayed a hyperbolic shape. This led Semlow to conclude that there was a marked increase in sales per one percent of potential as the territories decrease in potential.

Weinberg and Lucas (1974) formally represented Semlow's implicit model as a power function and used his data to estimate the parameters:

$$\ln (S_i/P_i) = 233 - .985 \ln P_i, \qquad R^2 = .79.$$
$$(t\text{-value}) \qquad (-9.66) \tag{5.12}$$

Although the fit of this equation appears to be good, Weinberg and Lucas found by considering alternative functional forms that the fit was spurious due to the presence of the same variable on both sides of the equation.

To determine whether specification error analysis would have revealed that something was amiss, we evaluated Eq. (5.12) using DATGENTH, a computer program authored by James B. Ramsey to calculate the regression specification error tests. The null hypothesis that the mean of the BLUS residuals is zero was tested using Eq. (5.10) with polynomial of degree 3. The F-statistic for this regression was 1.63 while the critical value of F with 3 and 19 degrees of freedom at the 0.05 level of significance is 3.13. Thus, the hypothesis of no specification error cannot be rejected. In the test against heteroscedasticity, Bartlett's M-statistic was .14 while the critical value of χ^2 with 2 degrees of freedom at the 0.05 level of significance is 5.99. Thus, the null hypothesis of homoscedastic errors could not be rejected. The Shapiro-Wilk W-test was employed to test the normality of the BLUS residuals. The null hypothesis was not rejected at the 0.05 level of significance. Thus, these specification error tests would not have required the researcher to revise the model.

General tests exist for most of the specification errors we might encounter. We now turn to a discussion of these tests. Each test is for one specification error *in the absence of other specification errors.*

Autocorrelation

The standard linear model assumes that successive disturbances are independent, that is

$$E(\epsilon_\alpha \epsilon_{\alpha+1}) = 0, \qquad \alpha = 1, \ldots, n - 1. \tag{5.13}$$

An alternative hypothesis is that the successive disturbances are positively (negatively) autocorrelated. Although under this alternative hypothesis the estimates of the regression coefficients are unbiased, the usual least-squares formula underestimates their sampling variances. Correspondingly the usual t-statistic will be overestimated. Therefore, the model will seem to fit the data better than it actually does.

The test against autocorrelation is the modified von Neumann ratio:

$$Q' = \frac{\sum_\alpha (\hat{\epsilon}_{\alpha+1} - \hat{\epsilon}_\alpha)^2}{(n - K - 1) s^2}, \tag{5.14}$$

where the summation is over the $n - K$ successive computed BLUS residuals and s^2 is the least-squares variance estimator. The significance table for Q' for values of $n - K$ between 2 and 60 are given in Theil [(1971), 728-729]. For values of $n - K$ greater than 60, a normal approximation for Q' with mean 2 and variance $2/(n - K)$ can be used.

A somewhat less powerful test, but one that is computationally simpler is the Durbin-Watson statistic.[4] The Durbin-Watson statistic uses least squares residuals instead of BLUS residuals:

$$d = \frac{\sum_{\alpha=1}^{n-1} (e_{\alpha+1} - e_{\alpha})^2}{\sum_{\alpha=1}^{n} e_{\alpha}^2} .$$ (5.15)

The null hypothesis of no autocorrelation is rejected in favor of the alternative hypothesis that the disturbances are positively (negatively) autocorrelated when d takes on a sufficiently small (large) value. Because of computational problems, bounds on the significance limits are used instead of an exact test. Therefore, the test of the null hypothesis against the alternative hypothesis of positive autocorrelation will reject the null hypothesis if the value of d is less than the lower limit, d_L, will not reject the null hypothesis if the value of d is greater than the upper limit, d_U, and will be inconclusive if d falls between the lower and upper limits. These bounds for sample sizes between 15 and 100 and for values of K between 2 and 6 are given in Theil [(1971), 724]. The Durbin-Watson statistic has been used in numerous marketing studies.

The Durbin-Watson test assumes that the independent variables are fixed. Thus, it can not be used when lagged values of the dependent variable are present among the predetermined variables. Durbin (1970) has proposed an alternative statistic to use in this situation. The statistic is given by

$$h = \hat{\rho} \left(\frac{n}{1 - nV(\lambda)} \right)^{1/2} ,$$ (5.16)

where $\hat{\rho}$ is the sample first-order autocorrelation coefficient of the residuals[5] and $V(\lambda)$ is the estimated variance of the coefficient of the dependent variable lagged one period. The Durbin h is asymptotically normally distributed with mean 0 and variance 1 under the null hypothesis that ρ is zero. This test statistic was used by Montgomery and Silk (1972).

When one of these tests indicates the presence of first-order autocorrelation, a two-step estimation procedure is required. The first step involves obtaining an estimate of ρ by means of ordinary least-squares (OLS) estimation. The second step requires that this estimate of ρ be used in a generalized least-squares (GLS) regression.

Nonlinearity

The modified von Neumann ratio can also be used to test for nonlinearity. The procedure involves rearranging the observations according to increasing values of the independent variable suspected of being nonlinear. Next Q' is computed for a set of $n - K$ BLUS residuals based on the first m and last $K - m$ rearranged observations where m is chosen optimally [Theil (1971), 217-218]. The presence of nonlinearity means that there is some order in the rearranged residuals. This order will result in successive values of these residuals being close to each other. Consequently, a low value of Q' suggests nonlinearity and a one-sided test against positive autocorrelation is used.

Heteroscedasticity

The variance of the disturbance term has been assumed to be constant. An alternative hypothesis is that this variance increases (decreases) with increases in an explanatory variable in a cross-section study or over time in a time series study. If the disturbances are heteroscedastic, OLS estimates of the coefficients of the model will be unbiased, but will not be efficient. The solution is to use GLS regression.

The test against heteroscedasticity is due to Goldfeld and Quandt (1965). This test [Johnston (1972), 219] involves:

1. Ordering the observations according to increasing values of the explanatory variable or time.

2. Omitting the c central observations. The value of c being chosen so as to maximize the power of the test.

3. Fitting *separate* regressions by ordinary least squares to the first $(n - c)/2$ observations and to the last $(n - c)/2$ observations.

4. Testing the ratio of the residual sums of squares from the two regressions using the F distribution with $(n - c - 2K)/2$ and $(n - c - 2K)/2$ degrees of freedom.

The use of separate regressions forces the numerator and denominator of the ratio to be independent so that the ratio has an F distribution under the null hypothesis. This would not be true if the residuals in a single equation were merely partitioned.

Multicollinearity

Multicollinearity occurs when the predetermined variables are strongly related to each other. In this case, the influence of one can not be separated from another. Consequently, the explanatory power of the regression is unaffected, but the estimates of the coefficients are not precise. The usual solution is to drop one or more of the offending variables from the equation. The risk of doing this is that the relationship between included and excluded variables might change over time. Thus, a better approach is to obtain new data or information which would resolve the multicollinearity issue. This might involve estimating some of the parameters in a time-series model by a cross-section study. Then these estimates would replace the corresponding unknown parameters in the time-series model. Finally, the remaining unknown parameters could be estimated using the time-series data. Another possible solution is to use *ridge regression.*

The mean-square error of an estimator is equal to its variance plus its bias squared. The least-squares estimator has zero bias, but has a large variance in the presence of multicollinearity. In ridge regression some bias is accepted in order to reduce the variance. This tradeoff is shown in Fig. 5.1. The ridge estimator is

$$\hat{\beta} = (\mathbf{X'X} + k\,\mathbf{I})^{-1}\,\mathbf{X'y}, \qquad (5.17)$$

where k is a nonzero scalar. Variance is a decreasing function of k while bias is an increasing function of k. Hoerl and Kennard (1970) discuss how k is chosen.

Farrar and Glauber (1967) developed a procedure for diagnosing multicollinearity problems. The procedure is based on careful examination of various correlation coefficients. The existance of

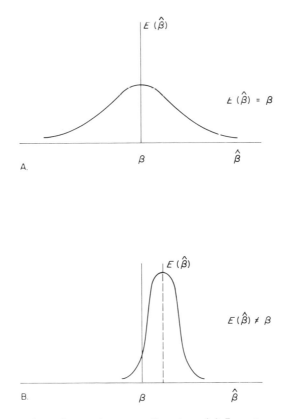

Fig. 5.1. Bias and variance in an estimator. (a) Least squares estimator: zero bias and large variance; (b) Ridge estimator: non-zero bias and small variance.

multicollinearity can be detected by transforming $|R|$, the determinant of the simple correlation matrix, into a chi-square statistic[6]:

$$\chi^2 = -\left\{n - 1 - [1/6][2(K-1) + 5]\right\} \log |R|. \tag{5.18}$$

Under the null hypothesis that the variables are orthogonal, this statistic is distributed $\chi^2 [(K-1)(K-2)/2]$.

If multicollinearity is detected, then the variables most strongly affected by interdependence must be determined. This localization is accomplished by regressing each independent variable against all remaining $K-2$ independent variables and evaluating the resultant coefficients of determination, R_i^2. Under the null hypothesis we know from Eq. (5.4) that the statistic

$$F = \frac{(n - K + 1) R_i^2}{(K - 2) (1 - R_i^2)}$$

(5.19)

is distributed as $F(K - 2, n - K + 1)$. Rejection of the null hypothesis indicates those variables which show a significant linear dependence with other predetermined variables.

The pattern of interdependence among the affected variables is further revealed by considering the pair-wise partial correlations of these variables. Under the null hypothesis, the corresponding partial t-statistic is distributed $t(n - K + 1)$. This and the previous tests have been implemented by means of a computer program by Bond and Montgomery (1970).

The multicollinearity tests of Farrar and Glauber assume that the variables under analysis constitute a multivariate normal distribution. This is a very tenuous assumption. Kumar (1975) and O'Hagan and McCabe (1975) demonstrate that the measures used by Farrar and Glauber can not be based on known statistical theory. Even so, our experience is that the measures provide useful insights of practical value.

Nonnormality

The previous specification error tests assume that the distribution of the disturbance terms is normal. One test for normality is the Shapiro-Wilk W-test:

$$W = \frac{\left(\sum_{i=1}^{n-K} a_i y_i \right)^2}{\sum_{i=1}^{n-K} (\hat{\epsilon}_i - \bar{\hat{\epsilon}})^2} \, ,$$

(5.20)

where the y_i are the order statistics obtained from the BLUS Residuals $\hat{\epsilon}_i$ and the a_i are weighting coefficients given by Shapiro and Wilk (1965, 603-604). The W-test can detect deviations from normality due to either skewness or kurtosis and is consequently superior to commonly used tests such as the chi-square and

Kolmogorov-Smirnov tests. These authors have tabulated critical values of W for values of $n - K$ between 3 and 50. For sample sizes larger than 50, one must use the D-statistic by D'Agostino (1971).

Systems of Equations

The analysis of specification error in simultaneous equation models involves two additional problems. First, when an estimation technique that incorporates more information than is contained in an isolated single equation is employed, the effects of specification error can be transferred across equations. Second, the inclusion of irrelevant variables or the omission of a relevant variable are specification errors that may affect the identifiability of one or more of the equations in the system. In general, the discussion of these problems is beyond the scope of this book. We will discuss just one test.

An *identifiability test statistic* should be used whenever the order and rank conditions for identifiability indicate an equation is over-identified. The purpose of the test is to determine if the *a priori* restrictions which caused the over-identifying condition are correct. Usually the over-identifying condition arises from variables in the system as a whole being excluded from a particular equation. Thus, a statistical test is required to judge if these extra exclusions are correctly specified in view of the evidence provided by the sample data. Basmann (1965a) discusses the construction of identifiability tests. Parsons (1968) gives a marketing application of such tests.

MODEL SELECTION

Theil (1971) defines the specification problem in econometric models as one of choosing the correct variables and the correct form of the relationship between them. It is thus a problem of choice, and a research strategy should be designed to aid in this decision process. We are, of course, seeking the true model of some marketing phenomena out of all possible models and so we are appropriately concerned with how the correct specification (if it were known) differs from any number of incorrect specifications. For econometric research, this issue becomes one of investigating alternative regression models according to some criterion. The criterion can either be an informal decision rule such as maximizing $\bar{R}^2$ or a formal decision rule involving hypothesis testing.

Informal Decision Rule

The most common decision rule for choosing among alternative linear models with nonstochastic exogenous variables is to select the model with the largest $\bar{R}^2$. $\bar{R}^2$ is an adjustment of R^2, the coefficient of determination:

$$\bar{R}^2 = R^2 - \frac{K-1}{n-K}(1 - R^2), \qquad (5.21)$$

where K is the number of exogenous variables and n is the number of observations. The adjustment approximately corrects for the bias caused by the fact that R^2 can be increased simply by adding more variables. An equivalent rule is select the model with the smallest residual variance. Moreover, the probability that the decision rule will choose a particular model when it is the correctly specified model can be calculated. Ideally, this probability should be large.

The problem is to choose between two alternative models:

$$(A1) \qquad y = X\beta + \epsilon$$

and

$$(A2) \qquad y = Z\gamma + \eta.$$

The number of independent variables in X is K_x and in Z is K_z. The number of observations is n. The dependent variable, y, is assumed to have a multivariate normal distribution with mean vector ξ and covariance matrix $\sigma^2 I_n$. The probability of choosing model A1 over model A2 by the maximum $\bar{R}^2$ criterion when model A1 is the correctly specified model is $\Pr(\bar{R}_x^2 > \bar{R}_z^2) = \Pr(y'Ay < 0)$. The symmetric matrix A is defined as $M_x - \alpha M_z$, where $M_x = I_n - X(X'X)^{-1}X'$, $M_z = I_n - Z(Z'Z)^{-1}Z'$, and $\alpha = (n - K_x)/(n - K_z)$. This result is due to Schmidt (1973) and Ebbeler (1974).

Imhof (1961) developed a procedure for calculating the distribution of quadratic forms in normal variables. The Imhof procedure can be implemented by modification of a computer program given in Koerts and Abrahamse (1969). This approach was utilized in a marketing study by Parsons (1976).

There are several good uses for goodness of fit, especially as measured by $\bar{R}^2$. It is a particularly appropriate measure of the extent to which the (true) model accounts for total variation or, in a sense, approximates the real phenomena. In this case, $\bar{R}^2$ is a measure of the degree of approximation by which a generalization holds. For testing theories, however, a more powerful criterion is necessary. These ideas do not appear to be widely understood in marketing or economics as has been argued, notably by Bass (1969).

The major weakness of this criterion is rather fundamental: It doesn't work when none of the alternative specifications are correct. Moreover, since it only holds "on the average" there is no small chance that the wrong specification prevails. Now since the objective of marketing econometrics is to identify true sales response functions and marketing decision rules, a criterion which relies on the fortuitous inclusion of the correct model as one of the set under evaluation seems to be an inefficient way of conducting research. It is inefficient because the process does not encourage the development of specification (models) which are otherwise readily falsifiable, and therefore incorrect models are more easily accepted.

Moreover, this criterion assumes that the dependent variables of the models are identical. Sometimes, however, a marketing researcher may want to explore regressions with sales, Q and log Q as alternative forms of the dependent variable. In this case, the $\bar{R}^2$ criterion does not obtain directly. In comparing a set of linear market-share models with a set of loglinear models, Weiss (1969) has used antilog conversions and then correlation of y with $\hat{y}$ to evaluate relative goodness of fit.

Hypothesis Testing

The maximum $\bar{R}^2$ selection rule discussed in the last section is a methodological convention. It involves an implicit assumption that disagreement between the theoretical model and observations is a monotone decreasing function of $\bar{R}^2$. However, this convention can be in conflict with classical statistical inference. In classical statistical inference, the disagreement between the theoretical model and observations is a monotone decreasing function of the probability with which the observed event is supposed to occur.

The two conventions necessarily yield similar conclusions only if the *population* coefficient of determination, P^2, is equal to 1.0. The probability density function of the *sample* coefficient of determination is noncentral F, with $K - 1$, $n - K$ degrees of freedom and noncentrality parameter nP^2. This reduces to the familiar central F (5.4) when the null hypothesis is $P^2 = 0$.

Basmann (1964) provides the following illustration of this distinction. Suppose we are able to derive, from a conjunction of the underlying behavioral marketing postulates and the given sample observations of size 20 on 3 exogenous variables, a statement that P^2 just lies between 0.3 and 0.4. Furthermore, suppose we obtain $R^2 = .75$ in our regression run. Under the first convention, we may well judge that this test statistic does not disagree with our model. However, since

$$\int_{.70}^{1.0} f(R^2 ; 20P^2 ; 2)d(R^2) \leqslant 0.05,$$

under the second convention, we would decide that the observed sample coefficient of determination is *too large* to be in good agreement with our marketing postulates.

Embedded Alternatives. One way to discriminate among linear models is to embed the specific alternative models within one general model. Hypotheses about the values of certain parameters of the general model can be deduced from the specific alternative models. For instance, suppose we want to choose between these two alternative specific models

$$y_\alpha = \beta_0 + \beta_1 x_\alpha + \beta_2 x_{\alpha-1} + \epsilon_\alpha, \tag{5.22}$$

and

$$y_\alpha = \beta_0 + \beta_1 x_\alpha + \beta_3 y_{\alpha-1} + \epsilon_\alpha. \tag{5.23}$$

Then, we can embed these two models in this general model

$$y_\alpha = \beta_0 + \beta_1 x_\alpha + \beta_2 x_{\alpha-1} + \beta_3 y_{\alpha-1} + \epsilon_\alpha. \tag{5.24}$$

If at least one, but not both, of the last two parameters (β_2, β_3) in the general model is zero, then we can discriminate between the two models. If $\beta_2 = 0$, we will reject the model of Eq. (5.22). If $\beta_3 = 0$, we will reject the model of Eq. (5.23).

A robust procedure for testing a regression model against a nested alternative model can be derived using the likelihood ratio method. A nested model implies that r of the variables in the full regression model with K variables will have zero regression coefficients. Kendall and Stuart [(1973), 257-261] show that the appropriate test statistic is

$$ F = \frac{n - K}{r} \left(\frac{\hat{\hat{\sigma}}^2 - \hat{\sigma}^2}{\hat{\sigma}^2} \right), \tag{5.25} $$

where $\hat{\hat{\sigma}}^2$ and $\hat{\sigma}^2$ are the least-squares residual sum of squares for the nested and full regression models, respectively. The nested model will be rejected if $\hat{F} > F_{\alpha, r, n-K}$. An application of this test is given in Chap. 8.

The nested approach to model discrimination has some limitations. It is difficult to use if the number of alternative models becomes too large. A large number of alternative models would likely require a general model with a large number of variables. This, in turn, would necessitate a large sample size as well as increase the potential for multicollinearity problems. Moreover, if one of the specific alternative models is the correct model, then the general model will involve specification error because of the presence of irrelevant variables.

Pooling.[7]   The F-statistic [Eq. (5.25)] can be used to test whether or not to pool T time periods and N cross sections of data (see Chap. 4). The problem is one of testing the conditions under which pooling is appropriate, since we know that the microparameter vectors (of the different sales territories) have to be equal to prevent aggregation or "pooling" bias. The basic procedure is described briefly. Perform *unconstrained* regression, viz.,

$$ \begin{bmatrix} y_1 \\ y_2 \\ \cdot \\ \cdot \\ \cdot \\ y_N \end{bmatrix} = \begin{bmatrix} X_1 & 0 & \cdots & 0 \\ 0 & X_2 & & \\ \cdot & & \cdot & \\ \cdot & & & \cdot \\ \cdot & & & \cdot \\ 0 & & & X_N \end{bmatrix} \begin{bmatrix} \beta_1 \\ \beta_2 \\ \cdot \\ \cdot \\ \cdot \\ \beta_N \end{bmatrix} + \begin{bmatrix} \epsilon_1 \\ \epsilon_2 \\ \cdot \\ \cdot \\ \cdot \\ \epsilon_N \end{bmatrix} \tag{5.26} $$

estimating $N \times K'$ parameters using $N \times T$ observations, and *constrained* regression, viz.,

$$
\begin{bmatrix} y_1 \\ y_2 \\ \cdot \\ \cdot \\ \cdot \\ y_N \end{bmatrix} = \begin{bmatrix} X_1 \\ X_2 \\ \cdot \\ \cdot \\ \cdot \\ X_N \end{bmatrix} \begin{bmatrix} \beta \end{bmatrix} + \begin{bmatrix} \epsilon_1' \\ \epsilon_2' \\ \cdot \\ \cdot \\ \cdot \\ \epsilon_N' \end{bmatrix} \tag{5.27}
$$

estimating K' parameters with $N \times T$ observations. The constrained regression amounts to pooling the observations from all sales territories, thereby constraining the coefficient vectors β_i, β_j for all i, j to be equal. This would imply that the sales territories exhibit equivalent sales responsiveness. Unconstrained regression, on the other hand, allows each sales territory to behave differently in this regard. The null hypothesis is

$$
H_0 : \beta_1 = \beta_2 = \cdots = \beta_N = \beta. \tag{5.28}
$$

To test the null hypothesis of equal response coefficients covariance analysis may be used. The general framework in which this testing can take place will be discussed briefly. In general, let the model under investigation be

$$
y_i = X_i \beta_i + \epsilon_i, \qquad i = 1, 2, \ldots, N \text{(territories)}. \tag{5.29}
$$

Making the usual assumptions, the OLS estimator of β_i is unbiased and efficient.

To determine whether the response coefficient vectors, β_i, β_j for all i, j differ significantly, we can proceed as follows. Assuming that $\sigma_{\epsilon_i}^2 = \sigma_{\epsilon_j}^2$ for all i, j, this hypothesis of overall homogeneity can be tested using the F-statistic [Eq. (5.25)] where $n = N \times T$, $K = N \times K'$, and $r = K' \times (N - 1)$.

A number of issues relevant to this procedure for investigating the homogeneity in the overall relationship should be considered, however. A lack of overall homogeneity may be the result of differences in only one or two of the parameters across sales territories. It is possible to use mixed models in the sense that all but one or a few of the parameters are constrained to be equal while the other parameters are allowed to be different. Similarly, it may be argued that some of the cross sections have the same relationship while others behave differently. Although it would be possible to segment sales territories according to similarity in the relationship using some heuristic [Wittink (1973)], it is not possible, in a strict sense, to test the appropriateness of such a procedure.

The F-statistic suggested to test the existence of homogeneity in the relationship is based on several assumptions. For one thing, the model is assumed to be correctly specified. If it is argued that it is never possible to include all relevant variables in a model then the null hypothesis of homogeneity can always be rejected as long as the sample size is large enough. Wallace has argued for constrained estimation (pooling) even when the null hypothesis is rejected because "... even if the restriction is strictly invalid, the constrained estimators have smaller variances and one might be willing to make a tradeoff, accepting some bias in order to reduce variances" [Wallace (1972), 690].

A second assumption involves the homogeneity of disturbance variances. When comparing the relationship across sales territories using covariance analysis, it is assumed that the variances are homogeneous. This assumption can be relaxed, but only asymptotic tests (using the estimated disturbance variances) can be used to investigate the homogeneity of relationships under conditions of heterogeneous variances [Swamy (1971), 124-126]. Furthermore, the appropriateness of the F-test for the purpose of comparing response coefficient vectors for each of the sales territories is also conditional upon the existence of homogeneity in the relationship over time. Thus, it is possible that a finding of significant differences for the sales territories is really the result of varying parameter values over time. The validity of each of these assumptions should be established. In addition different pooling methods should be considered and compared both from a theoretical and an empirical viewpoint [Bass and Wittink (1975)].

Predictive Testing. The notion of predictive testing, in which the theoretical premises of a theory are challenged with the possible inconsistency of their predictions with empirical data, falls within long-established traditions of scientific inquiry. For this reason, the fact that predictive tests are not used more widely in economics or marketing is somewhat surprising. The primary development of the ideas of predictive testing in econometric research is due to Basmann (1964, 1965, 1968). Initial studies involving predictive testing in marketing have been made by Bass (1969a) and Bass and Parsons (1969). The concept has been further discussed by Bass (1969b, 1971). The discussion below relies on Parsons (1968).

An explanatory marketing model, such as a sales response function, is comprised of theoretical marketing premises and justifiable factual statements of initial conditions. From the model, a set of prediction-statements that attribute definite probabilities to specified observable marketing events is deduced. Deductive analysis of an explanatory marketing model should result in a statement of the exact finite sample joint distribution function of parameter estimates and test statistics.

Discourses on the scientific method usually consider a predictive test conducted under experimental conditions. Often the assertion that initial conditions appropriate for a particular theory are thoroughly known is implicitly made. Ensuingly, an effective technology for controlling these initial conditions is assumed to exist and to have been used.

It is true, nevertheless, that explicit consideration of initial conditions cannot be omitted when developing a marketing model. Since the model can be falsified by unsuccessful predictions, close attention must be given to substantiating statements that claim that external influences are negligible during the historical period analyzed.

A statement of initial conditions is really a combination of three statements. One statement specifies the observed values of the exogenous variables explicitly included in the structural relations of the model. Another statement specifies the statistical distribution of the random disturbances explicitly included in the structural relations.[8] In addition, one statement asserts that relevant external conditions stay approximately constant during the historical period under consideration.

What we are saying is that the marketing environment is one in which uncontrollable changes can be anticipated to cause the structure of a relationship to change. Thus, we need to know how a theory can be tested in a situation where its structural form is not invariant to time. The necessary additional information is obviously a precise statement of the environmental conditions under which the theory is assumed to hold. In effect, we must guard against sampling from the wrong temporal population when testing a particular model; otherwise, we may falsely reject a theory.

The predictive test of an explanatory marketing model is implemented by specification of an observable event (the critical region for the test) which has a probability of occurring that is very small if the conjunction of initial conditions and economic premises is true. Occurrence of this theoretically improbable event implies that at least one, and maybe only one, of the assumptions about the initial conditions and marketing premises is discredited. If factual investigation justifies the statement of initial conditions, then at least one, and maybe only one, of the marketing premises is discredited.

Note that a forecast and prediction are not synonymous. Important and pragmatic statements about future occurrences can be made without deducing these statements from initial conditions with the aid of a model. A forecast is an extrapolation from statistical parameter estimates obtained in one historical period to observations generated *in another historical period*. Therefore, while forecasts *seem* to provide information concerning an hypothesis, Brunner (1973) points out that neither "good" nor "bad" forecasts supply any relevant evidence in themselves.[9] Forecasts do not satisfy the logical requirements of a test statement.

SUMMARY

Specification is a general problem of research strategy. It should be apparent that both scientific and creative forces are necessary to build marketing theories. Whether the origin of the theory is empirical or logical, or both, the result was shown to be a set of premises which specify that the model belongs to a small subset of all possible models, assuming that the model represents a true theory. The specification problem involves the procedures required to identify marketing variables and relationships. Specification analysis concerns the consequences of incorrect specifications on the interpretation of research results.

We have sought to show that specification analysis requires a criterion that provides for a rigorous test of the theory embodied by the model, that is, a test which preserves the degree of falsifiability of the theory. In this way, the test of the specification of the model becomes congruent with the test of the model as a theory.

FOOTNOTES

[1] Specification error could also be caused by sampling from the incorrect population.

[2] BLUS transformation.

[3]
$$v = \sum_{i=1}^{k} v_i = n - K.$$

[4] Laroche (1975) examined the reliability and sensitivity of this test in the context of marketing research.

[5] The correspondence to the Durbin-Watson statistic can be seen by substituting the relation $\hat{\rho} = 1 - d/2$ into Eq. (5.16).

[6] The intercept variable, a constant, is excluded from the analysis.

[7] This section is a digression from our main arguments concerning discrimination among alternative models and may be skipped without loss of continuity.

[8] Cunnyngham (1972) notes that "Not only must the stochastic properties of the variables in the invariant structural form of a marketing model be identified and deductively explained in terms of its associated marketing theory, but the stochastic properties so identified must be invariant; that is, they must represent stationary distribution functions."

[9] This is true notwithstanding the lengthy lists of nonparametric measures for model evaluation such as given in Dhrymes *et al.* (1972).

Part Three. Econometric Research in Marketing

Chapter 6

THE DEVELOPMENT
OF MARKETING MODELS

The creation of a marketing model is an artistic act within the domain of science. The reliance on science is most familiar and perhaps easiest to see. As a scientific endeavor, the model-building process is characterized by its method—careful planning, apparent objectivity, and rigorous procedures—all designed to produce some measure of truth. We evaluate the quality of science by evaluating its method; if the method is sound, then the result of the research, the finding, is presumably sound. As an exercise in art, the process is more difficult to assess. Art is judged by the result, not the process of developing it. The artistic *piece* is the test of quality, in this case, the model. Thus, the creation of a marketing model, or any model, requires two kinds of talents—the ability to investigate, which is a scientific trait and the ability to create, which is the definition of art. As this chapter will show, these two talents must be carefully nurtured, especially in marketing.

To be more specific, consider sales response models as a subclass of marketing models. As discussed in Chaps. 1 and 2, these models deal with relationships between measures of sales and marketing effort. Where do the relationships come from? How do we test them as theories of marketing behavior? These two questions raise the artistic and scientific issues noted above. They can only be answered by appealing to the creative and investigative talents of the researcher. The purpose of this chapter is to consider the process of developing marketing models, especially sales response models, which meet rigorous scientific standards. We argue that this process is a creative one and that these artistic considerations complement the scientific method.

MARKETING MODELS AND THEORIES

Sales response models represent theories of marketing behavior. For this reason it is important to examine the relationship between models and theory development. The scientific basis of marketing models is discussed in this section. In the next section, more operational considerations are raised.

Elements of Marketing Theory

Marketing theory is rather elusive. As a well-defined body of knowledge, it is possible to say that it doesn't exist. It would certainly be controversial to try to delimit marketing theory in this way. There are, however, certain hypotheses which have received support and which can be considered to hold under specified conditions and thus serve as generalizations of marketing behavior. Some of these have to do with group behavior of market segments, with effects of advertising on sales, with new product diffusion patterns, and so forth. These empirically supported hypotheses may not form a coherent, interdependent explanation or general theory of marketing behavior , but they do represent a beginning toward the development of systematic knowledge in marketing. They at least represent "islands of theory."[1]

One of the major obstacles to the development of marketing theory undoubtedly has been the *modus operandi* of its research. Marketing research has long connotated a set of rather specific techniques aimed at solving a collection of rather specific problems. Technique rather than substance to a great extent dominates extant marketing research. This situation and the pragmatic view of marketing research that it reflects has considerable merit in "marketing as a professional activity." In "marketing as a science," however, this state of affairs provides the nexus to the problem of marketing theory. The development of theory in marketing requires a broadened perspective of marketing research and an elaboration of the principles of scientific research. To an admirable extent, such issues are raised and discussed in Zaltman, Pinson, and Angelmar's *Metatheory and Consumer Research* (1973).

The setting of sales response models affords us an opportunity to explore aspects of model specification and development in relation to established procedures of econometric research and existing studies of sales behavior. We focus on the identification of sales response functions and marketing decision rules. To the extent that this process becomes theory construction, though, we must deal with a consideration of the origin of marketing hypotheses, at least briefly.

Marketing Generalizations. We define marketing theories (equivalent to marketing hypotheses) as constructs capable of being falsified by empirical data which is to say that they are constructs capable of being tested. The marketing proposition that sales is a function of advertising can be regarded as a marketing theory when the terms sales and advertising are precisely defined, variables arc chosen to represent these terms, the form of the function is specified, and the conditions under which the relation is expected to hold are elaborated. In addition, we may require that premises be made about the parameters of the model (where any logical connection of variables is a model). Marketing propositions that fall short of these requirements should not be regarded as theories because they are not capable of being tested in that form.

The sources of marketing theories are marketing generalizations. A generalization about some phenomena can be viewed as an approximate summary of the data which describe the phenomena. This view holds that the origin of generalization (and hence theory) is data and thus observation of the phenomena is a precondition to theory development. Simon (1968) describes this process as one involving three stages: first, "finding simple generalizations that describe the facts to some degree of approximation"; second, "finding limiting conditions under which the deviations of facts from generalization might be expected to decrease"; and, third, "explaining why the generalization 'should' fit the facts." This third stage, in which the notion of explanation appears, is crucial in defining the purpose of theory: Marketing theory seeks to explain marketing phenomena. Not all generalizations, however, originate from data. Another source of generalizations is from deductive reasoning.

This view holds that the origin of generalization is from *a priori* logic. *A priori* notions about the phenomena are employed to make generalizations and thus reason rather than data plays the central role. Both the empirical and *a priori* bases for generalizations are used in scientific research. We tend to be familiar with these traditions in some fields but not others. The theoretical sciences, for example, are not merely deductive. Physics is a good case where theoretic and correlational procedures are complementary. Margenau (1950) notes that "A theoretic, or deductive, science does not move wholly in the thin air of reason. It receives its validity by constant reference to what is empirically given."

These ideas are relatively unexplored in marketing and this undoubtedly explains some of the casualness of our research. Rigorous procedures are required to both develop and test theories of marketing behavior. Since we are primarily concerned with theory construction in this chapter, we cannot deal at length with theory testing. The topic, however, is closely related to the present argument because for a generalization to be falsifiable, or testable, it must (a) be extended beyond the data from which it was generated, or (b) be derived from an explanatory theory which has testable consequences beyond the original data [Simon (1968)]. This is true because the generalization itself by definition is not testable. Thus marketing generalizations evolve into marketing theories when these conditions (for theory testing) become effective. These principles in marketing are discussed more fully by Bass (1969b, 1971).

Marketing Premises. Premises are the building blocks of a marketing theory. Consider the advertising-sales proposition above. To qualify as a theory, a number of specific assertions or premises about the world must be embodied in the statement. One premise could be that advertising determines sales (where both terms are defined) and not the reverse and this assertion would be one of causality. Another premise could be that the functional relationship is linear in logarithms of the variables. A premise could be made about the parameter—an elasticity in this case—of advertising, specifying, for example, that it should fall in the interval 0 to +.5 which implies that the effect of advertising on sales is small, positive and inelastic. Finally, a premise could be made about the conditions under which the relation is expected to hold. These conditions might be for a class of frequently purchased branded goods sold predominantly in supermarkets. These premises taken together define a rather specific marketing theory which can be tested by examining its conformity with marketing data. If the theory survives this test, we continue to entertain it until further tests show it to be inconsistent with the evidence.

The rigor of the test, at least from a theoretical point of view, is defined by the degree to which the premises imply that the model (as the representation of the theory), on the condition that it is true, belongs to a small subset of all possible models. This concept is essentially what Popper (1961) calls the "degree of falsifiability" of theories which he equates with the simplicity of a theory. The simplicity of generalizations is an important point to be considered by marketing and other researchers. Simon (1968) makes a useful distinction between the implication of simplicity and the plausibility of theories. Popper desires hypotheses "to be simple so that, if they are false, they can be disconfirmed by empirical data as readily as possible." Simon argues that "a simple hypothesis that fits data to a reasonable approximation should be entertained, for it probably reveals an underlying law of nature." According to Popper, a simple hypothesis describes a highly particular state of the world which is easily falsified because it is improbable. According to Simon, a simple hypothesis summarizes a "highly unique (but actual)" state-of-the-world and thus it is highly plausible. But these positions are not incompatible. Simon seems to follow Hanson (1961) who argued for a logic of discovery (of hypotheses) that would result in *plausible conjectures*. Hanson felt that, while discovery was in part psychological (our "art") , it was also partly logical (our "science") in that some generalizations are more likely to succeed than others. These ideas of plausibility, falsifiability, and the confirmation of hypotheses are elegantly integrated in a Bayesian framework by Salmon (1967), making these notions quite practical for marketing scientists.

Two examples can serve to illustrate these different processes of model development and specification. The deductive approach to marketing generalization is rare; however, Bell, Keeney, and Little (1975) show, using such logic, that for certain assumptions market share is a simple linear normalization of attraction, viz., models of the sort

$$MS_i = \frac{A_i}{\sum_{i=1}^{N} A_i} \, , \tag{6.1}$$

where

MS_i = market share of firm i
A_i = advertising of firm i

can be logically derived from the definition of a set of "attractions" $(A_i, i = 1, \ldots, N)$ and several assumptions about the nature of the attractions. Together with other premises, Eq. (6.1) can express a theory of sales response where at least part of the theory (the premise that market share is a linear function of advertising share) was the result of *a priori* reasoning.

Empirical observation of marketing phenomena can also lead to marketing generalizations and hence premises for marketing theories. The leading example of such a process is in the work of Ehrenberg (1972). This work begins with an empirical search for regularities in the data. If regularities are found, then they can be compared with other sets of data to establish their generality. Only then does the analysis proceed to the search for interrelationships (how the regularities occur) and for explanations (why they occur).

This research paradigm, which is identical with the approach discussed in connection with Simon above, was used by Ehrenberg to develop the NBD-LSD theory of repeat buying. Empirical regularities were used to build the theory and the theory was employed to predict further conclusions to be checked against different data. Ehrenberg's description of the process as "from facts to theory, and back again" is quite apt.

Summary

The relationships described in this section are summarized in Fig. 6.1. Observation and/or reasoning about marketing phenomena (such as sales responses) can lead to marketing generalizations. These approximate summaries of the data or logical conclusions can be quite formal, reflecting explicit *laws* of marketing behavior [Ehrenberg (1972)], or definite *theorems* [Bell, Keeney, and Little (1975)] or quite informal, constituting merely our *notions* of how the facts fit together. Such marketing generalizations, expressed as a set of premises, are sharpened into marketing theories when they are made more precise and when they carry with them *explanations* of the phenomena. A simple parallel can be drawn with the physical sciences. Boyle's Law states that at constant temperature a fixed weight of gas occupies a volume inversely proportional to the pressure exerted on it. This statement is a

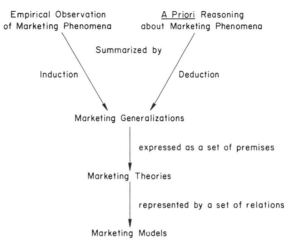

Fig. 6.1. Theory development in marketing.

generalization—a description of a physical relationship. It is not, by itself, an explanation (i.e., a theory), but can lead to a theory if certain premises are offered regarding molecular structure. Marketing generalizations and theories have just the same relationship.

The purpose of a marketing model is to *represent* a marketing theory. A theory of sales response, for example, can be represented by a set of mathematical relations, thus becoming a mathematical model. Although nothing precludes verbal models of theories, symbolic models—whether they are mathematical or logical flow types—are very efficient for theory building as well as for theory testing. So models in this scheme are tools for implementing research. They have long been regarded as "the central necessity of scientific procedure" [Rosenbleuth and Wiener (1945)].

Models, and the theories they represent, can be simple or complex depending upon their scope and the inherent complexity of the phenomena under study. A researcher's natural drive for completeness is offset by such practical considerations as degrees of freedom and such theoretical constraints as parsimony where the simplest model to "explain well" is to be preferred. The fact, first noted in Chap. 1, that econometric procedures are equally appropriate for simple or complex models suggests the fundamental importance of econometrics to theory building and to theory testing. And it should be noted that while the ultimate test of a theory is its validity, the ultimate test of a model is its utility in the research process itself.

MARKETING VARIABLES AND RELATIONSHIPS

Sales response models describe the relationship between certain marketing decisions and environmental variables and their effect on sales. Econometric methods have been used to estimate these models in a variety of marketing situations. The testing of econometric models is logically prior to their estimation, for as we have seen, testing involves the validity of a relation while estimation concerns the best representation of its parameters. The identification of econometric models, defined nonrigorously here as the specification of variables and their connection (a more specific meaning was given in Chap. 3), must precede testing and hence estimation. Thus, procedures for identifying marketing econometric models are of the first importance. This view is consistent with the argument that marketing theories originate from marketing generalizations which themselves must grow from some notion, either *a priori* or empirical, or the nature of marketing variables and their relationships. In the remainder of this section, we discuss the identification of sales response functions, marketing decision rules, and the question of whether or not they are interdependent.

Identifying Sales Response Functions

Virtually all sales response functions in marketing will grow from the investigator's knowledge of marketing data or at least his observation of the marketing situation under study. A typical scenario goes something like this: A market is selected for investigation; the investigator examines the nature of the market, including the position of the company or brand in the market (usually sales response studies *focus* on one brand or firm), the structure of competition, and the variables which seem to influence total market demand and company market share or simply company sales; the researcher looks at the dynamics of the market, i.e., changes in total market demand, competition, market shares, relative marketing effort, and so forth; finally, the investigator develops some theory about how the market works, expresses the theory as an econometric response model, and analyzes the model with formally collected empirical data; in the final step, the investigator reports his findings, although not typically in a manner that permits replication (which is an essential feature of scientific method) because of the proprietary nature of most marketing data.

The strategy of identifying sales response functions, then, relies heavily on close observation of marketing situations. By "close" we mean that the investigator observes firsthand, which itself implies observation *within* the organization. More than other areas of research, even other topics in marketing research, sales response studies require that the investigator have access to the company and its sales and marketing records. Investigation from *outside of* the organization is usually not possible because it does not allow the mechanics of market and firm behavior to be determined. Of course, if marketing theory was developed to the point where we could deduce certain sales response equations for specific marketing situations, then an alternative approach would be available.

This other approach, which is the deductive approach to marketing generalizations (as in Fig. 6.1) has been successfully applied to sales response functions by economists who are interested in price-quantity relationships and call them *demand curves*. Demand equations are the logical consequences of a theory of consumer choice which posits that consumers choose among goods so as to maximize their total utility-given prices and subject to a budget constraint.[2] The specification problem in this case is "solved" by the consumer theory which leads to a set of demand equations in which quantity purchased is a function of the good's own price, other prices, and individual incomes. Functions like these have been estimated for many years and substantial progress has been made in summarizing the effect of the marketing variable price. Most modern market situations, however, involve other marketing variables in addition to (or perhaps in place of) price. At this point, axiomatic theory in economics stops and none in marketing has been developed. This absence of a deductive source of marketing generalizations, rather than any inherent advantage of the empirical approach, accounts for the prevailing reliance on observation and data analysis.

We conclude from this state of affairs that research on sales response functions requires a considerable amount of creativity and that this artistic talent may determine the "success" of the sales response model. The identification of sales response functions without prior theory is an artistic act. Their testing and subsequent estimation turn more on standard principles of scientific and, in particular, econometric method. But the process of specifying the model and the theory of marketing behavior which it embodies is certainly a "frontier" of marketing science.

Identifying Marketing Decision Rules

There are at least two sources of ideas about marketing decision rules which correspond to the inductive and deductive paradigms discussed above. First, an investigator can observe how decisions are made in a company. This can be done by examining the relationship between the decision variables and measures of company performance or by investigating the behavioral process of decision making. The empirical approach attempts to relate, say, advertising expenditures to past revenue, profit, advertising, and other variables. Regression analysis is used to find significant relationships which "explain" total variance of the decision variable. The behavioral approach seeks to develop an information-processing theory of executive behavior from which decision rules for price, advertising, selling effort, etc. can be derived. Very few studies in marketing treat decision variables endogenously; among those that do are Bass and Parsons (1969), Schultz (1971), and Wildt (1974). Even these studies rely primarily on a combination of empirical evidence and management interviews to identify the decision rules without developing an explicit theory of executive decision making. The behavioral approach requires that a positive model of decision making be developed and that this serve as the source of generalizations about how specific marketing decisions are made. An initial effort along these lines is a study of marketing decision rules by Schultz and Dodson (1974b).

The second major source of ideas about marketing decision rules is normative theory in marketing. If firms are acting rationally (and optimally), we may attribute their decisions to models which show how to set optimal prices, optimal advertising budgets, and so forth. Consider advertising, for example. Dorfman and Steiner (1954), Nerlove and Arrow (1962), and others (cf. Chap. 9) have stated conditions under which a firm would maximize profits; extensions of their work show how these theories can be converted into operational decision rules [Kotler (1971), Chap. 7]. We may use the variables in these rules as those to include in our marketing decision rule functions. Then, investigation can proceed as to whether or not firms were acting in accordance with optimal rules. Comparisons of this sort have been made by a number of researchers as reported in Chap. 9.

As with sales response functions, the identification of marketing decision rules requires considerable reliance on the creative capacity of the investigator. In many ways this is a state-of-the-art problem, especially in that well-developed theories of executive decision making are not available, although initial work in this area has been done by Howard and Morgenroth (1968) and Hulbert, Farley, and Howard (1972). In the sense that managers know what they are doing and use established procedures for setting marketing decision variables, the problem of identifying decision rules may be less severe than that of identifying response functions. To the extent that managers deviate from these rules, however, the problem becomes much the same. Present evidence suggests that there is a considerable unexplained component in such models and thus new "pioneering" studies are necessary.

Simultaneous Relationships

The possible interdependence of sales response functions and marketing decision rules raises an important question of model specification and an important issue of model estimation. The connection between these specification and estimation problems is an additional problem for model testing. There may be reason to believe that sales and advertising are interdependent in the sense that sales is a function of current advertising and vice versa. This implies that a model of market behavior should be one of simultaneous-equations, or at least one that recognizes in its statistical assumptions the correlation among disturbances of the two types of equations.

The specification question involves whether or not the relations are interdependent, i.e., whether or not *both* sales and advertising are endogenous or simply interdependent in disturbances. The estimation issue is that, if they are interdependent, the single-equation specification and ordinary least-squares estimation of the model parameters will result in estimates which are not consistent. This bias is a well-known problem in econometrics and its solution is discussed in Chap. 3. A more interesting question (for this chapter at least) is how to test simultaneous—vs—single-equation specifications.

In a model of sales and advertising there are three mutually exclusive specifications in terms of the causal ordering of the model: either (a) advertising determines sales, (b) sales determines advertising, or (c) both advertising determines sales and sales determines advertising.. How does the investigator know which specification is correct? The answer to this question (the reader may guess by now) depends upon *a priori* knowledge, empirical evidence, or both. For example, the researcher may have independent reasons for hypothesizing the existence of both a sales response function, $S_\alpha = f(A_\alpha)$, and an advertising decision rule, $A_\alpha = f(S_\alpha)$. The sales response function may have originated in observation of the market; the advertising decision rule may have originated from interviews with management. The two relations taken together imply that both sales and advertising are contemporaneously correlated and thus they are both endogenous variables in period α. On the other hand, the researcher may have reason to believe that one relation holds but be uncertain about the other, mainly because he has no theory to explain the presence or absence of the other relation.

Suppose the investigator "knows" that management uses a percent-of-sales decision rule for advertising but is uncertain whether or not advertising influences sales. This problem, or its mirror image, has great significance in sales response research, but its solution does not seem to be well understood. However, the solution is straightforward: If sales and advertising are contemporaneously correlated, then they must be considered to be interdependent in a simultaneous-equation way because there is no reason to believe that one relation or the other is implausible. The simultaneous-equation estimation of such a model is, in a sense, a hedge against the possibility of simultaneous-equation bias.

Two other possibilities exist in our sales-advertising example. The first is that one relation or the other can be ruled out as implausible. Thus, even though advertising is significantly correlated with sales in period α, the investigator may have other evidence to exclude one of the relations. He may, for example, be dealing with monthly data and know that the advertising budget is set annually as a percent of sales. In this case he can proceed as if the causality ran from advertising to sales. The second possibility is that sales and advertising are not significantly correlated in period α, but that they are correlated across some (at least one) set of time periods. For example, the researcher may use cross-lag correlation analysis to show that $r(S_\alpha, A_{\alpha-1})$ is significant while $r(A_\alpha, S_{\alpha-1})$ is not or that $r(S_\alpha, A_{\alpha-1}) > r(A_\alpha, S_{\alpha-1})$, the inference being that advertising causes sales rather than vice versa. Notice that the first case is much stronger than the second and that the method is used not to test theory but to help specify the model so that it can be tested. The method of cross-lagged correlations is discussed by Campbell (1962) and demonstrated in marketing by Montgomery and Silk (1972). Neither of these studies indicates clearly, however, the appropriate use of cross-lagged correlations as an aid to model specification or, more importantly, the limitation of the technique in cases of significant contemporaneous correlation.

The question of causality raised here is not a simple one and yet some guidance is needed for practical econometric research. We are inclined to agree with Simon (1953) who argues that causal ordering is (or can best be treated as) a property of the model. Thus, in Chap. 1, we talk about the causal ordering of the model [Eqs. (1.3)-(1.4)]. Schultz (1971) discusses the causal ordering of his model and the revealed causal ordering; in both cases the word "causal" attaches to the model as a characteristic. When econometric work is done with experimental data, of course, causal implications can be drawn from the experiment itself. With the kind of data most often available for sales response research, however, the question must always retain an element of speculation. The basic issues surrounding causal inference in nonexperimental research are covered in Blalock (1964), although his particular suggestion that models be built as recursive systems is opposed to our more general view with such models as a special case. From a philosophical standpoint, we are persuaded by Hume's agrument that as scientists we can observe (or perceive) events but not the relation (or force) between events. One event can be called a cause and another event an effect as long as it is clearly understood that this means no more or no less than A is always followed by B [Kemeny (1959)]. In practice, since this notion of force can never be tested, causality must necessarily be treated in this more limited way. Thus, a functional relationship, e.g., between sales and advertising, $S = f(A)$, is treated here at most as the propositional statement, if A, then B, and typically only as the generalization or association between S and A implied by the function itself. In systems of relations, we employ Simon's framework of causal ordering to suggest the asymmetrical relationships in a model.

A final consideration of simultaneous relationships involves decision variables other than advertising. Personal selling expenditures, distribution expenditures, sales promotion budgets, prices, and other marketing factors may be set in relation to present or past sales. This means that in marketing mix models the problem of simultaneous relationships is also likely to occur.

THE ARTIST AND THE SCIENTIST

This chapter has stressed the dual nature of model building in marketing; the scientific enterprise and the artistic craft. Even such seemingly simple matters as data adjustment can be seen to involve quite fully the creative and technical talents of the researcher. The only way to prove this to yourself is to build a model. Then, even this book—with its emphasis on bringing out many of these subtleties—will fall short, as it must, of the experience of the laboratory and of the real world.

FOOTNOTES

[1] In Chap. 12, we argue that marketing theory can be defined by certain *elementary* marketing behavior.

[2] McGuire, Weiss, and Houston (1975) discuss the restrictions placed on various demand specifications by economic theory.

Chapter 7

SALES RESPONSE
MODELS

Until recently, the setting of marketing decision variables has been the least developed area of management in terms of research and practical decision models. The purpose of this chapter is to review advances that have been made in the measurement of sales response to marketing decision variables. These advances make possible the building and implementation of decision models to help managers make decisions on advertising appropriations, pricing, sales force effort, and so on.

In order for a marketing decision model to be useful, it must embody some mechanism for relating the effects of marketing expenditures on sales. This mechanism, usually called a sales response function, is the keystone of the model, and thus the quality of its measurement is an important determinant of the model's eventual success. In the last chapter we described a sales response function as a model of the relationship between sales and relevant marketing decision variables. For example, the dependence of sales on advertising can be estimated from marketing data using econometric methods. The result is a sales response equation which shows the effect of advertising on sales. Of course, sales response equations can be quite complex and often include the effects of marketing mix interactions, lagged responses, competition, and simultaneous relationships. The purpose of these more complex models is the same: to link marketing actions to market response.

Company marketing decisions lead to company sales. Two factors mediate this process: industry demand and competitive behavior. A number of variables may influence total industry demand including price, income, population, and others; advertising may also influence industry demand. In addition, a company's market share can be considered to be a function of the marketing efforts of competitors. A variety of methods for estimating industry demand

137

or predicting competitive behavior have been employed in sales response research and are reported in Chaps. 9 and 10.

Econometric models for the measurement of marketing effectiveness can be classified on the basis of three dichotomous elements: (1) Whether the dependent variable is the market share or sales. (2) Whether the model contains one or more than one equation. (3) Whether the parameters of the model are constant or time-varying. In the following review of empirical work (a summary of which appears in Table 7.1), attention is focused on how the models have become progressively more elaborate and better approximations of the actual market mechanism. This elaboration has been made possible through developments in computer technology and statistical techniques discussed in previous chapters. Our survey of the literature begins with single-equation market share models and ends with multiple-equation sales models. Then we turn to a discussion of models in which the parameters are no longer constant, but instead, vary over time.

MARKET SHARE RESEARCH

Many firms evaluate their relative success in terms of selective demand position or market share. Two reasons for this are suggested. One is that trends in primary demand are frequently out of the control of the firm and affect the industry as a whole. Another is that marketing instruments, in particular advertising, may have minimal impact on total industry sales. Instead, the managerial decision variables serve to allocate this total amount among the competing firms.

Single-Equation Models

The problem of isolating the effects of one instrument from the many other variables that affect sales is not primarily one of analysis, but rather is one of data collection. Once the data are available, econometric analysis permits evaluation of the relative effect of each of the elements of the marketing mix. Banks (1961) postulated a linear relationship between the managerial decision variables and market share:

Brand Share = β_1 [Price] + β_2 [Advertising] + $\cdots$ + β_7 [POP Effort] + ϵ.

$$(7.1)$$

The results of this study indicated that advertising was an important determinant of market share for coffee, but not for scouring cleanser. For scouring cleanser, price and promotional effort were important. These results are not very meaningful because of the small sample sizes available. The study was a cross-sectional one in which the individual entities were brands: 9 for cleanser and 21 for coffee. Moreover, since the relationship was based on cross-section data, the results apply to the market as a whole, but may not apply to an individual brand. A better understanding of market share behavior is obtained when time-series data are used.

The managerial decision variables in Bank's model are *absolute*. The influence of competitors' actions could be represented in such a model by separate exogenous variables expressed in absolute terms as well. The actions of each competitor can be treated individually or the efforts of all competitors can be treated together for each element of the marketing mix. For a marketing instrument such as advertising or sales-force expenditures, the values of it for each of the competing brands are simply summed together. For an instrument such as price or retail availability, the values are weighted by volume before summing. In any case, an "all other" brand is created. Competitive effects can be represented in alternative ways using this "all others" brand. A relative marketing variable can be created that is the ratio of the value for the brand to the value for the "all others" brand. A share marketing variable can be constructed that is the ratio of the value for the brand to the value for the total market (that is, the value for the brand plus the value for the "all others" brand). The treatment of competitive effects is considered in more detail in Chap. 9. The choice of whether to use absolute, relative, or share managerial variables can be critical in as much as they usually do not produce equivalent results.

Sales response functions are often formulated so that the influence of the predetermined variables is multiplicative rather than linear. Weiss (1968) examined a model to explain market share movement of three national brands of a low cost, frequently purchased consumer product. The influence of competitive factors was represented by transforming the independent variables through

Table 7.1

Econometric Sales Response Studies

Study (year)	Product or service	Sales variable S= Absolute sales MS= Market share	Marketing mix effects	Temporal effects 1. Inertia 2. Distributed lags carryover	Competitive effects 1. Exogenous 2. Endogenous	Simultaneous effects 1. Recursive 2. Interdependent
Banks (1961)	Scouring cleanser, coffee	MS	Yes	No	No	No
Buzzell (1964)	Various FPBG[a]	MS	No	Yes	No	No
Kuehn, McGuire, & Weiss (1966)	FPBG	MS	Yes	Advertising[2]	Yes[1]	No
Frank & Massy (1967)	FPBG	MS	Yes	Price[2] Deal Index[2]	No	No
Weiss (1968, 1969)	FPBG	MS	Yes	No	Yes[1]	No
Simon (1969)	Liquor	MS	Yes	Advertising[2]	No	No
Lambin (1970)	Small electrical appliance	MS,S	Yes	Advertising[2]	Yes[1]	No
Sexton (1970, 1972)	FPBS	MS,S	Yes	Advertising[2]	Yes[1]	No

Johansson (1973)	Women's hair spray	MS	Yes	No	No	No
McCann (1974)	Same as Bass and Parsons (1969)	MS	Yes	Yes[1]	No	No
Moriarity (1975)	FPBG	MS	Yes	Yes[1]	No	No
Wittink (1975)	Same as Moriarity (1975) [Different Brand]	MS	Yes	Yes[1] Advertising[2]	No	No
Schultz (1971)	Airlines	MS,S	Yes	Yes[1]	Yes[1]	Yes[2]
Lambin (1972)	Gasoline	MS,S	Yes	Advertising[2]	Yes[1]	Yes[2]
Beckwith (1972)	FPBG	MS	No	Advertising[2]	Yes[1]	Yes[2]
Clarke (1973)	Same as Bass and Parsons (1969)	MS	No	Yes[1]	Yes[1]	Yes[2]
Wildt (1974)	Specialty food product	MS	Yes	Yes[1]	Yes[2]	Yes[2]

(Table 7.1 continued on following page.)

Table 7.1 (*continued*)

Study (year)	Product or service	Sales variable S= Absolute sales MS= Market share	Marketing mix effects	Temporal effects 1. Inertia 2. Distributed lags carryover	Competitive effects 1. Exogenous 2. Endogenous	Simultaneous effects 1. Recursive 2. Interdependent
Houston and Weiss (1974)	Sames as Weiss (1968,1969)	MS	Yes	Advertising[2]	Yes[1]	Yes[2]
McGuire, Weiss, and Houston (1975)	Mayonnaise	MS	Yes	No	Yes[1]	Yes[2]
Telser (1962)	Cigarettes	S	Yes	Advertising[2]	Yes[1]	No
Palda (1964)	Lydia Pinkham vegetable compound	S	No	Advertising[2]	No	No
Urban (1969)	FPBG	S	Yes	No	Yes[1]	No
Bass and Clarke (1972)	Dietary weight control product	S	No	Advertising[2]	No	No
York and Mount (1975)	FPBG	S	Yes	Advertising[2]	No	No

Bass and Parsons (1969)	FPBG	S	No	Yes[1]	Yes[2]	Yes[2]
Samuels (1970/71)	Household cleansers	S	No	Advertising[2]	Yes[1,2]	Yes[2]
Frank and Massy (1971)	FPBG	S	Yes	No	No	Yes[2]
Parsons (1974)	Same as Bass and Parsons (1969)	S	Yes	No	No	Yes[1]

[a] Frequently Purchased Branded Good.

the operation of dividing them by the appropriate mean value for the period. Thus, his multiplicative model is

$$\text{Brand Share} = \left[\frac{\text{Price of Brand}}{\text{Average Price for All Brands}}\right]^{\beta_1} \left[\frac{\text{Advertising for Brand}}{\text{Average Advertising for All Brands}}\right]^{\beta_2} \cdots . \quad (7.2)$$

Taking the logarithm of both sides gives a linear model. Weiss estimated this model by ordinary least squares. The coefficient of price, β_1, turned out to be positive. This was contrary to *a priori* expectations. Weiss conjectured that this may have been because of one or more omitted variables such as product quality differences.

The parameters in the multiplicative model can be interpreted directly as elasticities. The elasticity of a decision variable is defined as the ratio of the percentage change in market share[1] (*MS*) associated with a percentage change in that managerial decision variable (*MDV*) or

$$\eta_{MDV} = \frac{dMS/MS}{dMDV/MDV} . \quad (7.3)$$

Elasticities are pure numbers and can be compared without concern about measurement units. Suppose we differentiate the sales response function (7.2) by any one of the predetermined variables; for instance, the ratio of price of the brand to the average price for all brands (*RP*).

$$dMS = \beta_1 RP^{\beta_1 - 1} RA^{\beta_2} \cdots dRP = \beta_1 (MS/RP)dRP. \quad (7.4)$$

By rearranging (7.4) to conform with (7.3) we find that $\beta_1 \equiv \eta_{RP}$ as we asserted.[2] This interpretation enables the model builder and the manager to interact more easily.

The managerial decision variables in linear sales response functions exhibit constant returns to scale. However, current marketing thought suggests that they exhibit diminishing returns to scale. This is possible, but not required, in multiplicative models.[3] A marketing instrument will display diminishing returns to scale if its elasticity is less than one in absolute value.

Kotler [(1973), 35-37] notes that sometimes demand may initially exhibit increasing marginal returns and then only subsequently show diminishing returns to scale with respect to various levels of marketing effort. The logistic function can depict such an S-shaped relationship. It can also take into account the market saturation level. One version of the logistic function is

$$y = y^o / \left\{ 1 + \exp\left[-(\beta_0 + \sum_{k=1}^{K} \beta_k x_k)\right] \right\}. \tag{7.5}$$

where y^o denotes the saturation level. This relationship can be rewritten as

$$\ln\left[\frac{y}{y^o - y}\right] = \beta_0 + \sum_{k=1}^{K} \beta_k x_k. \tag{7.6}$$

The inflexion point, at which the change from increasing to decreasing marginal returns occurs, is $y = y^o/2$.

A nonsymmetric S-shaped curve may be more appropriate in marketing applications. One such logistic model would be

$$\ln \frac{y - y_o}{y^o - y} = \ln\beta_0 + \sum_{k=1}^{K} \beta_k \ln x_k, \tag{7.7}$$

where y_o is the intercept ($0 \leqslant y_o \leqslant y^o$). The independent variables are assumed to be positive. The dependent variable y may vary between the lower limit y_o and the saturation level y^o.

The saturation level y^o must be specified *a priori* in both the log-linear model (7.6) and the double-log model (7.7). In the latter model, the intercept y_o must also be specified. When the dependent variable is a proportion such as market share, the most common assumption is that $y^o = 1$ and $y_o = 0$.

Johansson (1973) found that the double-log logistic function fit the data for women's hair spray:

$$\ln\left[\frac{\text{Brand Share} - \text{Proportion of Repeaters}}{\text{Trial Proportion} - \text{Brand Share}}\right]$$

$$= \ln\beta_0 + \beta_1 \ln[\text{Advertising Share}] + \beta_2 \ln[\text{Deal Proportions}] + \cdots. \tag{7.8}$$

In this case, survey data were used to estimate the intercept (proportion of repeaters) and saturation level (trial proportion).

Johansson discusses the estimation problems inherent in these models.

Implicit in these first models is the notion that all variables act contemporaneously. The presence of carryover effects, in which current marketing expenditures influence the sales in future periods, is ignored. The measurement of carryover effects is sufficiently important to warrant separate treatment in the next chapter. Carryover is represented in models by the use of lagged variables. The presence of a lagged dependent variable makes the model dynamic.

This market share model incorporating a lagged dependent variable was examined by Lambin (1970)[4]:

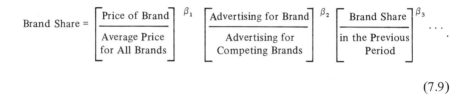

$$(7.9)$$

An analysis was accomplished for one of three brands of an electrical appliance that dominated the market. The lagged brand share variable was called goodwill. Both goodwill and relative advertising had a significant impact on sales.

The econometric approach permits intermedia advertising comparisons. Sexton (1970) developed a negative exponential model in which advertising expenditures in network television, spot television, magazines, and newspapers were each treated as separate variables. Again the model can be made linear through a logarithmic transformation:

$$\text{Brand Share} = 1 - 1\left(-\left[\begin{array}{c}\text{Brand Share}\\ \text{in the Previous}\\ \text{period}\end{array}\right]^{\beta_1}\exp\left(-\left[\begin{array}{c}\text{Advertising}\\ \text{in Network}\\ \text{Television}\end{array}\right]^{\beta_2}\left[\begin{array}{c}\text{Advertising}\\ \text{in Spot}\\ \text{Television}\end{array}\right]^{\beta_3}\cdots\right)\right.$$

$$(7.10)$$

For the particular product class studied, pricing and dealing were more important than advertising in explaining market share behavior.

The relatively more effective media were found to be magazines and newspapers.

Thus far, all of the models have been linear or transformable into linear versions. A nonlinear model with the acronym MATE has been formulated by Kuehn and Weiss (1965).

Brand Share $= \beta_1$ [Brand Share in the Previous Period]

$$+ [1 - \beta_1] \left\{ \beta_2 \left[\frac{[\text{Other Effects}] [\text{Price of Brand}]^{-\beta_3}}{\text{Sum Over All Brands } [\text{Other Effects}] [\text{Price of Brand}]^{-\beta_3}} \right] \right. \quad (7.11)$$

$$\left. + [1 - \beta_2] \left[\frac{[\text{Other Effects}] [\text{Price of Brand}]^{-\beta_3} [\text{Advertising of Brand}]^{-\beta_4}}{\text{Sum Over All Brands } [\text{Other Effects}] [\text{Price of Brand}]^{-\beta_3} [\text{Advertising of Brand}]^{-\beta_4}} \right] \right\}$$

There have been two empirical studies of this model. Both begin by assuming that the parameter describing habitual repurchase behavior, β_1, is zero. The parameter β_2 linearly allocates the effect of price and price-advertising "interaction" on market share. Weiss (1969) estimated that 95.7% of the influence on market share resulted from the relative price term.

Kuehn, McGuire, and Weiss (1966) extended the model so that it included the effect of lags on the effectiveness of advertising expenditures. They assumed a distributed lag formulation which produced the following equation for the effective shock of advertising:

$$\begin{bmatrix} \text{Advertising Shock} \\ \text{of Brand} \end{bmatrix} = \beta_0 \begin{bmatrix} \text{Advertising Shock} \\ \text{of Brand in the} \\ \text{Previous Period} \end{bmatrix} + \beta_i \begin{bmatrix} \text{Advertising} \\ \text{Of} \\ \text{Brand} \end{bmatrix} . \quad (7.12)$$

The parameter β_0 is rate of advertising carryover. The parameter β_i is the intrinsic relative effectiveness of the advertising copy and use of the media by the ith brand. If data on advertising expenditures are available by media, the authors note that estimates can be developed of the relative effectiveness of those media. In an empirical study of a grocery product, expenditures for brand 1 were more than twice as effective as expenditures for brand 2 and over twenty times as effective as those for brand 3.

The parameters of the model were estimated by a direct search technique developed by Hooke and Jeeves. Van Wormer and Weiss (1970) explain this methodology. A major problem with regression market share models is that forecasting is usually not possible since the requirement that the estimates of market share sum to one is not fulfilled. The direct search technique permits estimation subject to this restriction.

Multiple Equation Models

Reservations must be held about the single equation models because of the unidirectional flow of influence implicit in them. Although sales is a function of advertising expenditure, advertising is also a function of sales. Frequently the demand curve shifts while the firm's advertising budgeting practices remain rigid. In such situations, there will be a series of different intersection points, but they will merely trace out the advertising budget line. One danger lies in mistaking the advertising budget line for the demand curve. Kuehn and Rohloff (1967) cite an example of a leading advertising agency that made this error. In econometrics, this is known as the identification problem. Processes which involve multiple relationships must be represented by a system of equations.

Schultz (1971) investigated one two-city air-travel market. Four equations were necessary to describe the basic marketing system. Besides an equation to explain market share, additional equations explained the company's advertising share in each of the two cities and its share of nonstop flights between the two cities. Separate from the market share model was a regression equation to explain total demand. The combination of these two models made calculation of optimal flights and optimal advertising expenditures possible.

Lambin (1970) explored the gasoline retail market. A single-equation regression model was used to identify the determinants of total gasoline consumption. The influence of advertising on primary demand was found to be negligible. Instead, the role of advertising was to increase selective demand. A two-equation model described the systematic dependence between advertising and market share.

Lambin was able to do two interesting things with his model.

First, he was able to examine to what extent there were significant differences between three media—press, radio, and TV. Press advertising was clearly the most important medium. Second, he was to examine to what extent the introduction of an advertising-quality variable improves the model. Two brands ran campaigns of very different types, but both were considered very creative and successful. The first was a promotional game, the second, an image-building type of campaign. A dummy variable was used to evaluate the impact of each campaign. The effect on market share of the promotional game was found to be more than three times higher than that for the image-building campaign.

Other market share models include those of Beckwith (1972), Clarke (1973), and Wildt (1974). The importance of their work is in demonstrating that market share relationships should be estimated simultaneously even when these relationships are seemingly unrelated. Their efforts do much to undermine the credibility of previous single-equation studies.

Beckwith (1972) studied a frequently purchased, inexpensive consumable good. This product class was at the maturity stage of the product life cycle. The top five brands accounted for 98% of the industry sales. All brands were sold at uniform retail and wholesale prices. No price changes occurred during the period investigated. Advertising was the predominant marketing instrument. Letting MS = market share and AS = advertising share, Beckwith's model assumed that for each brand i,

$$MS_{\alpha i} = \beta_{1i} MS_{\alpha-1,i} + \beta_{2i} As_{\alpha,i} + \epsilon_{\alpha i} \qquad i = 1, \ldots, 5. \qquad (7.13)$$

Ordinary least-squares estimation of these equations revealed that only two of the five advertising coefficients were significantly different from zero. However, Beckwith recognized that the contemporaneous covariance matrix was not diagonal. The sales shares of Brands "A" and "B" varied together as did those of "D" and "E". Moreover, the shares of "A", "B", and "C" were affected by the disturbances oppositely from "D" and "E". Consequently, he reestimated the equations by the iterative seemingly unrelated equations approach (see Chap. 3). Four out of the five advertising coefficients were now significantly different from zero.

Clarke (1973) elaborated upon the seemingly unrelated equations model used by Beckwith by postulating autocorrelated as well as contemporaneously correlated disturbances. He also used relative advertising instead of advertising share. The specific assumption was that the disturbances have first-order autocorrelation.[5] Clarke's equation is

$$\epsilon_{\alpha i} = \rho \epsilon_{\alpha-1,i} + \xi_{\alpha i}. \tag{7.14}$$

Autocorrelation can occur because of the lagged effect of temporary shocks distributed over a number of time periods, an incorrect functional form specified for the model, or the omission of variables from the relationship. Clarke argued that the presence of the first-order autoregressive process is due to the first cause. We think the last two explanations are more likely. Clarke performed a reanalysis of the Bass and Parsons (1969) data, but used a simpler model than they did (their model will be discussed in the sales response section). Bass and Parsons did not find any significant autocorrelation in the disturbance terms of their equations.

Wildt (1974) investigated the market for a specialty product sold predominantly in retail food outlets. The product is purchased by the consumer on an irregular and infrequent basis. Wildt focused on the competitive behavior of the three major firms in the industry. Unlike Beckwith and Clarke, Wildt assumed that advertising was also endogenous. His structural model was block recursive so that it could be decomposed into two subsystems—the market share equations and the managerial decision variables equations. Each subsystem in a block recursive model can be treated in isolation and its parameters can be estimated by whatever method seems appropriate in the context of that particular subsystem. In Wildt's model, the market share subsystem was estimated by the seemingly unrelated equations technique and the managerial decision variables subsystem by two-stage least squares. The empirical evidence supported his contention that the firms in this industry compete on the basis of advertising, promotion, new varieties, and price.

McGuire, Weiss, and Houston (1975) show how a special case of the MATE model (7.11) can be reformulated so that it is a *multinomial logit model* [Theil (1969)].[6] The brand shares of each of the N brands in a market might be represented as

$$MS_{\alpha i} = \frac{\beta_i \, X_\alpha \, P_{\alpha i}^{-\beta-1} e^{\epsilon \alpha i}}{\sum\limits_{j=1}^{N} \beta_j \, P_{\alpha j}^{-\beta}} \,, \tag{7.15}$$

where X is total expenditures for the product class, P_i is the price of brand i. The own and cross elasticities will be functionally identical for all brands. A more general version would be

$$MS_{\alpha i} = \frac{\gamma_i \beta_i \, X_\alpha^{\beta_i+1} \, P_{\alpha i}^{-\beta_i-1} \, e^{\epsilon \alpha i}}{\sum\limits_{j=1}^{N} \gamma_j \, \beta_j \, X_\alpha^{\beta_j} \, P_{\alpha j}^{-\beta_j}} \,. \tag{7.16}$$

The elasticities are no longer functionally identical.

These models can be transformed into linear models by taking the logarithms of the ratio of any two equations. The ratio of the ith to the jth equation for Eq. (7.15) would be

$$\frac{MS_{\alpha i}}{MS_{\alpha j}} = \frac{\beta_i}{\beta_j} P_{\alpha i}^{-\beta-1} \, P_{\alpha j}^{\beta+1} \, e^{\epsilon \alpha i - \epsilon \alpha j} \tag{7.17}$$

and for Eq. (7.16)

$$\frac{MS_{\alpha i}}{MS_{\alpha j}} = \frac{\gamma_i \beta_i}{\gamma_j \beta_j} X_\alpha^{\beta_i-\beta_j} \, P_{\alpha i}^{-\beta_i-1} \, P_{\alpha j}^{\beta_j+1} \, e^{\epsilon \alpha i - \epsilon \alpha j} \,. \tag{7.18}$$

The log-linear models can be estimated by the seemingly unrelated equations technique.

McGuire, Weiss, and Houston applied this approach to the market for mayonnaise and other mayonnaise-like dressings and spreads. The brands were Kraft Miracle Whip, Hellman's Mayonnaise, and "All Others." The "All Others" category served as the denominator in each ratio equation. They concluded that the general model (7.16) was more appropriate than the restricted model (7.15) as the representation for this product class. Another application of this approach is given in Weiss and Houston (1974).

Estimation Problems

The specification of market share as the dependent variable incurs estimation problems. There are two reasons for these problems. First, market share, when expressed as a fraction, is constrained to lie between zero and one. Second, the sum of these market shares for all brands in any given period must equal one. Violations of these constraints expose the internal inconsistencies of a model.

Whenever the dependent variable is stated as a proportion, as market share is, the risk is run of violating the assumption that the variance of the disturbance term is constant. A well-known result is that the variability of a proportion p is given by $p(1 - p)/n$ (n is sample size). This variation depends upon p with the maximum variation occurring when $p = 0.5$ and the minimum when $p = 0$ or 1. The arc sin transformation will stabilize the variance of a proportion. This transformation involves calculating the angle in degrees of the square root of the proportion, the arc sin $\sqrt{p}$. This approach was used by Parsons (1974) when his dependent variable was retail availability, the fraction of retail stores (weighted by sales volume) handling the product. The use of the arc sin transformation is atypical. The attractiveness of the double-log transformation predominates. The hope is that the actual changes in market share would be confined to a narrow range so that they would not materially affect the variance of the disturbances.

More importantly, the application of the standard linear model to marketing data will often yield some *estimated* values of market share which are negative or greater than one. This could be avoided by changing the assumptions about the behavior of the disturbance term, although this approach has not proved practical [McGuire *et al.* (1975)].

McGuire *et al.* (1968), clarified by McGuire *et al.* (1975), have specified conditions under which the sum of estimated market shares must equal one. They term such a model *logically consistent.*[7] The reader should refer to these two references before building any market share model.

SALES RESEARCH

A more direct approach to estimating sales response functions is to use sales itself as the dependent variable. Probably the best-known single-equation study is one by Palda (1964) on a proprietary medicine. The product had no close substitutes, eliminating the usual complications produced by competitive marketing activities. His monograph made popular the use of distributed lags to express the mechanism by which advertising influences sales over a period of time. Palda concluded that evidence existed for the presence of cumulative advertising effects. Lambin (1969) concurred after performing a very similar investigation on a frequently purchased food product.

Bass and Parsons (1969) required four equations to explain the market structure of a product belonging to the general class of frequently purchased products sold predominately in supermarkets. The sales and advertising for both the brand and all other brands were described.

$$
\begin{bmatrix} \text{Current} \\ \text{Sales} \\ \text{Brand} \end{bmatrix} = \gamma_{21} \begin{bmatrix} \text{Current} \\ \text{Advertising} \\ \text{Brand} \end{bmatrix} + \gamma_{41} \begin{bmatrix} \text{Current} \\ \text{Advertising} \\ \text{Remainder} \end{bmatrix} + \beta_{11} \begin{bmatrix} \text{Lagged} \\ \text{Sales} \\ \text{Brand} \end{bmatrix} + \beta_{31} \begin{bmatrix} \text{Lagged} \\ \text{Sales} \\ \text{Remainder} \end{bmatrix}
$$

$$
+ \beta_{51} \begin{bmatrix} \text{Current} \\ \text{Sales} \\ \text{New Brands} \end{bmatrix} + \beta_{61} \begin{bmatrix} \text{Current} \\ \text{Advertising} \\ \text{New Brands} \end{bmatrix} + \sum_{j=1}^{5} \beta_{j+6,1} D_j + \beta_{12,1} + \epsilon_{\alpha 1} , \tag{7.19}
$$

$$
\begin{bmatrix} \text{Current} \\ \text{Advertising} \\ \text{Brand} \end{bmatrix} = \beta_{12} \begin{bmatrix} \text{Lagged} \\ \text{Sales} \\ \text{Brand} \end{bmatrix} + \beta_{22} \begin{bmatrix} \text{Lagged} \\ \text{Advertising} \\ \text{Brand} \end{bmatrix} + \beta_{32} \begin{bmatrix} \text{Lagged} \\ \text{Sales} \\ \text{Remainder} \end{bmatrix} + \beta_{42} \begin{bmatrix} \text{Lagged} \\ \text{Advertising} \\ \text{Remainder} \end{bmatrix}
$$

$$
+ \sum_{j=1}^{5} \beta_{j+6,2} D_j + \beta_{12,2} + \epsilon_{\alpha 2} , \tag{7.20}
$$

$$
\begin{bmatrix} \text{Current} \\ \text{Sales} \\ \text{Remainder} \end{bmatrix} = \gamma_{23} \begin{bmatrix} \text{Current} \\ \text{Advertising} \\ \text{Brand} \end{bmatrix} + \gamma_{43} \begin{bmatrix} \text{Current} \\ \text{Advertising} \\ \text{Remainder} \end{bmatrix} + \beta_{13} \begin{bmatrix} \text{Lagged} \\ \text{Sales} \\ \text{Brand} \end{bmatrix} + \beta_{33} \begin{bmatrix} \text{Lagged} \\ \text{Sales} \\ \text{Remainder} \end{bmatrix}
$$

$$
+ \beta_{53} \begin{bmatrix} \text{Current} \\ \text{Sales} \\ \text{New Brands} \end{bmatrix} + \beta_{63} \begin{bmatrix} \text{Current} \\ \text{Advertising} \\ \text{New Brands} \end{bmatrix} + \sum_{j=1}^{5} \beta_{j+6,3} D_j + \beta_{12,3} + \epsilon_{\alpha 3} , \tag{7.21}
$$

$$
\begin{bmatrix} \text{Current} \\ \text{Advertising} \\ \text{Remainder} \end{bmatrix} = \beta_{14} \begin{bmatrix} \text{Lagged} \\ \text{Sales} \\ \text{Brand} \end{bmatrix} + \beta_{24} \begin{bmatrix} \text{Lagged} \\ \text{Advertising} \\ \text{Brand} \end{bmatrix} + \beta_{34} \begin{bmatrix} \text{Lagged} \\ \text{Sales} \\ \text{Remainder} \end{bmatrix} + \beta_{44} \begin{bmatrix} \text{Lagged} \\ \text{Advertising} \\ \text{Remainder} \end{bmatrix}
$$

$$
+ \sum_{j=1}^{5} \beta_{j+6,4} D_j + \beta_{12,4} + \epsilon_{\alpha 4} . \tag{7.22}
$$

The D_j's are dummy variables representing seasonality in the bimonthly data. The nonconstant variables have been deflated by population and are expressed in logarithmic form. The remainder brand was defined as the total market less the brand and less new brands. New brands were operationally defined as brands on the market for less than a year.

This model was the first one capable of explaining the behavior of competing brands as well as the brand studied. The advertising decision rules are based on marketing actions and results in the *previous* period.[8] The multiple-equation system can be rearranged so that it is recursive. However, Bass and Parsons specified that the contemporaneous covariance matrix was not diagonal. Consequently, three-stage least squares should have been used by them, but it was not. Among other findings, they discovered that competitive advertising activities appeared to stimulate primary demand in this industry. Samuels (1970/71) tested a similar model using information on household cleansers and toilet soaps.

Clarke (1972, 1973) reanalyzed the data of Bass and Parsons. The major goal of his study was to measure the competitive effects of advertising. The Bass and Parsons model provides direct estimates of the effect of advertising of the remainder on sales of a brand. Their model could be extended by unbundling the remainder into its constituent individual brands. On the other hand, Clarke's simple market share model provides only bounds on sales-advertising cross-elasticities.

McCann (1974) provides a different perspective on this market by integrating the advertising data with Market Research Corporation of American (MRCA) panel data rather than with Neilson store audit data. Again market share is the dependent variable. The cross-section and time-series data were pooled and dummy variables were used to represent individual differences in both intercept and slope coefficients. (This dummy variable technique is covered in Chap. 4.) Next, McCann combines estimates of the coefficients for individual brands into those for market segments. This aggregation involves weighting the estimates for each individual brand in accordance with its share of the segment. McCann calls his method the *average coefficient regression method*. We are not convinced of the viability of this approach and view his results with some skepticism because of the ad hoc nature of the procedure.

Parsons (1974) examined the introductions of 22 new brands in this industry over a sixteen-year span. By pooling cross-section and time-series data, he found that both current advertising and retail availability in the previous period have positive effects on current retail availability and that, in turn, current advertising and current retail availability positively influence current sales. These results demonstrated the necessity of making an investment in advertising in order to achieve retail distribution.

TIME-VARYING PARAMETER STRUCTURES

The coefficients of the controllable marketing instruments and the uncontrollable environmental variables in sales response functions are almost invariably assumed to be constant for the analysis period. However, the longer that the time interval is, the more tenuous this assumption is likely to be. Our interest in this section is consequently on the time effectiveness of managerial decision variables.

If structural changes occur at *known* points in time, then the changes in the coefficients of the relevant variables can be represented by dummy variables [Gujarati (1970)].[9] Palda (1964) assumed that restrictions placed upon Lydia Pinkham's advertising copy by the Food and Drug Administration in 1914 and again in 1925 and by the Federal Trade Commission in 1940 could be captured by dummy variables. These dummy variables, which were discussed in Chap. 3, affect only the intercept of the sales response function. A somewhat more appropriate approach might have been to use the dummy variables to model changes in the slope coefficient, i.e., the effectiveness of advertising.

Basically this approach means that segments of a sales response function can be fit separately by linear regression. This method is called piecewise regression [McGee and Carleton (1970)]. A more elegant counterpart of this methodology can be found in the theory of splines [Poirier (1973)]. The major problem with these approaches is the difficulty in defining the segments since the timing of structural changes is rarely known. A procedure has been developed by Farley and Hinich (1970) for determining if exactly one structural change has occurred. And if so, Chow (1960) provides a way to identify when. Beckwith (no date) extends Chow's test for equality of regression coefficients for two subsets of observations to many subsets.

Coefficients in a response function might vary between each time period rather than only between a few time periods. If cross-sectional observations were also available, we could use the random coefficients model (see Chap. 4). Otherwise, some *a priori* constraint must be imposed so that we might obtain unique estimates of the coefficients. Parameter variation might be *stochastic* but, for instance, required to follow an autoregressive process of low order such as first-order Markov. Alternatively, parameter variation might be *systematic* with the parameters themselves being functions of observable variables.

Stochastic Parameter Variation

Any model of stochastic parameter variation which involves some assumption of an autoregressive parameter process is called a *sequentially varying parameter model*. Little (1966) was the first to propose such a sales response function. The coefficients of promotion rate was assumed to be generated by a stochastic process.

$$\beta_{1\alpha} = (1 - \phi)\bar{\beta}_1 + \phi\beta_{1,\alpha-1} + \xi_{1\alpha}, \tag{7.23}$$

where $0 \leqslant \phi \leqslant 1$. The value of the parameter β_1 in any time period will be a weighted average of its value in the previous period and its long-run average value plus a random disturbance.[10] The term $1 - \phi$ represents a tendency to converge toward the mean value $\bar{\beta}_1$. As $\phi \to 1$, $\beta_{1\alpha}$ becomes more dependent on $\beta_{1,\alpha-1}$ and wanders more freely from its mean value. On the other hand, as $\phi \to 0$, β_1 becomes equal to the mean value plus a random variable as in a random coefficient model.

Little's work antedated econometric developments in this area. Recently, Cooley and Prescott (1973) developed a model in which the parameters were assumed to adapt to permanent and transitory changes. The transitory change of the parameter vector can be represented as

$$\beta_\alpha = \beta_\alpha^* + \tau_\alpha \qquad \alpha = 1, \ldots, T, \tag{7.24}$$

where β_α^* is the permanent component of β_α and τ_α is the vector of transient change in period α. In addition to transient changes which are in effect for only one period, there are permanent changes which persist into the future.

$$\beta_\alpha^* = \beta_{\alpha-1}^* + \xi_\alpha \qquad \alpha = 1, \ldots, T, \qquad (7.25)$$

where ξ_α is the permanent change vector.

The vectors τ_α and ξ_α are identically and independently distributed normal variables with mean vectors zero and *known* covariance structures. These convariance structures are written as

$$E(\tau\,\tau') = (1 - \phi)\sigma^2 \Sigma_\tau \qquad (7.26)$$

and

$$E(\xi\,\xi') = \phi\sigma^2 \Sigma_\xi, \qquad (7.27)$$

where Σ_τ and Σ_ξ are known up to scale factors. The parameter ϕ indicates how fast the parameters are adapting to structural change. It is restricted to fall within the range $0 \leqslant \phi \leqslant 1$. In this formulation if $\phi = 1$, then all change is permanent. Whereas if $\phi = 0$, we once again have a random coefficients model.

Cooley and Prescott discuss estimation techniques for this type of model. Certain simplifying assumptions are often made. In the absence of information to the contrary, first, the relative importance of permanent and transitory changes is assumed to be the same for all random parameters. Thus, $\Sigma_\tau = \Sigma_\xi$. Second, these changes are assumed to be not correlated between parameters. Consequently, the covariance matrices will be diagonal. The variances of the estimated parameters under the assumption of no temporal changes provide an estimate of the variances in these matrices.

Winer (1975) applied this approach to Palda's Lydia Pinkham data. While Palda maintained that the regulatory actions should produce discrete changes in the constant of the sales response function and should leave the effectiveness of advertising otherwise unchanged, Winer argued that the shock is likely to induce some continuous change in the constant and, in any event, the assumption of parameter constancy for the other coefficients is not valid. Winer estimated the sales response function

$$S_\alpha = \beta_{0\alpha} + \beta_{1\alpha} A_\alpha + \beta_{2\alpha} S_{\alpha-1} + \epsilon_\alpha \qquad (7.28)$$

subject to Eqs. (7.24)-(7.27), and the simplifications covered in the last paragraph. His empirical results indicated that the intercept $\beta_{0\alpha}$ showed a strong nondiscrete tendency to change over time, that advertising coefficient $\beta_{1\alpha}$ showed an upward trend, and that the coefficient of sales in the previous period $\beta_{2\alpha}$ declined over time. The proportion of permanent parameter change, ϕ, was about 0.75 for these data.

In Chap. 8 we will show that an equation similar to Eq. (7.28) can be derived from a geometric advertising lag model provided that the coefficients are constant. In such a model, the coefficient of lagged sales will be equal to the advertising carryover parameter. It is not transparent that the same correspondence holds if the coefficients are time varying. Since we consider the measurement of advertising carryover difficult in even favorable circumstances, we think that superimposing time-varying parameters on top of distributed lag models may well create insurmountable problems.

The notion of sequentially varying parameters can be incorporated into a cross-section, time-series model. This combination is known as a *convergent parameter model* [Rosenberg (1973b)]. The individual coefficient vectors follow first-order Markov processes subordinated to a tendency to converge to the population mean vector. The population mean vector will also evolve over time.

The individual parameter vector may contain both cross-varying parameters which vary across the population and cross-fixed parameters which are the same for all individuals in any time period. The F cross-fixed parameters obey the relation

$$\beta_\alpha = \beta_{\alpha-1} + \tau_{\alpha-1} \qquad \alpha = 2, \ldots, T. \tag{7.29}$$

The number of cross-fixed parameters, F, may be zero. The V cross-varying parameters are assumed to obey the relation

$$\beta_{\alpha i} = \bar{\beta}_{\alpha-1} + \Delta_\phi (\beta_{\alpha-1,i} - \bar{\beta}_{\alpha-1}) + \nu_{\alpha-1,i} \tag{7.30}$$

$$i = 1, \ldots, N; \alpha = 2, \ldots, T.$$

The convergence matrix Δ_ϕ is diagonal with entries ϕ_ν. Each ϕ_ν $(0 \leqslant \phi_\nu < 1)$ is the proportion of the individual divergence from the population mean which persists into the next period. The properties of the disturbances and the estimation procedure are discussed in Rosenberg (1973b). If there are no cross-fixed parameters and the divergence rates are set equal to zero, the model reduces to a version of a random coefficient model.

Johansson (1974) represented the margarine market by a convergent parameter model. The individual, or cross-sectional, units were the fifteen largest brands in the margarine market. The time units were 52 weeks. He focused on the relationship between the price of the product and the quantity purchased.

$$(Q_{\alpha i} - Q_{\alpha-1,i}) = \beta_{1\alpha i} (P_{\alpha i} - P_{\alpha-1,i}) + \beta_{2\alpha i} (P_{\alpha i}/\bar{P}_\alpha - P_{\alpha-1,i}/\bar{P}_{\alpha-1}) + \epsilon_{\alpha i},$$

$$(7.31)$$

where

$Q_{\alpha i}$ = per capita quantity (in pounds) of brand i at time α
$P_{\alpha i}$ = price (in dollars) of brand i at time α
P_α = mean price in the market at time α.

Both coefficients in this model were postulated to be cross-varying parameters and to obey (7.30). The empirical results indicated that this model should be rejected. The coefficients were rarely significantly different from zero and, contrary to theory, often were positive in sign. Johansson suggested that one cause of these results might be misspecification, the omission of a deal promotion variable.

Systematic Parameter Variation

The parameter vector β in some model such as $y = f(\beta, X)$ may exhibit variation and this variation may be systematic rather than stochastic. Systematic variation implies that the parameter vector can be written as $\beta = f(\lambda, Z)$. The parameters β are expressed as a function of other parameters λ and observable variables Z. This set of variables may include some of the variables in X. In contrast, stochastic parameter variation is assumed to be uncorrelated with the predetermined variables. In systematic parameter variation, least squares procedures are usually applicable although they are quite likely to be nonlinear rather than linear. For a more detailed discussion see Belsey (1973).

We have already seen that Winer (1975) attempted to model the nonconstancy of the parameters in a sales response function for Lydia Pinkham (7.28) by means of a sequentially varying parameter model. Beckwith (no date) assumed that the parameters in this response function varied systematically as a polynomial function of time. For instance, if the polynomial is of degree one, then the model is

$$S_\alpha = \beta_0 + (\beta_{11} + \beta_{12}\tau)A_\alpha + (\beta_{21} + \beta_{22}\tau)S_{\alpha-1} + \epsilon_\alpha, \qquad (7.32)$$

where the time τ was scaled to be one-tenth of the number of years after the year 1900. The major difficulty in using a polynomial formulation is the likelihood of multicollinearity. Beckwith encountered this problem. His results were similar to Winer's in that both found that advertising effectiveness was increasing through the later years.

One source of systematic variation in marketing is the product life cycle. Marketing theory, as propounded by Mickwitz (1959) for instance, states that the demand elasticities of the managerial decision variables change over the product life cycle. These changes in elasticities are both absolute and relative. In general, the absolute magnitudes of these elasticities decline over time. Differential rates of change among the various elasticities mean that the relative importance of each of the decision variables is altered in successive periods.

The product life-cycle theory does not make any statement about the behavior of elasticities of environmental variables over time. A key environmental variable is buyer behavior. The main factor of interest is habit patterns. At the aggregate level this factor is represented by sales in the previous period. The marketing premise is that the longer a brand has been on the market (more mature), the greater the brand's own lagged unit sales elasticity. Empirical evidence has generally supported this premise.

Parsons (1975) tried to model the product life cycle of Sappolio, a quality household cleanser [Tull (1955)]. The only information available on marketing decision variables was for advertising. The advertising expenditures were deflated by a general price index. The advertising elasticity was postulated to be an exponential function of time, while the elasticity of sales in the previous period was postulated to be a modified exponential function, that is

$$\ln Q_\alpha = (\beta_1 e^{-\beta_2 \tau} + \beta_3)\ln(A_\alpha/P_\alpha) + [\beta_4(1 - e^{-\beta_5 \tau}) + \beta_6]\ln S_{\alpha-1} + \epsilon_\alpha.$$

$$(7.33)$$

Thus, at $\tau = 0$, the elasticities are $\eta_{A/P} = \beta_1 + \beta_3$ and $\eta_{S_{\alpha-1}} = \beta_6$. As $\tau \to \infty$, $\eta_{A/P} \to \beta_3$ and $\eta_{S_{\alpha-1}} \to \beta_4 + \beta_6$.

An important feature of this model is that the constant elasticity model is a special case. The parameters β_3 and β_6 can be set equal to zero to avoid the problem of multicollinearity in the event that the elasticities are constant. This restricted model can be estimated. If the constant elasticity model is true, then the empirical results should indicate that $\beta_2 = 0$ and $\beta_5 = \infty$. Thus, the model does not force the elasticities to be time varying.

Representation of a parameter as an exponential function of time means that it is a special case of the polynomial function of time. The exponential series expansion is

$$e^{-\beta\tau} = 1 - \beta\tau + (1/2!) \beta^2 \tau^2 - (1/3!) \beta^3 \tau^3 + (1/4!) \beta^4 \tau^4 + \cdots . \qquad (7.34)$$

This may open an avenue for testing the model if the problem of multicollinearity can be overcome. Ridge regression is one option (see Chap. 5).

Parsons estimated (7.33) by means of nonlinear least squares [see Goldfeld and Quandt (1972)]. Perhaps because annual observations were used, the structure was found to be much simpler than postulated.

$$\ln Q_\alpha = 1.0252\exp(-.07841\tau)\ln(A_\alpha/P_\alpha)$$
$$\quad (.0237) \quad\quad (.01540)$$

$$(7.35)$$

$$+ .99435 \; [1 - \exp(-.07841\tau)] \ln S_{\alpha-1},$$
$$\quad (.00226)$$

where the numbers in parentheses are asymptotic standard deviations of the parameters. The time index is equal to 0 in 1869, 17 in 1886, and 46 in 1915. The time-varying elasticities are plotted in Fig. 7.1. The advertising elasticity was initially 1.0252, declined to .2703 by 1886, and ended up at .0278 in 1915. Conversely, the lagged sales

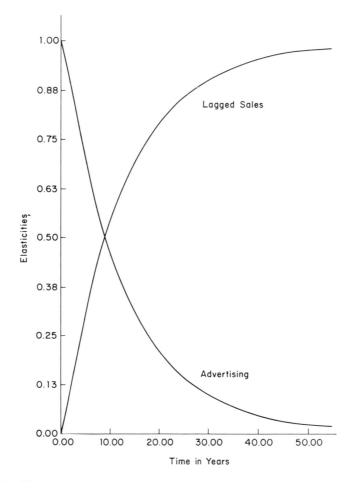

Fig. 7.1. Time-varying elasticities. Source: Parsons (1975).

elasticity began at .0000 increased to .7321 by 1886, and finished up at .9674 in 1915.

The elasticities in the sales response function were expressed as explicit functions of time. This is still only an approximation. Future research must be directed at expressing these elasticities as functions of controllable marketing instruments and external environmental factors. Even ignoring the product life cycle, marketing theory suggests that such an approach is necessary. For example, increased advertising is supposed to decrease the buyer's price sensitivity. Thus, the price elasticity in a sales response function should be related to advertising expenditures.

Representation of certain types of marketing systems also reveal systematic parameter variation. Consider the simple two-equation model in which the quantity of sales, Q, is a function of advertising expenditures, A, and retail availability, D, and simultaneously these advertising expenditures are a function of sales revenue, S, and consumer income, X.

$$Q_\alpha = \gamma_{21}A_\alpha + \beta_{11}D_\alpha + (0)X_\alpha + \beta_{31} - \epsilon_{\alpha1}, \tag{7.36}$$

$$A_\alpha = \gamma_{12}S_? + (0)D_\alpha + \beta_{22}X_\alpha + \beta_{32} - \epsilon_{\alpha2}. \tag{7.37}$$

Usually, lags in information gathering and decision making would cause this system to be recursive. That is, the advertising decision rule would be based on sales revenue in the prior period, $S_{\alpha-1}$. However, sometimes the system may be, or appear in the data to be, simultaneous because of the "continual adjustment process" of bringing advertising into its historical relationship to actual sales. In this case, the decision rule would use sales revenue in the current period, S_α.

Sales revenue is defined as the product of unit price times unit sales or $S_\alpha = P_\alpha \cdot Q_\alpha$. If price is constant over the time period studied, then we have a conventional constant parameter model. However, price is likely to be variable. Then the decision rule can be expressed as

$$A_\alpha = (\gamma_{12}P_\alpha)Q_\alpha + \beta_{22}X_\alpha + \beta_{32} - \epsilon_{\alpha2}. \tag{7.38}$$

The coefficient of unit sales varies systematically with price. Consequently, in this case, all the reduced-form coefficients will as well.

Systematic parameter variation need not be evaluated over time, but rather it could be evaluated over individuals. Wittink (1975) studied the sales behavior of one brand over N sales territories and T months. Market share was a function of relative price, advertising share, and market share in the previous period.

$$MS_{\alpha i} = e^{\beta_0 i} MS_{\alpha-1,i}^{\beta_1 i} RP_{\alpha i}^{\beta_2 i} (AS_{\alpha i} + \lambda AS_{\alpha-1,i})^{\beta_3 i} e^{\epsilon_{\alpha i}} \tag{7.39}$$

$$i = 1, \ldots, N; \alpha = 2, \ldots, T.$$

The presence of the lagged dependent variable is in the sense of a partial adjustment model (see Chap. 8). Lagged advertising effects are captured by adding a portion, λ, of the previous period's advertising share to the current advertising share.

In addition, Wittink proposed that the parameters in Eq. (7.39) were themselves dependent on observable variables, that is

$$\beta_{ji} = Z_{ji}\lambda_j + \xi_{ji} \qquad j = 0,\ldots,3; i = 1,\ldots,N, \qquad (7.40)$$

where the exogenous variables included demographic variables as well as the mean levels of advertising share and market share. Although β_{ji} is unknown, $\hat{\beta}_{ij}$ is available from applying ordinary least squares to Eq. (7.39). Because of the covariances among the parameter estimates, estimation of the new parameters by means of seemingly unrelated equations regression was required.

Wittink found that the demographic variables were insignificant. However, he did determine that relative price was inelastic and that advertising share, although significant, was inelastic. Furthermore, relative price became more elastic as advertising share increased. This suggests that advertising tended to increase the price competitiveness of the brand.

SUMMARY

Econometric models like the ones discussed above will be shown in Chap. 9 to permit determination of the optimal marketing budget. Features that have been shown to be feasible with econometric models are:

1. Isolation of the effects of one marketing instrument from those of other factors
2. Characterizations of
   a. carryover and feedback effects.
   b. nonlinearities
   c. simultaneous interactions
   d. intrinsic relative effectiveness of advertising
   e. impact of different campaigns
   f. time-varying effectiveness of marketing instruments

3. Comparison of various media
4. Prediction of
   a. behavior of brand advertising and sales
   b. competitive advertising and sales behavior

Although each of these features is not present in every model, the capability to incorporate them exists. The lack of appropriate data is the primary reason for the omission of a particular feature. This problem is diminishing as the input requirements have become more widely appreciated. After a representative sales response equation is obtained through econometric research, the next question concerns the use of this mechanism in a marketing decision model. This issue is addressed in Chap. 9.

FOOTNOTES

[1] In which case we have a "market share" elasticity. We could use sales in place of market share and have a "sales" elasticity. We usually speak of an elasticity without any qualifier attached, but with the qualifier being implicitly understood from the context in which it is used.

[2] The elasticities in a linear model are functions of the level of the managerial decision variables. Suppose, the linear response function (7.1) is differentiated with respect to price (P) or $dMS = \beta_1 dP$. Then the price elasticity can be expressed as $\eta_p = \beta_1 (P/MS)$.

[3] Other models permit diminishing returns to scale. For instance, Little (1966) proposed the quadratic sales response function: $S = \beta_0 - \beta_1 A - \beta_2 A^2$.

[4] Equation (7.9) is the reduced form of the geometric distributed lag model (see Chap. 8).

[5] This type of model will be discussed in more detail in the next chapter.

[6] The general multinomial logit model can be written as

$$\frac{y_{\alpha i}}{y_{\alpha j}} = e^{\beta_{oi} - \beta_{oj}} \prod_{h=1}^{H} Z_{\alpha h}^{\beta_{hi} - \beta_{hj}} \prod_{k=1}^{K} \left(\frac{X_{k\alpha i}}{X_{k\alpha j}} \right)^{\gamma_k} e^{\epsilon_{\alpha i} - \epsilon_{\alpha j}}.$$

[7] Naert and Bultez's (1973) contributions to this area were demonstrated to be wrong by Beckwith (1973), who produced a counter example.

[8] Clarke's [(1972), 154-158] interpretation is not accurate on this point.

[9] This approach to seasonally time-varying parameters is discussed in Chap. 4.

[10] In finance, Rosenberg and Ohlson have proposed such a stochastic model of the "beta" for any security [Rosenberg (1973b), 401].

Chapter 8

THE MEASUREMENT
OF CARRYOVER EFFECTS

Current expenditures on marketing instruments usually do not have their full impact on sales in the same accounting period. Moreover, their impact on sales may extend well into the future. The influence of current marketing expenditures on sales in future periods is called a carryover effect.

Two forms of carryover effects have been identified by Kotler (1970). The delayed response effect arises when there is an interval between making the marketing expenditure and realizing the associated sale. For instance, a salesman may wait some time between making an initial call and consummating the deal. The customer holdover effect arises because the marketing expenditure may create a new customer who not only will make an initial purchase, but also will repurchase it in future periods. Thus, the current marketing effect must receive some credit for these subsequent sales.

Sales may not react fully and immediately to changes in marketing inputs, but may do so in a more gradual manner. Advertising can create new customers. However, the timing of the first purchase of these new customers will vary according to each buyer's shopping and usage behavior. Moreover, repeat purchases will also depend on usage rates.

In order to properly assess the effectiveness of marketing instruments, the fraction of total sales in the current period and each succeeding period which are attributable to the current marketing effort must be measured. The duration of the carryover effect induced by this effort must also be determined. The purpose of this chapter is to discuss alternative specifications for representing carryover effects and the estimation of the parameters in these formulations.[1]

Sales (y_α) may respond to marketing expenditures with lag t. A linear model of this relationship might be

167

$$y_\alpha = \beta_0 + \beta_{t+1} x_{\alpha-t} + \epsilon_\alpha. \tag{8.1}$$

This model represents a *simple* lag of the exogenous variable (x_α). The effect of a marketing expenditure in period $\alpha - t$ occurs only, and completely, within period α. Often, the effect of a marketing variable is *distributed* over several time periods. Consequently, sales in any period is a function of the current and previous marketing expenditures:

$$y_\alpha = \beta_0 + \sum_{t=0}^{\infty} \beta_{t+1} x_{\alpha-t} + \epsilon_\alpha , \tag{8.2}$$

where

$$\sum_{t=0}^{\infty} \beta_{t+1} = \text{constant} < \infty.$$

This restriction ensures that while a finite change in the level of marketing expenditures will persist indefinitely, it will cause only a finite change in sales.

The general distributed lag model can not be estimated because it contains an infinite number of parameters. Even if the maximum lag is known *a priori* to be finite so that

$$y_\alpha = \beta_0 + \sum_{t=0}^{T} \beta_{t+1} x_{\alpha-t} + \epsilon_\alpha, \tag{8.3}$$

the exact value of the maximum lag, T, is rarely known. In any case, the number of parameters to be estimated still may be large and the exogenous variables highly collinear.[2] Additional assumptions usually must be imposed to obtain estimates.

THE LAG STRUCTURE AS A SET OF PROBABILITIES

A very useful assumption to make, and one that is usually plausible in marketing situations, is that the coefficients all have the same sign.[3] The general distributed lag can now be rewritten as

$$y_\alpha = \beta_0 + \beta_1 \sum_{t=0}^{\infty} \omega_t x_{\alpha-t} + \epsilon_\alpha, \tag{8.4}$$

where

$$\omega_t \geqslant 0 \text{ and } \sum_{t=0}^{\infty} \omega_t = 1. \tag{8.5}$$

The sequence of ω's describes the shape of the lag over time. More importantly, the ω's can be regarded as probabilities of a discrete distribution.

This probability formulation permits easy interpretation of some of the properties of the empirical response function. Properties such as the average lag between making a marketing expenditure and obtaining a sales response or the degree to which the impact is concentrated in an interval of short duration or diffused over an extended period can be calculated using the moments of the probability distribution.

Geometric Distribution

The geometric is the most commonly used distributed lag model in marketing. The maximum impact of marketing expenditures on sales is registered instantaneously. Then, the influence declines geometrically to zero. This approach was popularized in marketing by Palda (1964) in his attempt to measure the cumulative effects of advertising.

The geometric distribution gives

$$\omega_t = (1 - \lambda) \lambda^t \qquad t = 0, 1, 2, \ldots, \tag{8.6}$$

where $0 < \lambda < 1$. Thus, the specification of the sales response function becomes

$$y_\alpha = \beta_0 + \beta_1 (1 - \lambda) \sum_{t=0}^{\infty} \lambda^t x_{\alpha-t} + \epsilon_\alpha. \tag{8.7}$$

This relationship is nonlinear in the parameter λ. Thus, ordinary least squares can not be used as the estimation method. Consequently, Koyck (1954) proposed a transformation. First, multiply λ times the sales response function in the previous period, $\alpha - 1$:

$$\lambda y_{\alpha-1} = \lambda \beta_0 + \beta_1 (1 - \lambda) \sum_{t=1}^{\infty} \lambda^t x_{\alpha-t} + \lambda \epsilon_{\alpha-1}. \tag{8.8}$$

Now, subtract this expression from the original sales response function and obtain the result that

$$y_\alpha = (1 - \lambda)\beta_0 + (1 - \lambda)\beta_1 x_\alpha + \lambda y_{\alpha-1} + (\epsilon_\alpha - \lambda\epsilon_{\alpha-1}). \tag{8.9}$$

The original Eq. (8.7) might contain one or more independent variables which do not exhibit any lagged effects. Price may be such a variable, particularly if we are concerned with a frequently purchased branded good. Each of these variables will appear in the original equation as $\beta_i x_{\alpha,i}$ and in the transformed Eq. (8.9) as $\beta_i(x_{\alpha,i} - \lambda x_{\alpha-1,i})$.

Ordinary least-squares estimators of the parameters in this relationship will be inconsistent unless the error term follows a first-order Markov process with parameter λ.

Palda (1964) in his well-known study of the cumulative effects of Lydia Pinkham Vegetable Compound advertising found when using annual observations that

$$S_\alpha = 212 + .537A_\alpha + .628\,S_{\alpha-1} - 102D1 + 181D2 - 203D3 \quad R^2 = .92,$$
$$(.143) \quad\ (.085) \quad\ \ (98) \quad\ \ (68) \quad\ \ (70)$$
$$\tag{8.10}$$

where the D's are dummy variables representing copy changes and the numbers in parentheses are the estimated standard errors of the coefficients. Unfortunately this model has proved to be inappropriate as we will discuss later in this chapter. Others employing the geometric distributed lag model include Simon (1969), Lambin (1969, 1970, 1972), Samuels (1970, 1971), and Bass and Clarke (1972). Much of the statistical evidence has failed to support the geometric lag hypothesis although the researchers themselves have frequently not recognized this phenomenon. Surprisingly, the coefficient of the marketing instrument in the reduced form equation is often not statistically significant.

Testing. One alternative to the geometric lag model is the partial adjustment model. In the partial adjustment model, sales in the current period are similar to sales in the previous period except for a response to the marketing instrument.

$$y_\alpha = \beta_0 + \beta_1 x_\alpha + \beta_2 y_{\alpha-1} + \epsilon_\alpha. \tag{8.11}$$

This model tends to fit any time series with inertia very well. The only difference between the partial adjustment model (8.11) and the reduced form of the geometric lag model (8.9) is that the partial adjustment model has a simpler disturbance term. Establishment of the presence of carryover effects requires that the linkage between the reduced form model (8.9) and the underlying structural model (8.7) be shown.

Griliches (1967) pointed out that it is possible to discriminate between the geometric lag model and a simple first-order autoregressive model. The disturbances in an autocorrelated errors process obey the relationship

$$\epsilon_\alpha = \rho \epsilon_{\alpha-1} + \xi_\alpha, \quad \text{where } |\rho| < 1. \tag{8.12}$$

Marketing carryover effects are presumably the reason for the presence of an autoregressive process. The parameter, ρ, is thus a measure of carryover strength. This relationship is then substituted into the simple model

$$y_\alpha = \beta_0 + \beta_1 x_\alpha + \epsilon_\alpha$$

$$= \beta_0 + \beta_1 x_\alpha + \rho \epsilon_{\alpha-1} + \xi_\alpha$$

$$= (1 - \rho)\beta_0 + \beta_1 x_\alpha + \rho y_{\alpha-1} - \beta_i \rho x_{\alpha-1} + \xi_\alpha. \tag{8.13}$$

Thus when we estimate the equation

$$y_\alpha = b_0 + b_1 x_\alpha + b_2 y_{\alpha-1} + b_3 x_{\alpha-1} + \xi_\alpha, \tag{8.14}$$

if the autoregressive model of current effects is true, $\hat{b}_3 = -\hat{b}_1 \hat{b}_2$. Whereas, if the geometric lag model of cumulative effects is true, $\hat{b}_3 = 0$ and $\hat{b}_2 = \hat{\rho}$.

Clarke and McCann (1973) reappraised Palda's Lydia Pinkham results using this approach. The current effects model could not be rejected. However, in two other product classes, the opposite conclusion was found. Both Bass and Clarke (1972) and Montgomery and Silk (1972) determined that the cumulative effects model could not be rejected, but that the current effects model could be rejected.

A fourth product class produced mixed results. Lambin (1972) found that two brands seemed to exhibit cumulative effects whereas two other brands did not.

Houston and Weiss (1975) argued that while past pricing policy, physical product characteristics, retail availability, as well as advertising, all contributed toward repeat purchase of Lydia Pinkham tonic, advertising had a unique role. Consequently, they postulated a model of the form

$$y_\alpha = \beta_0 + \beta_1 x_\alpha + \lambda y_{\alpha-1} + \epsilon_\alpha, \tag{8.15}$$

wherein the lagged sales term was explicitly introduced rather than being introduced as a result of an autocorrelated error process. *Then* they superimposed a first-order autoregressive process which yielded

$$y_\alpha = (1 - \rho)\beta_0 + \beta_1 x_\alpha - \rho\beta_1 x_{\alpha-1} + (\lambda + \rho)y_{\alpha-1} - \rho\lambda y_{\alpha-2} + \xi_\alpha. \tag{8.16}$$

If $\lambda = 0$, this will reduce to the simple autoregressive model (8.13). The results found by Houston and Weiss are shown in Table 8.1. The current effects model of Clarke and McCann was rejected in favor of the Houston-Weiss generalized carryover model.

Table 8.1

Parameter Estimates for Lydia Pinkham Models

Models[a]	$\hat{\lambda}$	$\hat{\rho}$	$\hat{\beta}_1$	$\hat{\beta}_0$
Palda Geometric lag (8.15)[b]	.609 (7.40)	—	.531 (3.86)	254. (2.62)
Clarke and McCann Current effects (8.13)	—	.821 (13.2)	.562 (4.63)	1330. (5.77)
Houston and Weiss Generalized carryover (8.16)	.333 (1.48)	.644 (2.70)	.548 (4.17)	744. (1.69)

[a]These parameter estimates are from Houston and Weiss [(1975), 477] and are based on the same number of observations. The numbers in parenthesis are asymptotic t statistics. The estimates for the dummy variables are not shown.
[b]The restriction on the error term imposed by the geometric lag structure is not taken into account, i.e., (8.15) is estimated instead of (8.9).

Duration of Carryover Effect

The average lag between making a marketing expenditure and obtaining a sales response for the geometric lag is $\lambda/(1 - \lambda)$. The extent to which the marketing effects are concentrated or diffused is indicated by the variance of the geometric distribution $\lambda/(1 - \lambda)^2$. Typical values of these statistics for advertising carryover are given in Table 8.2.

Table 8.2

Some Geometric Lag Studies of Advertising

Study	Product	Data interval	Retention rate $(\hat{\lambda})$	Lag (in months)	
				Mean	Std. Dev.
Palda (1964)	Lydia Pinkham	Annual	.628	20.28	25.56
Simon (1969)	Ancient Age Bourbon	Annual	.670	24.36	29.76
Lambin (1969)	FPBG	Annual	.443	9.6	14.28
Lambin (1970)	Small electrical appliance	Annual	.678	25.2	27.76
Samuels (1970/71)	Washing Up Liquid A	Monthly	.458	.85	1.25
	Washing Up Liquid B	Monthly	.528	1.11	1.54
	Household cleanser	Monthly	.508	1.03	1.45
Bass and Clarke (1972)	Dietary weight control Product	Monthly	.621	1.64	2.07

The number of periods necessary to achieve a given fraction θ of the total long run effect can also be calculated.[4] The total effect of the marketing expenditure is

$$Q_\alpha = \beta_1(1 - \lambda) \sum_{t=0}^{\infty} \lambda^t x_\alpha = \beta_1 x_\alpha. \qquad (8.17)$$

The sales generated by this marketing expenditure in the first N periods is

$$Q_N = \beta_1(1 - \lambda) \sum_{t=0}^{N-1} \lambda^t x_\alpha = \beta_1(1 - \lambda^N)x_\alpha. \qquad (8.18)$$

Now, N can be found such that $Q_N/Q_\infty \geqslant \theta$. By substitution, this inequality is

$$1 - \lambda^N \geqslant \theta. \qquad (8.19)$$

This relationship can be solved for th , implied duration level, N:

$$N \leqslant \frac{\log(1 - \theta)}{\log \lambda}.$$

The .5 and .9 implied duration levels are plotted as a function of λ in Fig. 8.1. For example, Samuels found that the retention for a household cleanser was .508. For this product, 50% of the total long

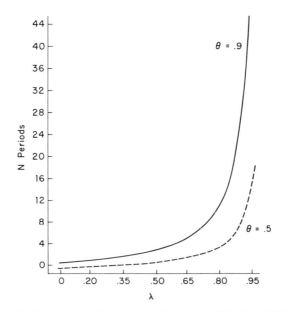

Fig. 8.1. Implied duration intervals. Source: Clarke (1975, p.7).

run advertising effect occurs within 1.0 month and 90% of the effect within 3.4 months.

Extensions. The geometric distributed lag model can be extended in several different ways. Perhaps the geometric decline does not start immediately in the first period, but rather starts at the kth period. This modification can be represented by

$$y_\alpha = \beta_0 + (1 - \lambda) \sum_{t=0}^{k-2} \beta_{t+1} x_{\alpha-t} + \beta_k (1 - \lambda) \sum_{t=k}^{\infty} \lambda^{t-k} x_{\alpha-t+1} + \epsilon_\alpha. \quad (8.20)$$

This formulation permits the lag structure to be nonmonotonic. Application of a Koyck-type transformation results in

$$y_\alpha = (1 - \lambda)\beta_0 + (1 - \lambda)\beta_1 x_\alpha + (1 - \lambda) \sum_{t=1}^{k-1} (\beta_{t+1} - \lambda \beta_t) x_{\alpha-t} \quad (8.21)$$
$$+ \lambda y_{\alpha-1} + (\epsilon_\alpha - \lambda\epsilon_{\alpha-1}).$$

This generalization increases the likelihood of encountering the problem of multicollinearity because of the k successive values of the independent variable. Bass and Clarke (1972), Lambin (1972), and Montgomery and Silk (1972) have incorporated this extension into their models.

Bass and Clarke (1972) felt that the geometric decay in advertising a dietary weight control product did not begin with the initial month but was delayed until month two. Consumers of the product belong to one of two segments: (1) light users who consume it once a day to help control their weight and (2) heavy users who are on a diet and consume little else but the product. Since these groups have different average interpurchase times, the modal total sales response time to an advertising input will depend on the relative proportions of these two segments. The modal response time was conjectured to be three weeks or more.

The maximum likelihood estimates of the traditional geometric lag model,

$$Q_\alpha = 272.6 + .157A_\alpha + .585 Q_{\alpha-1}, \quad R^2 = .650 \quad (8.22)$$
$$(.002) \quad\;\; (.083)$$

can be compared with the estimates of the modified geometric lag model,

$$Q_\alpha = 286.2 + .127A_\alpha + .081A_{\alpha-1} + .399 Q_{\alpha-1}, \quad R^2 = .686, \quad (8.23)$$
$$(.026) \quad\;\; (.043) \quad\quad\;\; (.144)$$

where the numbers in the parentheses are the estimates of the standard errors of the coefficients.

Since the traditional model is nested within the modified model, the traditional model can be tested using the estimates of the parameters of the modified model. If the traditional model is true, then the coefficient of advertising in the previous period in the modified model should be equal to zero. Bass and Clarke judge that this is not the case. Computation of the likelihood ratio test statistic [Eq. (5.25)] given in Chap. 5 yields

$$F = \frac{n-K}{r}\left(\frac{\hat{\sigma}^2_{8.20} - \hat{\sigma}^2_{8.21}}{\hat{\sigma}^2_{8.21}}\right) = \frac{33-4}{1}\left(\frac{65,211 - 58,516}{58,516}\right) = 3.31 \, ,$$

which is greater than the critical value of $F_{.10,1,30} = 2.88$. Thus, the nested model was rejected by Bass and Clarke at the .10 level of significance. However, at the more conventional .05 level of significance, the traditional geometric lag model could not have been rejected.

Another direction for extension is to allow more than one independent variable to experience the same geometric distributed lag:

$$y_\alpha = \beta_0 + \beta_1(1-\lambda)\sum_{t=0}^{\infty}\lambda^t x_{\alpha-t,1} + \beta_2(1-\lambda)\sum_{t=0}^{\infty}\lambda^t x_{\alpha-t,2} + \epsilon_\alpha. \qquad (8.24)$$

Although the decay rate is assumed to be identical for all of the independent variables, the magnitudes of the effects need not be identical. Once again a Koyck-type transformation is applied to yield

$$y_\alpha = (1-\lambda)\beta_0 + (1-\lambda)\beta_1 x_{\alpha,1} + (1-\lambda)\beta_2 x_{\alpha,2} + \lambda y_{\alpha-1} + (\epsilon_\alpha - \lambda\epsilon_{\alpha-1}). \qquad (8.25)$$

Marketing studies that employ this formulation include those by Frank and Massy (1967) and Montgomery and Silk (1972).

Frank and Massy (1967) investigated the effects of price and dealing on the market share of one brand in a frequently purchased food item product class. The variables in their model were market share of the brand (MS), an index of the base price of the brand relative to the base prices of all the other brands in the market (P), and index of the deal magnitude of the brand relative to the deal magnitudes of all the other brands in the market (D), the proportion of the brand's unit sales that were moved under a consumer deal (PD), and the expected share for the brand based on the long-run purchase probabilities of those prospects who actually bought during the period (ES). The base price is the normal shelf price of the brand when not on deal. The deal magnitude is then the amount of discount from this base price. All variables were expressed in logarithms.

The price and deal variables were assumed in the model to experience identical decay rates. Moreover, the geometric decay in both variables was assumed not to begin until the third period. Weekly panel data were used to estimate the parameters of the model

$$MS_\alpha = -.027 - 2.368\, P_\alpha + .437\, P_{\alpha-1} + .435\, P_{\alpha-2}$$
$$\quad\quad\quad\quad (.44)\quad\quad (.47)\quad\quad\quad (.39)$$

$$\quad + .048\, D_\alpha + .002\, D_{\alpha-1} + .004\, D_{\alpha-2} + .027\, PD_\alpha \quad\quad (8.26)$$
$$\quad\quad (.02)\quad\quad (.02)\quad\quad\quad (.02)\quad\quad\quad (.03)$$

$$\quad + 1.014\, ES_\alpha - .257\, ES_{\alpha-1} + .124\, MS_{\alpha-1} \quad\quad R^2 = .59,$$
$$\quad\quad (.18)\quad\quad (.21)\quad\quad\quad (.11)$$

where the numbers in the parentheses are the estimates of the standard errors of the coefficients. Incredibly Frank and Massy consider this model a reasonable representation of the market mechanism. Our interpretation of these results is that the impact of the marketing instruments is instantaneous. The coefficient of market share in the previous week is not large relative to its standard error suggesting that the hypothesis that $\lambda = 0$ can not be rejected. A similar statement can be made about each of the coefficients of the lagged exogenous variables. Therefore, the empirical evidence does not support the distributed lag formulation.

Montgomery and Silk (1972) provide some empirical evidence of a nonmonotonic lag structure in marketing instruments. They measured the market share response of an established ethical drug to its communications mix. The instruments in the communications mix included journal advertising (JA), direct mail advertising (DM), and samples and literature (SL). Geometric decay was assumed to set in at different points of time for each instrument. However, once decay begins, each instrument experiences the same decay rate. In addition, a major competitive product was removed from the market during the period for which observations were available. This necessitated inclusion of a dummy variable (CO) which had the value one when the competitor was present and zero otherwise.[5] All variables except the dummy variable were expressed in logarithms. The ordinary least squares regression results were

$$MS_\alpha = -2.75 - .28\,CO_\alpha + .002\,DM_\alpha + .010\,DM_{\alpha-1}$$
$$(-6.83) \quad (-3.95) \qquad (.71) \qquad (2.86)$$

$$+ .015\,SL_\alpha + .025\,SL_{\alpha-1} + .010\,SL_{\alpha-2} + .157\,JA_\alpha$$
$$(2.17) \qquad (3.68) \qquad (1.51) \qquad (6.48)$$

$$- \quad .053\,JA_{\alpha-1} + .026\,JA_{\alpha-2} + .068\,JA_{\alpha-3} + .348\,MS_{\alpha-1}$$
$$(-1.71) \qquad (1.00) \qquad (2.61) \qquad (3.66)$$

$$(8.27)$$

where the numbers in parentheses are the estimated t-ratios. The value of R^2 was 0.891.

The peak sales effects of direct mail and of samples and literature occur one period after these expenditures are made. The peak effect of journal advertising occurs in the same period that the expenditure is made. There is a substantial sales response to journal advertising, a lesser response to samples and literature, and a very small response to direct mail . Moreover, the company was allocating its communications expenditures in inverse relation to the actual market response!

All these authors recognized that there was no reason to believe that the effects of the variables will tend to decay in accordance with the same law. However, they did not implement this modification. One could allow different rates of decline to apply to various variables:

$$y_\alpha = \beta_0 + \beta_1(1-\lambda_1)\sum_{t=0}^{\infty}\lambda_1^t x_{\alpha-t,1} + \beta_2(1-\lambda_2)\sum_{t=0}^{\infty}\lambda_2^t x_{\alpha-1,2} + \epsilon_\alpha.$$

$$(8.28)$$

Repeating twice the Koyck-type transformation leads to

$$y_\alpha = (1-\lambda_1)(1-\lambda_2)\beta_0 + \beta_1(1-\lambda_1)(x_{\alpha,1} - \lambda_2 x_{\alpha-1,1})$$

$$+ \beta_2(1-\lambda_2)(x_{\alpha,2} - \lambda_1 x_{\alpha-1,2}) + (\lambda_1+\lambda_2)y_{\alpha-1} - \lambda_1\lambda_2 y_{\alpha-2}$$

$$+ [\epsilon_\alpha - (\lambda_1+\lambda_2)\epsilon_{\alpha-1} + \lambda_1\lambda_2\epsilon_{\alpha-2}].$$

$$(8.29)$$

Peles (1971) used such a model in a study of the demand for beer. Advertising expenditures by the firm and advertising expenditures by competitors exhibited different carryover effects on the firm's demand. The estimated coefficients of demand lagged one year and demand lagged two years were 0.938 and -0.218, respectively. Using the relationships that $\lambda_1 + \lambda_2 = .938$ and $-\lambda_1\lambda_2 = -0.218$, we find that $\lambda_1 = 0.425$ and $\lambda_2 = 0.218$. The corresponding average lags are 0.739 years and 0.279 years.

Negative Binomial Distribution

The monotonically decreasing sequence of coefficients in the geometric lag structure may be inappropriate in some marketing situations. The effect of marketing expenditures may be small, initially, increase to a peak, and then decline. The negative binomial distribution is a flexible two-parameter distribution which can represent such an effect:

$$\omega_t = \frac{(r + t - 1)!}{(r-1)!t!}(1 - \lambda)^r\lambda^t, \qquad t = 0,1,\ldots, \tag{8.30}$$

where $0 < \lambda < 1$ and r is a positive integer. The mean lag is $\lambda r/(1 - \lambda)$ and the variability is $\lambda r/(1 - \lambda)^2$. For $r = 1$, the negative binomial reduces to the geometric distribution. Mann (1975) fit the negative binomial to monthly Lydia Pinkham data. He tried values of r from 1 through 10. The best fit was achieved for $r = 4$.

POLYNOMIAL LAG STRUCTURES

A more flexible approach to estimating a finite general distributed lag model involves expressing the coefficients, β_{t+1}, in terms of some function $f(t)$. The function $f(t)$ is not known. However, the Weierstrass theorem states that all continuous functions can be approximated by polynomials on any finite interval with arbitrarily small error. Thus, the function $f(t)$ can be approximated by a polynomial in t. These two successive approximations can be written

$$\beta_{t+1} \simeq f(t) \simeq \sum_{i=0}^{p} \lambda_i t^i, \qquad t = 0,1,2,\ldots,T. \tag{8.31}$$

This polynomial lag model is said to be of order T and degree p. Presumably p is less than T so that there are fewer parameters to estimate in the restricted version.

One advantage of a polynomial lag structure is that the set of predetermined variables does not contain any lagged values of the dependent variable. Consequently, some of the estimation problems inherent in geometric lag models and other such similar models do not occur and ordinarily least-squares regression can be used.

Incorporating *A Priori* Knowledge

Some *a priori* information about the shape of the lag structure may be known. Perhaps marketing theory suggests that the lag structure should exhibit a humped shape. A means of incorporating such *a priori* knowledge usually involves specification not only of the degree of the polynomial, but also of either the roots of the polynomial or the boundary conditions on the $[0,T]$ interval.

Johansson (no date) provides an example of this approach. Suppose that the nonzero coefficients of a finite lag model of order T are approximated by a second-degree polynomial:

$$\beta_{t+1} \simeq \lambda_0 + \lambda_1 t + \lambda_2 t^2, \qquad t = 0, 1, 2, \ldots, T. \qquad (8.32)$$

In addition, the roots of the polynomial might be specified to be located at $t = -1$ and $t = T + 1$. Thus

$$\lambda_0 + \lambda_1(-1) + \lambda_2(-1)^2 = 0 \qquad (8.33)$$

$$\lambda_0 + \lambda_1(T + 1) + \lambda_2(T + 1)^2 = 0,$$

and consequently $\lambda_0 = -\lambda_2(T + 1)$ and $\lambda_1 = -\lambda_2 T$. The polynomial approximation is now

$$\beta_{t+1} \simeq -\lambda_2[T + 1 + Tt - t^2]. \qquad (8.34)$$

If, as would be expected, λ_2 is assumed to be negative, then the coefficients of the finite lag model increase from $t = 0$ to a maximum at $t = T/2$ and subsequently decline. Johansson set $T = 4$ in his investigation of a nonseasonal consumer product which had a monthly average purchase frequency.

Lagrangian Interpolation

The Lagrangian interpolation polynomial provides a convenient form which is amenable to incorporating *a priori* restrictions [Dhrymes (1971), 40-43, 229-234); Johnston (1972), 294-297]. If $p + 1$ points, t_i, are arbitrarily specified between 0 and T, this approximation can be written as

$$\beta_{t+1} \simeq \sum_{i=0}^{b} b_i \, s_i \, (t), \qquad t = 0, 1, 2, \ldots, T. \tag{8.35}$$

The $s_i(t)$'s are *known* weights[6]:

$$s_i \, (t) = \frac{\prod\limits_{j \neq i} (t - t_j)}{\prod\limits_{j \neq i} (t_i - t_j)}, \qquad j = 0, 1, 2, \ldots p. \tag{8.36}$$

Then the equation to be estimated is

$$y_\alpha = \beta_0 + \sum_{t=0}^{T} \beta_{t+1} x_{\alpha-t} + \epsilon_\alpha \tag{8.37}$$

$$= \beta_0 + \sum_{t=0}^{T} \sum_{i=0}^{p} b_i s_i(t) x_{\alpha-t} + \epsilon_\alpha$$

$$= \beta_0 + \sum_{j=0}^{p} b_i \sum_{t=0}^{T} s_i(t) x_{\alpha-t} + \epsilon_\alpha$$

$$= \beta_0 + \sum_{i=0}^{p} b_i z_i,$$

where the z_i's are the new set of predetermined variables.

The two polynomial approximations (8.31) and (8.35) give identical estimates of the lag structure. Use of the first formulation permits easier testing of the degree of the polynomial (to wit, test the hypothesis that $\lambda_p = 0$). Use of the second permits easier incorporation of *a priori* constraints.[7] In addition, the latter approach may involve less multicollinearity.

Yon and Mount (1975) applied a polynomial lag model of order

7 and degree 3 to monthly data for a branded food product sold in France. The impact of advertising expenditures experienced the distributed lag. The model also included price. All variables were expressed in logarithms.

The lag values at which the Lagrangian interpolation polynomial is unity were assumed to be $t_0 = 1$, $t_1 = 3$, $t_2 = 5$, and $t_3 = 7$. The results of estimation are

$$Q_\alpha = \begin{array}{cccc} 6.66 & -.00006\,Z_0 & + .0032\,Z_1 & + .00283\,Z_2 \\ (18.98) & (0.54) & (6.19) & (1.37) \end{array}$$

$$\begin{array}{cc} + .0014\,Z_3 & -.641 P_\alpha, \qquad R^2 = .649, \\ (1.40) & (-8.82) \end{array}$$

(8.38)

where the numbers in parentheses are estimated t-values. The distributed lag coefficients can be calculated from Eqs. (8.35) and (8.36); for instance

$$\hat{\beta}_1 = \frac{(0-3)(0-5)(0-7)}{(1-3)(1-5)(1-7)}(-.00006) + \frac{(0-1)(0-5)(0-7)}{(3-1)(3-5)(3-7)}(.0032) \qquad (8.39)$$

$$+ \frac{(0-1)(0-3)(0-7)}{(5-1)(5-3)(5-7)}(.00283) + \frac{(0-1)(0-3)(0-5)}{(7-1)(7-3)(7-5)}(.0014)$$

$$= -.00385.$$

The other distributed lag coefficients can be calculated similarly. These coefficients are shown in the first column of Table 8.3.

Table 8.3

The Lag Structure for Advertising

Variable	Estimated coefficients	
	Unconstrained polynomial	Constrained polynomial
A_α	$-.00385$	.00000
$A_{\alpha-1}$	$-.00006$	.00000
$A_{\alpha-2}$	$-.00218$	.00166
$A_{\alpha-3}$	.00320	.00310
$A_{\alpha-4}$	.00331	.00399
$A_{\alpha-5}$	.00283	.00400
$A_{\alpha-6}$	.00209	.00278
$A_{\alpha-7}$	.00140	.00000

The lag structure displays a humped shape. This rules out the possibility that the lag structure is geometric. However, several of the estimates of the coefficients of the lagged advertising variables are negative. Marketing theory suggests that all these coefficients should be nonnegative. In order for all the coefficients to be nonnegative, Yon and Mount imposed the constraints that the parameters β_1, β_2, and β_8 be equal to zero. The estimated coefficients of the third-degree polynomial were

$$Q_\alpha = 7.0321 - .6491P_\alpha + .0031W_1 + .0040W_2, \qquad R^2 = .55, \qquad (8.40)$$
$$ (19.99) \ \ (9.22) \qquad (6.47) \qquad (3.84)$$

where the numbers in parentheses are the estimated t ratios. The corresponding distributed lag coefficients are shown in the second column of Table 8.3.

The specification of the zeros of the polynomial is a key determinant of the shape of the lag structure. One check is to estimate the unrestricted formulation in which the zeros of the polynomial remain unspecified.

RATIONAL LAG STRUCTURES

Advanced work with distributed lags is facilitated by the use of the lag or delay operator. The lag operator L is the transformation

$$Lx_\alpha = x_{\alpha-1}, \qquad (8.41)$$

and it can be applied k successive times so that

$$L^k x_\alpha = x_{\alpha-k}. \qquad (8.42)$$

Then the general rational lag structure [Jorgenson (1966)] can be written as

$$y = \beta_0 + \frac{A(L)}{B(L)} x_\alpha + \epsilon_\alpha, \qquad (8.43)$$

where

$$A(L) = \sum_{i=0}^{m} a_i L^i, \quad B(L) = \sum_{j=0}^{n} b_j L^j, \quad b_0 = 1.$$

In addition, the error terms ϵ_α are independently and identically distributed random variables with $E(\epsilon_\alpha) = 0$ and $E(\epsilon_\alpha^2) = \sigma^2$.

The finite lag function and the negative binomial lag function are special cases of the general rational lag. In the former, the correspondence is

$$B(L) \equiv I, \tag{8.44}$$

where I is an operator which when applied to an element yields that element, while in the latter

$$A(L) = \beta(1 - \lambda)^r \quad \text{and} \quad B(L) = (1 - \lambda L)^r. \tag{8.45}$$

Setting $r = 1$ reduces Eq. (8.45) to the geometric distributed lag function:

$$y_\alpha = \beta_0 + \frac{\beta_1(1 - \lambda)}{(1 - \lambda L)} x_\alpha + \epsilon_\alpha. \tag{8.46}$$

To see the correspondence with Eq. (8.9), multiply Eq. (8.46) by $(1 - \lambda L)$ and apply the lag operator.

Higher-Order Lags

The general rational lag structure provides a framework for extending the Koyck-type model to represent higher-order lag functions. For example, a second-order lag function can be expressed by setting

$$A(L) = \beta_1(1 - \lambda_1 - \lambda_2) \quad \text{and} \quad B(L) = (1 - \lambda_1 L - \lambda_2 L^2) \tag{8.47}$$

The resultant equation after applying the lag operators and rearranging terms is

$$y_\alpha = \beta_0(1 - \lambda_1 - \lambda_2) + \beta_1(1 - \lambda_1 - \lambda_2)x_\alpha + \lambda_1 y_{\alpha-1} + \lambda_2 y_{\alpha-2} \tag{8.48}$$

$$+ \epsilon_\alpha - \lambda_1 \epsilon_{\alpha-1} - \lambda_2 \epsilon_{\alpha-2}.$$

For this relationship to imply a nonnegative lag distribution for x, λ_1 and λ_2 must satisfy the restrictions: (1) $0 < \lambda_1 < 2$, (2) $|\lambda_2| < 1$,

(3) $1 - \lambda_1 - \lambda_2 > 0$, (4) $\lambda_1^2 \geqslant - 4\lambda_2$ [Griliches (1967), 27]. These restrictions can be deduced from the requirements for the stability of the difference equation [Goldberg (1961), 169-175]. Bass and Clarke in their dietary weight control product study found that the fourth restriction was violated in such a second-order lag function in advertising. In particular, they found that $\beta_0 = 725.56$, $\beta_1 = .342$, $\lambda_1 = .910$, and $\lambda_2 = -.305$.

Frank and Massy (1971) posited a second order lag function in order to capture the carryover effect of a promotion in one week on sales in future weeks. Two opposing influences were thought to be at work. A positive carryover effect would be present if the promotion led to repeat purchases by new buyers of the brand. A negative carryover effect would occur if the promotion was causing current buyers to stock up on the brand. This would merely shift the timing of the sales without increasing long-run sales. On the basis of their own experience, Frank and Massy thought that the stocking-up effect would dominate. Their results did not support this contention. They found that there were no negative coefficients of the lagged demand variable of any magnitude for the major brands. Moreover, many of these coefficients were not statistically significant. Thus, Massy and Frank did not include these variables in their final model.

In their ethical drug study, Montgomery and Silk (1972) also examined second- and third-order lag functions. They concluded that the first-order geometric lag was more plausible than either the second- or third-order lag model.

Estimation

Unfortunately OLS regression can not be used in the estimation of the rational lag structure [Eq. (8.43)]. Suppose one attempted to apply OLS to the model

$$B(L)y_\alpha = \beta_0 B(L) + A(L)x_\alpha + U_\alpha. \tag{8.49}$$

The first problem is that application of the lag operator results in lagged values of the dependent variable appearing in the set of predetermined variables and these variables are not uncorrelated with the error term. In the absence of serially correlated disturbances, the OLS estimators will be consistent although biased in small samples.

The second problem occurs because the errors in Eq. (8.49) must obey

$$U_\alpha = B(L)\,\epsilon_\alpha. \tag{8.50}$$

Although autocorrelated disturbances in absence of lagged values of the dependent variable do not produce biased OLS estimators, the combination of these two problems usually means that the OLS estimators are inconsistent. Moreover, a fundamental identification problem occurs in OLS estimation because the parameters of the lag structure can not be separated from those of the probability structure of the error term.

The estimators of the rational lag structure are obtained by minimizing

$$Q = \left[y - \left(\beta_0 + \frac{A(L)}{B(L)}x\right)\right]' \left[y - \left(\beta_0 + \frac{A(L)}{B(L)}x\right)\right]. \tag{8.51}$$

Differentiating Q with respect to the parameters results in a system of highly nonlinear equations. The reader is referred to Dhrymes [(1971), 248-249)] for a procedure for solving this system.[8] If the disturbances are distributed $N(0, \sigma^2 I)$, then minimization of Q corresponds to finding the maximum of the likelihood function.

RESERVATIONS

The three goals of the various approximations to the actual general distributed lag structure are (1) to come as near to the true lag coefficients as possible, (2) to accomplish this with as few parameters as possible, and (3) to require a relatively simple estimation technique. However, we should not adopt a deficient model simply because of its manageability. The marketing content of the model along with those properties of the market mechanism it attempts to represent must remain preeminent.

Some approximation techniques such as the Lagrangian interpolation polynomial are limited to situations in which the finiteness of the lag structure is reasonably well known. There must be some assurance that the neglected tail of the lag structure is of negligible proportions. Furthermore, Dhrymes [(1971), 52] points out that while an approximation might exist which would mathematically reproduce the beginning portion of the underlying true lag structure,

> ... when the parameters of the estimating scheme are estimated ... if the general infinite lag structure is true, then by using the approximating structure we are committing a misspecification error of unknown proportions. Moreover, ... such approximation schemes are likely to affect the mean lag and other summary characteristics of the lag distribution.

This is true regardless of how large the sample is or how loose the *a priori* assumptions seem to be.

Another source of specification error is temporal aggregation. Marketing analyses are often performed on data collected at intervals much longer than the intervals at which buyers are affected by marketing instruments. The application of a model appropriate for a short time interval to a longer time interval might result in a large bias. For example, compare in Table 8.2 the average lags derived from annual data with those from monthly data. Beckwith (no date) postulated a monthly distributed lag model from which an equivalent annual sales model was deduced. He found for Lydia Pinkham that the estimated monthly and annual relationships were inconsistent.

The appropriate time interval for marketing studies would seem to be approximately equal to the average interpurchase interval for the product. For frequently purchased branded goods, the correct time interval is more likely to be a month rather than a year. Use of shorter time intervals creates another problem, seasonality. The reader is referred to Sims (1974) for an introduction to the treatment of this problem.

While different models may have similar reduced functional forms, for instance, the geometric lag and the autoregressive models, these models have very different marketing implications. Along this line, the sensibility of interpreting the coefficient of sales (or market share) in the previous period as the advertising decay rate must be questioned. We agree with Weiss and Houston (1974) that this coefficient measures a confounding of the effects of habitual purchasing behavior and the effects of past marketing efforts including, but not confined to, advertising expenditures. Even within the same model, for instance, the negative binomial, rather small differences in the coefficients may imply very different lag structures. In this regard, Griliches [(1967), 30] concludes, "This sensitivity raises the question whether generalization to more complicated shapes of the lag distribution is worth the trouble if we can not determine this shape with any degree of accuracy."

Notwithstanding the inherent plausibility of concepts such as the cumulative effects of advertising, distributed lag models in marketing have little or no *theoretical* foundation. In particular, in none of the marketing models has the form of the lag structure been derived as an implication of a given set of behavioral propositions. Taken in conjunction with our previous discussion, this suggests that the distributed lag models employed to date in marketing should be viewed with no small degree of skepticism.

FOOTNOTES

[1] The works of Griliches (1967) and Dhrymes (1971) influenced the development of this chapter greatly.

[2] Preliminary findings on the use of ridge estimators for distributed lag models have not been promising [Maddala (1974)].

[3] An exception to this generalization was raised by Frank and Massy [(1967), 167] who claimed "In fact there were grounds for expecting that the lagged effects of one or both variables (price, deal index) might eventually assume a sign opposite to that of the current effect, ..."

[4] For a geometric progression, if a is the first term, r, the common ratio, n, the number of terms, and s, the sum of n terms, then

$$s = a \frac{(1 - r^n)}{1 - r} .$$

Moreover, if n is infinity and r^2 less than unity, $s = a/(1 - r)$.

[5] If βCO_α is the term in the distributed lag formulation, then the Koyck-type transformation yields $\beta CO_\alpha - \lambda \beta CO_{\alpha-1}$. But since $CO_\alpha = CO_{\alpha-1}$, except at one data point, this formulation can not be estimated. Consequently, bCO is estimated instead and thus $\hat{\beta} \cong \hat{b}/(1 - \hat{\lambda})$.

[6] Note that $s_i(t = t_i) = 1$.

[7] The degree of the polynomial is usually not known. The choice of too low a degree will lead to biased and inconsistent estimators. The choice of too high a degree will result in unbiased and consistent estimators, but at a loss in efficiency. Godfrey and Poskitt (1975) have proposed a method for determining the degree of the polynomial.

[8] Dhrymes [(1971), 260] proposed another procedure for use when the model has been extended to include autocorrelated errors. The presence of autocorrelation creates substantial convergence problems.

Chapter 9

EMPIRICAL DECISION MODELS

Our major premise in discussing the applied nature of this work is that the development and implementation of decision-making technology known as *marketing decision models* will result in better marketing decisions. We have up to this point focused primarily on the sales response function component of decision models. In this chapter, we consider the objective function of a decision model and, more generally, the manner in which optimal (or better) decisions can be made with such models. We will also consider how a model can, when conjoined with a method of information processing, become part of a *marketing decision system*. Since the empirical basis of such models and systems has been established (in Chaps. 6-8), the decision models discussed here will be those with empirical sales response functions and possibly empirical competitive reaction mechanisms.

The chapter is divided into four sections. First, the nature of marketing planning and forecasting is discussed. Second, optimal marketing decisions are considered. Third, competitive behavior is analyzed as it affects optimal marketing decisions. And, fourth, the evolution of marketing decision systems is discussed. Considerations about the implementation and actual use of such models are deferred to Chap. 11.

MARKETING PLANNING AND FORECASTING

There is a natural hierarchy between planning and forecasting: Marketing plans should precede sales forecasts. Meaningful forecasts can only be made on the basis of a firm's plans and expectations regarding competitive reactions. For example, suppose the sales response equation shows a relationship between market share and advertising share. To forecast market share, the firm's plans and the plans of competition with respect to advertising appropriations must be known or at least estimated. If the total industry (market) demand is known, then the firm can forecast its sales from these data. Although this prescription may seem straightforward, many firms reverse the functions, first forecasting sales and then setting advertising appropriations. Familiar "percent of sales" advertising decision rules imply this reverse order. It is only when plans precede forecasts that the logical nature of the dependence is maintained.

Schultz (1971) suggests how an econometric model should be incorporated into a planning process. Figure 9.1 is a flow chart of the planning process. The process involves four primary steps: (1) Set market objectives; (2) forecast demand; (3) set marketing plan and forecast market share; and (4) check plan against objectives. The process assumes a two-phase procedure for estimating company sales through separate equations for total industry demand and company market share. In addition, competition is treated as an exogenous variable. Sales response equations which estimate sales directly (in one phase) can also be used as can models with endogenous competition. In both cases, the planning procedure is similar.

The third step in the process refers to setting the marketing plan "using decision rules for managerial decision variables and competition assumptions." The decision rules can be of two kinds—old and new. The old rules are the ones used by the firm before model implementation. For example, a firm may set its advertising budget as a percent of expected sales. The purpose of an advertising decision model is to derive new decision rules by solving the model. The model can be formulated in such a way that an optimal solution can be obtained using mathematical analysis or programming. An alternative approach would be to formulate a simulation model and "experiment" with alternative advertising appropriations strategies. The choice between the two approaches depends on a number of factors including the complexity of the model and the characteristics of the organization. The important point is that, however the model is solved, it produces not only a specific solution (e.g., an optimal price and advertising budget) but also a general solution method (i.e., optimal decision rules). The general solution to a marketing decision model is a decision rule which can be used again in the future to solve the same problem. These new rules can then be used in place of the old rules and there is both a theoretical and empirical rationale

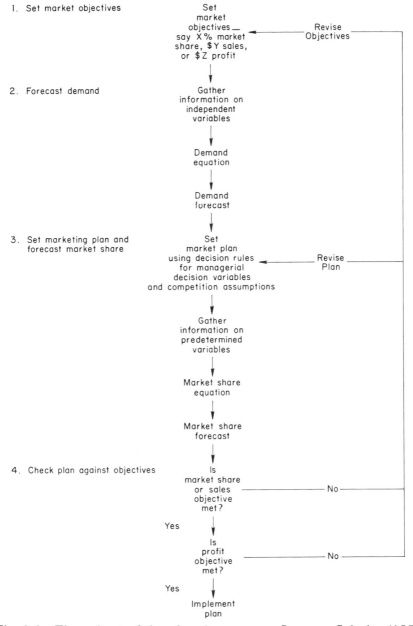

1. Set market objectives

    Set market objectives — say X% market share, $Y sales, or $Z profit ← Revise Objectives

2. Forecast demand

    Gather information on independent variables

    Demand equation

    Demand forecast

3. Set marketing plan and forecast market share

    Set market plan using decision rules for managerial decision variables and competition assumptions ← Revise Plan

    Gather information on predetermined variables

    Market share equation

    Market share forecast

4. Check plan against objectives

    Is market share or sales objective met? — No

    Yes

    Is profit objective met? — No

    Yes

    Implement plan

Fig. 9.1. Flow chart of the planning process. Source: Schultz (1971, p.159).

for believing them to be an improvement in marketing decision making.

The planning process in Fig. 9.1 requires that the manager combine the model output with his own judgment. In particular, he is asked to develop certain "plans" and "anticipations." The *plans* are statements concerning the firm's own actions in the future. The *anticipations* are statements concerning events over which the firm has no control, such as competitive and environmental behavior. Plans are dependent upon anticipations and so predictions of competition and environment are important ingredients in the planning process. Where competition is handled exogenously, the manager must anticipate competitive reaction to his plans. This is one of the key points where his judgment enters the model. In endogenous competition models, the model itself estimates competitive behavior and the manager presumably relies on this "explanation" of the interdependency of plans and anticipations using his judgment later in evaluating the model's recommendations. The combination of model output and judgment that a manager uses depends not only on the nature of the model (e.g., endogenous or exogenous competition), but also on the manager's attitudes toward the planning process. Schultz (1973) has proposed a strategy for handling competition in such models that considers the costs of developing and implementing the models. He concludes that behavioral considerations, such as attitudes toward the planning process, should be an important factor in model design. In this way, decision models can be developed that will have a greater chance of being used.

OPTIMAL MARKETING DECISIONS

The method of developing optimal decision rules, as noted above, depends on various factors. A reasonable criterion of choice would be appropriateness of the decision situation. Is an optimal solution desired or merely an evaluation of alternative policies? Both analytical and simulation approaches can be used to "solve" marketing decision models depending upon the answer to this question. The following discussion centers on several prototype models which offer promise as practical solutions to the optimal marketing policy problem.

Analytical Models

Theory. Analytical models can state either the conditions under which some objective is met or the value of the decision variable or both. The profit-maximizing conditions for advertising expenditures have been available for some time. Stigler (1961) argued that advertising was like any other productive resource and thus should be employed to the point where the marginal revenue product of advertising equals its marginal cost. Rasmussen (1952) showed that at this level the advertising elasticity would equal the ratio of advertising expenditures to sales. Dorfman and Steiner (1954) developed a solution for a demand function with price, advertising, and product quality as decision variables, thus showing conditions for an optimal marketing mix. In this case the optimality conditions are

$$\begin{bmatrix} \text{Price} \\ \text{Elasticity} \end{bmatrix} = \begin{bmatrix} \text{Marginal Revenue} \\ \text{Product of} \\ \text{Advertising} \end{bmatrix} = \begin{bmatrix} \text{Product Quality} \\ \text{Elasticity of} \\ \text{Demand} \end{bmatrix} \quad (9.1)$$

Nerlove and Arrow (1962) extended this analysis to account for the decay of advertising. They suggest that goodwill represents the effect of past and current outlays on demand. A dollar spent on advertising increases goodwill by a similar amount. Goodwill depreciates over time; perhaps this depreciation occurs at a constant proportional rate. Thus, the net investment in goodwill over a specified time interval is the difference between current advertising expenditures and the depreciation of the stock of goodwill. If the rate of interest is fixed, then the optimal policy can be shown to be found by solving these two equations simultaneously:

$$[\text{Unit Price minus Production Costs}] \begin{bmatrix} \text{Price Elasticity} \\ \overline{\text{Price}} \end{bmatrix} = 1. \quad (9.2)$$

and

$$[\text{Unit Price minus Production Costs}] \, [\text{Goodwill Elasticity}] \begin{bmatrix} \text{Quantity Demanded} \\ \overline{\text{Goodwill}} \end{bmatrix}$$

$$= [\text{Interest Rate plus Depreciation}]. \quad (9.3)$$

The Dorfman-Steiner condition is just a special case of the second equation in which the interest rate is zero and the depreciation rate is one.

Lambin, Naert and Bultez (1975) have generalized the Dorfman-Steiner theorem to the case of an oligopoly with multiple competitive reactions and expansible industry demand. They identify *simple competitive reaction* where competitors react with the same marketing decision variable as the one that causes their reactions and *multiple competitive reaction* where competitors react with the same or different marketing decision variables. Their marketing mix optimality conditions are:

$$
\begin{bmatrix} \text{Decision Variable } u \\ \text{Elasticity of} \\ \text{Company Demand} \end{bmatrix} = \begin{bmatrix} \text{Decision Variable } u \\ \text{Elasticity of} \\ \text{Industry Demand} \end{bmatrix} + \begin{bmatrix} \text{Matrix } R \text{ of} \\ \text{Reaction} \\ \text{Elasticities} \\ \eta_{U_j, u_i} \end{bmatrix} \begin{bmatrix} \text{Decision Variable } U \\ \text{Elasticity of} \\ \text{Industry Demand} \end{bmatrix}
$$

$$
+ \begin{bmatrix} \text{Decision Variable } u \\ \text{Elasticity of} \\ \text{Company} \\ \text{Market Share} \end{bmatrix} + \begin{bmatrix} \text{Matrix } R \text{ of} \\ \text{Reaction} \\ \text{Elasticities} \\ \eta_{U_j, u_i} \end{bmatrix} \begin{bmatrix} \text{Decision Variable } U \\ \text{Elasticity of} \\ \text{Company} \\ \text{Market Share} \end{bmatrix} \qquad (9.4)
$$

In this formulation, u represents a vector of company decision variables and U represents a vector of competitor's decision variables; industry sales less company sales equals competitor's sales; and

$$
\eta_{U_j, u_i} = \frac{\partial U_j}{\partial u_i} \cdot \frac{u_i}{U_j} ,
$$

a decision variable cross-elasticity.

Lambin, Naert, and Bultez show how a number of market competition situations are special cases of Eq. (9.4). In monopoly, company sales equals industry sales and so U and R do not exist; in monopolistic competition, each firm faces its own demand curve and no industry demand is defined. In oligopoly, no competitive reaction implies that $R = 0$; simple competitive reaction implies that $R = R_d$, i.e., the off-diagonal elements of R are zero; multiple competitive reaction implies the full matrix R. Stable industry demand implies that elasticities with respect to industry demand equal zero; expansible industry demand implies that these elasticities are nonzero. The Dorfman-Steiner condition is also a special case of Eq. (9.4) in which $R = 0$ for stable industry demand.

In models that take into account the lagged effect of advertising and other marketing mix variables, it is possible to derive the short- and long-run effects of marketing decision variables on sales. In the last chapter, we found that the reduced-form relationship of the geometric distributed lag was

$$Q_\alpha = (1 - \lambda) \beta_0 + (1 - \lambda) \beta_1 X_\alpha + \lambda Q_{\alpha-1} + (\epsilon_\alpha - \lambda \epsilon_{\alpha-1}), \qquad (9.5)$$

where

$$Q_\alpha = \text{sales at time } \alpha$$
$$X_\alpha = \text{marketing effort at time } \alpha.$$

The short-run marginal effect of X on Q is just $dQ_\alpha/dX_\alpha = (1-\lambda)\beta_1$. Long-run sales are given by

$$Q_\infty = \beta_1 X_\alpha, \qquad (9.6)$$

where Q_∞ is the sum of a converging geometric series since $0 < \lambda < 1$. The long-run marginal effect of X on Q is thus $dQ_\infty/dX_\alpha = \beta_1$. Similarly, we can derive these effects in terms of elasticities, the short-run elasticity being

$$\eta_{QX} = (1 - \lambda)\beta_1 \frac{X}{Q} \qquad (9.7)$$

and the long-run elasticity being

$$\eta_{QX}^\infty = \beta_1 \frac{X}{Q}. \qquad (9.8)$$

Prominant applications of marginal analysis have been made by Telser (1962a, 1962b), Palda (1964), and in several studies by Lambin.

These results show how optimal marketing decisions can be made given certain inputs such as relevant elasticities of marketing mix variables, competitive behavior and, in some cases, total market demand. As noted in Chap. 2, marketing decision models can be subjective or empirical, or both, depending upon whether these inputs are subjective or empirical, or both. We choose to characterize empirical decision models as those with empirical sales response functions, such as those discussed in Chap. 7, whether or not, for example, competition is handled subjectively or empirically (see below). Empirical marketing decision models, then, must be able to accommodate rich empirical sales response functions. It will be shown below that these general optimality conditions lead to just such models.

A number of theoretical solutions have been offered to the optimal advertising problem beyond these general conditions although most have necessarily been developed with highly simple or general sales response functions. In a study of optimal advertising policy, Melrose (1969) reanalyzed Palda's (1964) Lydia Pinkham data from the perspective of advertising decision rules suggested by Nerlove and Arrow (1962). Three of his four decision rule models, however, can not be distinguished on the basis of R^2 and none can be directly compared with Palda's sales response equations. As the author notes, from a behavioral standpoint the evidence on optimal advertising is "far from conclusive." Gould (1970) overcomes one main problem with the Nerlove-Arrow model by examining optimal policy with nonlinear costs for adding to goodwill. He also redefines the goodwill concept in terms of diffusion theory, thus recognizing how information spreads throughout a market. Although his model examines extreme cases, it does suggest the shape of optimal paths of advertising expenditures. Gould himself notes that the analysis is subject to rather unrealistic assumptions about competition and industry demand.

Mann (1975) generalizes the Nerlove-Arrow model to include model-delayed or "inverted V" distributed lag functions governing the time relationship between advertising expenditures and sales response. This more general lag is consistent with the empirical findings of Bass and Clarke (1972) and of Mann (1973). He finds, using Lydia Pinkham data, that the exponential-decay models overvalue the marginal physical product of advertising, thereby overspecifying the optimal level of advertising stock.

Sethi (1973) considers an optimal-control problem for the dynamics of the Vidale-Wolfe (1957) advertising model. The objective function is the present value of the profit stream up to a finite time horizon; the optimal control is the rate of advertising expenditure necessary to achieve a terminal market share within specified limits in a way that maximizes this objective. Horsky (1974) extends this work by including competition. His optimal-control solution is based on a Markov sales response process with transition probabilities as a linear function of the advertising goodwills of the firm and of its competitors. Tested on cigarette data, it advocates an optimal policy of "slicing" market share away from competitiors at a rate that at each point in time is not sufficient to cause a competitive reaction as opposed to earlier suggestions to "pulse" advertising and jump market share up to the optimal level.

Other contributions include the game theoretic approaches of Friedman (1958) and of Shakun (1965), the dynamic programming approach of Sasieni (1971), and the work of Rao (1970). In all of these cases, problems of estimating sales response functions have been repressed in order to allow analytical solutions. The problem of simultaneity between sales and advertising, for one, calls into question the empirical (hence practical) relevance of much of this work.

Application. Although these optimality conditions are interesting, they do not give us the optimal values of marketing decisions. To find optimal values it is necessary to have an estimated sales response function and data on costs. *A sales response equation is a necessary condition for determining optimal marketing decisions.* Together with data on costs, it is sufficient to show profit-maximizing levels. A number of analytical models have been developed for setting optimal marketing decisions. One of the earliest was the well-known study by Vidale and Wolfe (1957). Using a nonlinear sales response equation, they were able to determine the optimal advertising budget for a specific campaign. The study is of limited generality, however, since it deals exclusively with advertising and omits competition. There are few market situations where both marketing mix interactions and competitive effects can be ignored. On the other hand, in many FPBG markets, advertising is the dominant competitive variable and the assumption that its optimal value can be found without explicit consideration of other marketing variables may not be untenable.

We now examine a number of analytical marketing decision models that are based on econometric measurement of sales response. They are summarized in Table 9.1. In each case the output is an optimal marketing decision or set of definitions. The first model was developed by Lambin (1969). One of his models for FPBG showed that:

Sales = a + b[Logarithm of Advertising] + [Decay Rate] [Sales in the Previous Period] .

$$(9.9)$$

It is possible to solve this equation algebraically for the advertising appropriation which would meet some sales objective, given that sales objective, the prior period's sales, the elasticity of advertising, and the decay rate of advertising goodwill. The constant a summarizes the influence of other environmental and decision variables. In this case a planned level of sales is related to an implied level of advertising. A somewhat different view would be to examine expected sales for a planned level of advertising. In addition, a profit equation could have been constructed if data on costs were available. Lambin did not extend his work along these lines until later (see below).

In his study of an airline passenger market, Schultz (1971) developed a marketing mix decision model based on econometric measurement of sales response. The two key decision variables were number of flights and dollars of advertising. He assumed a planning horizon of one year with separate decisions for each quarter although the analysis could be extended to any number of periods. The company's current revenue function for a given city pair (e.g., New York-London) was

$$\text{Revenue} = [\text{Price}] \begin{bmatrix} \text{Total} \\ \text{Market Demand} \end{bmatrix} \begin{bmatrix} \text{Company's} \\ \text{Market Share} \end{bmatrix} \qquad (9.10)$$

and its corresponding cost function was

$$\text{Cost} = \begin{bmatrix} \text{Cost of} \\ \text{One Flight} \end{bmatrix} \begin{bmatrix} \text{Number of} \\ \text{Flights} \end{bmatrix} + \begin{bmatrix} \text{Advertising} \\ \text{Expenditures} \end{bmatrix} \qquad (9.11)$$

The total profit was found by summing the differences between these two relationships over the planning horizon.

The demand equation was available through the empirical research. The market share equations showed that current frequency (flight) share and lagged advertising share influenced market share. Two market share equations, one linear and the other linear in logs, provided a good fit to the data. Solving the linear objective function (not shown) for first-order optimality conditions using the calculus yielded two optimal decision equations for each period except that advertising in the last period would theoretically be zero since it acted on market share through a one-period lag. In practice, the airline would never reach the end of its planning horizon.

The set of quadratic equations can be solved by the quadratic formula to find optimal values for number of flights and dollars of advertising. Schultz did this and compared the model's optimal decisions with the company's actual decisions for 32 previous

Table 9.1

Empirical Marketing Decision Models

Model (year)	Criterion variable	Information output: Optimal marketing decisions	Method of solution	Information input: [In addition to the marketing elasticities (required)]
Lambin (1969)	Sales	Advertising for the next period	Algebra	Constant summarizing other influences
Schultz (1971)	Current profit	Flights and advertising for n periods (quarters)	Calculus	Estimates of competitive advertising Estimates of total market demand Planned prices
Beckwith (1972)	Discounted profit	Advertising for n periods (months)	Calculus	Estimates of competitive advertising Estimates of total market demand Profit margins Cost of capital
Parsons and Bass (1971)	Discounted profit	Advertising for n periods (bimonths)	Nonlinear programming	Equations for competitive advertising Profit margins Cost of capital

(*Table 9.1 continued on following page.*)

Table 9.1 (continued)

Model (year)	Criterion variable	Information output: Optimal marketing decisions	Method of solution	Information input: [In addition to the, marketing elasticities (required)]
Parsons (1974)	Total profit	Advertising and distribution for n periods (bimonths)	Nonlinear program- ming	Profit margin
Clarke (1973)	Current profit	Advertising for n periods (bimonths)	Calculus	Estimates of competitive advertising Estimates of total market demand Planned gross margin
Wildt (1974)	Current profit	Advertising and price for n periods (bimonths)	Calculus	Estimates of competitive advertising and price Estimates of total market demand
Lambin, Naert and Bultez (1975)	Discounted profit	Advertising, price and prod- uct quality for n periods (years)	Calculus	Equations for competi- tive price, advertising and product quality Estimates of total market demand
Wittink (1975)	Current profit	Advertising and price for n periods (months)	Calculus	Estimates of competitive advertising and price Estimates of total market demand
Lambin (1972)	Sales or rate of return	Advertising and distribution for n periods (quarters)	Simulation	Estimates of competitive advertising Estimates of total market demand Planned advertising

quarters. He found that the airline scheduled a near-optimal number of flights, but spent considerably less than the optimal amount on advertising. His analysis shows how an airline (or any firm) can set optimal advertising appropriations in the short run. In this case, the advertising decision model requires as input the estimate of advertising elasticity, estimates of competitive advertising expenditures, estimates of total market demand, and planned prices. The model combines empirical findings with managerial judgment to obtain optimal advertising and optimal settings of other decision variables.

Beckwith (1972a) determined the optimal advertising levels necessary to maximize a brand's discounted earnings stream. His model requires as input the estimate of advertising elasticity, estimates of competitive advertising, the decay rate of advertising, estimates of total market demand, profit margins, and cost of capital. The output is optimal advertising for n periods (months). Beckwith measured the elasticities and decay rates for all brands in a market according to the following model:

$$
\begin{bmatrix} \text{Market} \\ \text{Share} \end{bmatrix} = \begin{bmatrix} \text{Decay} \\ \text{Rate} \end{bmatrix} \begin{bmatrix} \text{Market Share} \\ \text{in the Previous} \\ \text{Period} \end{bmatrix} + \begin{bmatrix} \text{Advertising} \\ \text{Elasticity} \end{bmatrix} \begin{bmatrix} \text{Advertising} \\ \text{Share} \end{bmatrix} + \begin{bmatrix} \text{Seasonality} \\ \text{. Factor} \end{bmatrix}
$$

$$(9.12)$$

Although each competitive brand's advertising elasticity and decay rate can be obtained through empirical research, only the brand's own response parameters are necessary for the profit maximization. Like Schultz's model, this one assumes that any competitive reaction to a firm's advertising can be estimated exogenously. The optimization is obtained by using management's best evaluation of competitive advertising levels and their best estimate of total market demand.

Parsons and Bass (1971) do not require these assumptions to find the optimal advertising expenditure strategy implied by their model. Since their statistical system is dynamic, the optimization problem is multiperiod in character. Sales and profit in a single period depend not only upon the advertising for that period but also upon advertising in previous periods. Moreover, since their system involves simultaneous dependencies, the advertising and sales of all other brands influence and are influenced by the sales and advertising for a brand. Parsons and Bass applied nonlinear programming techniques to calculate the unconstrained optimal decision strategy. This calculation showed that the firm was significantly overspending for some brands while significantly underspending for others.

The key feature of the Parsons and Bass model is that competition is handled endogenously. They developed a four-equation system which included four jointly dependent variables: sales of brand B, advertising of brand B, sales of the remainder (all other established brands), and advertising of the remainder. Since sales is the dependent variable, total market demand is also essentially endogenous. This sales response model provides information on advertising elasticities, decay rates, and competitive advertising. This is combined with information on profit margins and cost of capital as input to the decision model. The output of the advertising decision model is an advertising appropriations strategy that maximizes discounted profit. The strategy is obtained with maximum reliance on the econometric sales response equations.

Parsons (1974) determined the sequence of advertising expenditures which would achieve management's distribution and sales goals for a new brand introduction with minimum profit loss. Again nonlinear programming techniques were required to find the solution. However, the goals brought into the problem are constraints which the solution must satisfy. Without these constraints, the optimal solution would be to not advertise at all. Clearly, advertising is an investment for new products related to retail availability.

Several other models use essentially the same information inputs and model-solving techniques to produce optimal marketing decisions. Clarke (1973) argues that since most of the effects of advertising being measured in his study last less than two years, advertising can be considered to be an expenditure. Thus, he defines an objective function in terms of current profit. He is only able to obtain a "rough estimate" of optimal advertising, however, since gross margin is unknown (historically, but not, of course, for planning). Of 18 brands investigated, 8 overadvertised on average, 7 underadvertised, and 3 were "about right." Wildt (1974) estimates a sales response function with four marketing decision variables (advertising, promotion, new variety activity and price) for three brands, but is unable to include promotion and new variety in his (current) profit function. He proceeds, using calculus, to solve for optimal advertising expenditures. (Optimal prices are not reported.) Comparison of the ratio of optimal to observed advertising for the period covered by the study showed that for all firms the actual ratio exceeds the optimal ratio by as little as 50% in the case of Firm 1 to as much as 300% in the case of Firm 3. Wildt goes on to examine the long-term effects of advertising and concludes that Firm 2 has been consistently overspending, Firm 1 is near optimal, and Firm 3 is below optimal. Both Clarke and Wildt assume that estimates of competitive reaction and total market demand can be supplied exogenously.

Lambin, Naert, and Bultez (1975) employ their optimality theorem discussed above to analyze short- and long-run optimal advertising in a marketing mix model. (Other optimal decisions are not reported; to obtain optimal advertising, price is assumed to be optimal.) They find that the firm under study is near optimal on average, but overspent during a significant part of the period under study.

Wittink (1975) estimated market share response functions in static and dynamic form. Using the Dorfman-Steiner theorem to determine optimal advertising-to-revenue ratios for each territory studied, he found a correlation of 0.72 between the actual ratio and the implied optimal ratio for the static model and a correlation of 0.65, for the dynamic model. On the average, however, the company appeared to be overspending since the actual ratio of 0.10 exceeded the optimal ratio of 0.06 for the static model and 0.04 for the dynamic model.

Other studies have led to optimal conditions or optimal estimates of advertising expenditures that are not dealt with in detail here. The classic article by Telser (1962b) was important in directing economic analysis to advertising and marketing. Research by Lambin (1970, 1972b) offers examples of analytical solutions to optimal advertising with a profit objective. There are undoubtedly other studies as well. What we have tried to do here, however, is focus on studies where a main objective was to aid firms in marketing planning and hence where emphasis was placed on decision making.

The eleven analytical models discussed above are case-examples of a general approach to solving the optimal marketing decisions problem. Different alternative solutions to this problem are shown in Fig. 9.2. Lambin's model was (essentially) a market share maximization. Schultz, Beckwith, Clarke, Wildt, Lambin, Naert and Bultez, and Wittink solved unconstrained linear profit maximization models using the calculus. Bass and Parsons used nonlinear programming (a search technique) to maximize unconstrained profit. Parsons used

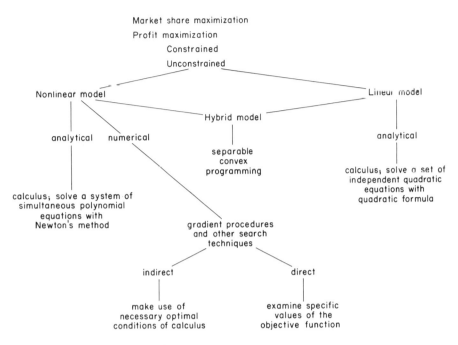

Fig. 9.2. Alternative solutions.

the same technique to maximize constrained profit. It is evident that other solution techniques can be employed as well, as suggested by the theoretical advances in control theory. Analytical models can be quite flexible with respect to assumptions and information input and have the advantage of leading to optimal solutions of the model. When the model itself is a good representation of the real world problem, then the solution to the problem is also indicated.

Simulation Models

Simulation models provide a means for evaluating alternative marketing strategies in cases where analytical models are not appropriate or cannot be solved. In addition, this class of models permits a great deal of interplay between empirical and subjective inputs, such as combining managerial judgment on competitive behavior with estimated parameters of sales response. An example of an advertising simulation based on econometric measurement of sales response is provided by Lambin (1972a).

Lambin suggests that the econometric models can be made more flexible by treating the regression coefficients as prior estimates to be adjusted on the basis of the manager's own judgment. In this way, new factors such as the entry of new competition and qualitative factors such as new advertising themes can be incorporated. On-line conversational· computing facilitates this integration. His planning model requires as input estimates of advertising elasticity and the decay rate, estimates of competitive advertising, estimates of total market demand, and planned advertising. He asks the decision maker to give expected (mean), pessimistic (0.10), and optimistic (0.90) values for the firm's decision variables and those of competition. Various advertising appropriations strategies are evaluated in the simulation and response parameters are updated as desired. The output is expected sales for the company. Another version of his model considers rate of return as the criterion variable [Lambin (1970)].

Lambin argues that the simulation approach reduces risk since "changes in the current program can be adopted more rapidly in response to an anticipated event or market reactions" [Lambin, (1972a), 124]. Lambin's work is only representative of the potential of marketing simulation models.[1] These models can be extended in a number of directions including the specific evaluation of current or discounted profit, the direct estimation of total market demand, and the endogenous treatment of competition, as in the simulation model developed by Schultz and Dodson (1974) reported below. As research progresses, the distinction between analytical and simulation solutions to marketing decision models is likely to blur. Models which are empirical, adaptive, on-line, and capable of producing optimal marketing decisions are possible and, given the momentum of current research, are just over the horizon. For now, the prototype models discussed in this section are strong indications that, with current technology, firms can implement such methods to make better marketing decisions.

Besides prices and cost of capital, two main information inputs to empirical marketing decision models are (1) estimates of competitive decisions and (2) estimates of total industry (or market) demand. In the next section, we discuss how these estimates of competitive behavior can be obtained and what effect they have on how the model is used. The analysis of total industry demand is discussed in Chap. 11.

THE ANALYSIS OF COMPETITIVE BEHAVIOR

In highly competitive markets, the problem of predicting the reaction of a firm's competitors to its own marketing plans must rank as one of the firm's most complex and pressing dilemmas.[2] To solve this problem, most firms rely on the judgment of marketing managers in making predictions about competitive response. Even under the best conditions, however, where managers possess considerable practical experience and marketing savvy, these judgments on competitive behavior embody a good deal of uncertainty about the *process* of competitive decision making as well as actual competitive *decisions*. Although this informal procedure may seem "workable" in many cases, it does not provide the firm with a very rigorous approach to a crucial determinant of its marketing success.

Despite the compelling nature of this problem, formal theories of competitive behavior ranging from classical economic models to modern game theoretic approaches are of only limited usefulness in this practical situation. Moreover, as scientific (real world) explanations of competitive behavior, they leave much to be desired. Most traditional economic models focus solely on price competition. A prominant oligopoly model, for example, posits that competitors will follow price reductions and ignore price increase, resulting in "sticky" price changes and "kinked" demand curves, but the limitations of such a model in markets where there is substantial nonprice competition should be apparent. In analyzing "oligopolistic interdependence" Baumol (1965) concludes that these markets are characterized by the recognition of interdependent decision making by all firms and by emphasis on advertising and other aggressive marketing tools. Yet the theory of imperfect competition remains largely unchanged from the basic contributions of Robinson and Chamberlin in 1933 [Dewey (1969)]. Since the appearance of *Theory of Games and Economic Behavior* in 1944, there has been a great deal of work on game theory, but its operational relevance has been highly limited [Telser (1972)]. Thus, a theoretical basis for understanding the dynamics of marketing competition remains to be developed.

In marketing research on sales response, the effect of competition is clearly an important factor, but very few studies deal with competitive behavior in an explicit way. There are three basic methods that have been used to model competitive effects in sales response research: no competition, exogenous competition, and endogenous competition. In addition, there have been a few comparative studies of these various methods. Most of the studies make methodological contributions although some important substantive findings are reported as well. In this section, these various approaches to handling competition in empirical decision models are discussed. It should be recalled that all of the optimal decision models that we have presented depend upon expected competitive behavior. This fact justifies looking into the matter in some detail. Models with no competition are included here for their historical not practical or even theoretical relevance.

Models With No Competition

The first sales response equations were simple regression models showing the influence of price and other marketing variables and/or socioeconomic variables on some measure of sales. The general form of these models is

$$\text{Sales}_A = f(\text{marketing decision variables}_A, \text{ socioeconomic variables}).$$

Some of the models include specific treatments of marketing mix effects and delayed responses, but there is no attempt to explicitly handle competitive effects. In this class of models, then, competition is embodied in the parameters of the model in an implicit way. No direct adjustment of the model is possible to reflect changes in competition and no direct inferences can be made about competitive behavior. Although the estimated sales response equations may pass statistical tests and rank as good predictive tools, they are necessarily limited as scientific explanations and planning models because of their limited treatment of competition.

The investigation of sales response has produced a number of models with no competition. Banks (1961) studied the markets for scouring cleanser and coffee using a model with market share as the dependent variable and only marketing mix interactions. Palda's well-known dissertation on Lydia Pinkham vegetable compound includes carryover effects but no others [Palda (1964)]. Lambin (1969) examined the demand for a frequently purchased branded good (FPBG) with only carryover effects explicitly covered. A recent study by Montgomery and Silk (1972) treats marketing mix and carryover effects but not competition in a market for ethical drugs. The lack of competition in these representative studies does not mean that they are not valuable contributions. In the case of Lydia Pinkham, for example, there was no "direct" competition to be modeled. A model for ethical drugs, however, may be *more* valuable if competition is included in some fashion.

Models With Exogenous Competition

A model which explicitly considers the settings of competitive marketing variables but does not explain them handles competition in an exogenous way. The general forms of these models are

$$\text{Sales}_A = f(\text{marketing decision variables}_A, \text{marketing decision variables}_B),$$
$$(9.13)$$

$$\text{Market share}_A = f(\text{marketing decision variable shares}_A), \qquad (9.14)$$

and

$$\text{Market share}_A = f(\text{marketing decision variable shares}_A) \qquad (9.15)$$

$$\text{Market share}_B = f(\text{marketing decision variable shares}_B). \qquad (9.16)$$

In the first formulation, subscript B usually ascribes all competition to a summary variable, say advertising of the remainder of firms or brands. In the second formulation, the ratio of company marketing effort to total marketing effort can be employed or each variable can be expressed as a separate ratio. The latter approach proves to be more convenient in using linear transformations. Besides ratios, deviations of A's settings of marketing decision variables from B's have also been used [Weiss (1968)], as have relative variables defined as the ratio of A's decision variable to B's. The third formulation is a system of seemingly unrelated regressions with variables defined similarly to those in the second formulation.

Several models with exogenous competition have been developed and tested. Weiss (1968, 1969) studied the market for a FPBG considering both marketing mix effects and (exogenous) competitive effects. Sexton (1970) investigated the demand structure for a FPBG and included marketing mix, carryover, and competitive effects. In research on airline passenger demand, Schultz (1971) handled marketing mix, carryover, and competitive effects in a simultaneous-equation model. Lambin (1972a) reports on the development of a single-equation sales response model including each of the other effects. Another version of his model handles simultaneity [Lambin (1972b)]. Clarke (1973) analyzed the effect of one brand's advertising on the sales of another brand for several FPBG brands. Beckwith (Eqs. 9.15-9.16) finds that the covariance matrix of structural disturbances is nonspherical. In particular, he discovers that in a five-brand market the market shares of brands A and B and D and E varied directly together while market shares of brands A, B and C were influenced oppositely from brands D and E. It is possible to draw conclusions about the nature of competition from the other studies as well. Despite the attractiveness of this approach, there are some important limitations. For prediction, the models require knowledge of competitors' sales and marketing efforts as input and these data may be difficult to obtain or very costly. Beckwith's procedure for setting optimal brand advertising does not require the response parameters of other brands, but only the sum of advertising expenditures for all other brands. He also notes that where a firm can estimate competitor's advertising expenditures, it does not need to know their response coefficients.

Models with exogenous competition have also proved to be useful as explanations of market behavior and as planning and forecasting devices. Although as "complete" theories of behavior, sales response functions may require endogenous treatment of competition, special circumstances and other considerations (discussed below) may make the exogenous method just as functional if not complete. Schultz shows that even under the assumption of no competitive reaction, his model can be solved for optimal values of the decision variables without violating a simple competitive constraint [Schultz (1973)]. Lambin creates a simulation model to explore policy alternatives in his model which requires estimates of competitive settings of marketing decision variables [Lambin (1972a)]. In both cases competition is "explained" outside the sales response model by combining managerial judgment with model output. In fact, this class of models is best viewed as one utilizing *direct* management judgment about competitive reaction to firm decisions.

Models With Endogenous Competition

An endogenous model of competitive behavior explains both the company's and competition's settings of marketing decision variables. The general forms of these models are[3]

$\text{Sales}_B = f(\text{marketing decision variables}_B, \text{marketing decision variables}_A, \text{sales}_{B,\alpha-1}, \text{sales}_{A,\alpha-1})$

$$(9.17)$$

$\text{Sales}_A = f(\text{marketing decision variables}_A, \text{marketing decision variables}_B, \text{sales}_{A,\alpha-1}, \text{sales}_{B,\alpha-1})$

$$(9.18)$$

Marketing decision variables$_A$

$= f(\text{sales}_{A,\alpha-1}, \text{marketing decision variables}_{A,\alpha-1}, \text{sales}_{B,\alpha-1}, \text{marketing decision variables}_{B,\alpha-1})$ (9.19)

Marketing decision variables$_B$

$= f(\text{sales}_{B,\alpha-1}, \text{marketing decision variables}_{B,\alpha-1}, \text{sales}_{A,\alpha-1}, \text{marketing decision variables}_{A,\alpha-1})$, (9.20)

Market share$_A$ $= f(\text{marketing decision variables}_A, \text{marketing decision variables}_B)$ (9.21)

Market share$_B$ $= f(\text{marketing decision variables}_B, \text{marketing decision variables}_A)$ (9.22)

Marketing decision variables$_A$

$= f(\text{marketing decision variables}_{A,\alpha-1}, \text{marketing decision variables}_{B,\alpha-1})$

$$(9.23)$$

Marketing decision variables$_B$

$$(9.24)$$

$= f(\text{marketing decision variables}_{B,\alpha-1}, \text{marketing decision variables}_{A,\alpha-1})$.

In equations (9.13-9.16) the subscript B is usually interpreted as the remainder. Unless noted by a lag (e.g., $\alpha-1$) a variable is in the current time period (α). The application of the "hybrid" model (9.21-9.24) by Wildt (1974) does treat each competitor separately, however. System (9.17-9.20) is a simultaneous-equation model when cast in stochastic form without the assumption of independent disturbances between equations. It is not simply the fact that this system explains competitive behavior that makes it simultaneous. As noted above, a system can be simultaneous without explaining competitive behavior. System (9.21)-(9.24) can be considered to be block recursive if the disturbances of (9.21)-(9.22) are independent of (9.23)-(9.24).

Studies of FPBG markets have been conducted by Bass (1969),

Bass and Parsons (1969), and Wildt (1974). In addition, another FPBG investigation was carried out by Frank and Massy (1971). Since competition is endogenous, some interesting substantive findings regarding competitive. behavior have emerged from this research. For example, Bass and Parsons [model (9.17)-(9.20)] report that advertising expenditures for the brand are extremely responsive to sales increases of other brands, although the responsiveness to other brands' advertising or an explanation of the remainder's advertising is not reported. Wildt's model is even more of a hybrid than the mixture of share and absolute variables suggests since it includes one current marketing decision variable of a competitor in one brand's decision rule equation. Wildt finds significant interactions among competitors in the market share response as well as the decision rule equations, suggesting that competitive behavior should be an important element in marketing decision models.

Models such as these with endogenous competition are "fully" empirical in the sense that both sales response and decision rule functions are estimated for the firm and for its competitors. If the models are not rejected, then managerial judgment plays, strictly speaking, no role in the use of such models for setting optimal decisions. Judgment appears only later when the decision is made to implement the optimal decisions or not. We discuss below an alternative to fully empirical models that still relies on empirical estimates of competitive reaction. It may be thought of as an endogenous competition/management judgment method of dealing with the problem.

Comparative Studies of Various Methods

At least four studies have been completed that compare various methods for handling competiton although it was the express purpose of only two. In a paper on "Advertising and Competitive Behavior" Lambin (1970) tests several econometric models of competitive interdependence, including absolute sales models, market share models, and simultaneous equation (recursive) models. These are equivalent to models (9.13), (9.14), and (9.17)-(9.20) above. The setting for Lambin's work is the market for a small electrical appliance with three major competitors. The absolute sales models indicate that competitive advertising influences a brand's sales for two of three brands. The market share models, which more explicitly cover competition, provide better fits to the data and support the finding of competitive interdependence. In the recursive models, a firm's advertising is shown to be determined by its lagged market share and competitive advertising, again supporting the finding of strong competitive interaction among brands. Lambin concludes that simultaneity was not a serious problem in this case and that a version of the market share model provided as good results as any. Of course, competitive decision rules were only revealed through the recursive model analysis. These are used to show that a substantial part of advertising is self-cancelling in this market. Lambin's study is interesting but not particularly definitive on the value of the various methods.

Sasser and Vernon (1970) compared the forecasting accuracy of sales response models with and without competition using a simulation approach. They adopted Bass and Parson's endogenous competition model and tested it against a similar single-equation model without competitive variables. On the criterion of minimum forecast variance, the model without competition was found to outperform the structural model. Of various test cases (different decision rules and forecast periods), only one supports the more complex model. According to the authors, this is a surprising result since the influence of competition was known to be true. All it really shows, however, is that in some situations a misspecified model will be a better forecaster than a correctly specified model. Although this may be a good "warning" as the authors put it to future model builders, it hardly seems like a good research strategy. We know that a spurious correlation can lead to a good forecast, but this knowledge does not justify the development of spurious models. The test of a model must be based on a number of factors, not only forecasting ability. On the other hand, Sasser and Vernon make a strong point about the cost of competitive data versus its value. Perhaps this study also leads to a "middle" position where competition is handled exogenously for theoretical as well as practical reasons.

Samuels (1970, 1971) and Rao (1972) also shed some light on the question of which approach to use. The study by Samuels on household cleansers and other products demonstrates (like Lambin) that models with competition can be valuable, although none of his models are without competition. He weakly asserts that the simultaneous-equation models (after Bass and Parsons) are the best, but the argument is not convincing. Rao examined five methods of estimation and four ways of specifying dependent variables in sales-advertising models for cigarette data. His research produced an implicit test of the no-competition—exogenous-competition—endogenous-competition methods. On the basis of adjusted R^2, the no-competition model estimated by OLS ranks above the exogenous-competition model in loglinear form, but the positions are reversed in linear form. Both rank substantially above the endogenous competition model in terms of adjusted R^2. On the basis of mean average percentage error, a version of the no-competition model ranks first (lowest error) followed by a version of the exogenous-competition model for OLS estimation. The 2SLS or endogenous-competition model again finishes last.

The comparative studies discussed above do not unequivocally answer the question of which method of handling competition is best. It is not clear either that goodness of fit or forecasting ability are the appropriate criteria on which to base an answer. A strong argument can be made, in fact, that the criterion ought to be a *behavioral* one reflecting how managers will actually *use* the model.

Managerial Models of Competition

The use of a marketing decision model depends upon how well the model represents a real market and also upon how compatible the model is with the organization. Representation of the market is usually measured by goodness of fit, predictive tests, and forecasting ability. These are quantitative (statistical) measures of validity. Compatibility with the organization is generally not measured at all although this fit between the model and the organization can be a crucial determinant of the model's success. An approach to model building and implementation called *behavioral model building* calls for the development of models which maximize both market and organizational validity [Schultz and Slevin (1972)]. This approach emphasizes the importance of paying attention to the model's internal environment, the organization, as well as its external environment, the market. These ideas are discussed more fully in Chap. 11.

The fit between a model and its human organizational environment is multidimensional. One of the most important behavioral factors of implementation is the attitudes of individual users toward the model. Marketing decision models have a number of dimensions which imply certain attitudes for compatibility of model and user. Two of the more interesting dimensions are use of data and use of computers. The use of data in models ranges from those which require only subjective inputs of marketing executives to those which require only empirical inputs of actual market data. Models which fall in between combine subjective and empirical data in some appropriate fashion. On this continuum, no-competition models are purely subjective (with respect to competition), exogenous-competition models are largely subjective, and endogenous-competition models are purely empirical. The use of computers in models ranges from those that require the computer for data processing and/or analysis without the direct interaction of the user to those which require the user to interact with the computer via conversational-type programs. Sales response decision models can be constructed in either way and so this factor doesn't affect the handling of competition although it can affect the probability of successful implementation.

The amount of attitude change necessary to implement a model depends upon the initial attitudes of potential users toward dimensions of the model. Since organizational attitudes may be initially oriented toward empirical data or subjective data, attitude change may be required in either direction. Because of the present dominance of subjective assessment of competition, however, we could expect that empirical-competition models (i.e., endogenous-competition models) would require more attitude change [but see Schultz, Slevin, and Keith (1975)]. Behavioral factors of implementation at the small group and organizational levels may also be important in choosing the way competitive effects should be handled, but they are not considered here.

Schultz and Dodson (1974b) report on a model designed to overcome some of the problems associated with fully empirical models, especially the fact that the manager must essentially either accept or reject them. The development of an endogenous competition model depends to a large extent on the availability of data on competitive sales and marketing actions [Schultz (1973)]. In many cases these data are not available or cannot readily be obtained. In these cases, the model builder must rely on subjective estimates by management of competitor's marketing actions if competition is to be included in the model.

If competitive data are available it is possible in principle to obtain explanatory or predictive competitive decision rules. The ability of the model builder to specify such rules depends upon the extent to which these rules are known and the extent to which they are stable. Where advertising is set as a constant percent of sales, competitive advertising expenditures can be estimated fairly well. Constant markup pricing, price leadership, regulated pricing, and going rate pricing can lead to good price estimates for competition. In airline markets, flights may be set according to trend or seasonality. In these and other situations it may be rather straightforward to obtain predictive equations which can be used to estimate competitors' marketing mix variable levels. Then planned firm marketing mix levels and estimated competitive mix levels can be used to forecast company sales and/or market share. In practice, the search for competitive decision rules may be more difficult. It may be only possible to identify a set of *possible* decision rules for competitors. This is the approach taken by Schultz and Dodson (1974b) and later by Little and Schultz (1975). These models utilize a combination of empirical estimation and managerial judgment within the framework of decision theory.

The argument of Schultz and Dodson proceeds from the question: What kind of information does a firm have about its competition? The answer, it is assumed, is (a) the firm is uncertain about competitive decisions but (b) the firm has some knowledge about *possible* competitive decision rules. As opposed to the exogenous competition approach wherein the actual decision is sought, and as opposed to the endogenous competition and fully empirical approach wherein the actual decision rule is sought, Schultz and Dodson explore the consequences of competitive reaction by recognizing the uncertainty of both the decisions and of the process.

There are two major aspects to their model, which is a simulation of competitive behavior. First, it is a conditional optimization. The firm (under study) makes an assumption about the decision process of its competitors and then it optimizes its marketing mix variables as if the competition will react in one of several ways with certainty. The optimization is conditional because it depends upon whether or not the assumed competitive response actually occurs. The payoffs (in profit) to the firm thus result from some combination of assumed and actual behavior. Second, it is an optimization accommodating uncertainty since the payoff matrix can be examined for *optimal assumptions* about competitive behavior. In this case, optimal assumptions are equivalent to optimal strategies because they dictate the nature of competitive interaction and consequent market performance.

The model utilizes a sales response equation and a set of equations representing decision rules for the firm and for competitors. Thus, the form of the model is similar to Eqs. (9.21)-(9.24). Instead of attempting to find one "true" decision rule for each competitor, however, the procedure is to estimate a set of plausible decision rules on the assumption that each is true. In Schultz and Dodson's model, management judgment is employed first to identify the set of competitive decision rules and later to provide a criterion for evaluating the payoff matrix.

The model was tested on airline passenger data where the control variable was number of flights [Schultz and Dodson (1974a)]. The simulation utilizes a market share equation, the competitive decision rules, and such inputs as price, industry demand, and unit cost of a flight. Given the inputs and an estimate of competitors' flights for the next planning period, the firm can compute analytically the number of flights that will maximize its profit. The output generated for each run is based on an *assumed* and an *actual* set of decision rules for competitors.

The model is used in planning by presenting managers with the payoff matrix of assumed and actual competitive behavior. Schultz and Dodson report that, for the airline data, if competitors set their flights based on time-dependent or flight-dependent (both nonre-active) decision rules, the best the firm can do is to have as good an estimate of competitors' flights as possible. If, on the other hand, competitors set their flights based on a competitive adaptive policy, then an aggressive marketing strategy on the part of the firm (induced by assuming competitive aggressiveness) will result in higher levels of competition, lower load factors, and reduced firm profit. Managers can also explore the consequences of other criteria such as maximin, maximax, and Bayesian strategies. Extensions of this work to include optimal strategies for competitors is reported by Little and Schultz (1975) and by Schultz and Little (1975), and to include optimal marketing mix decisions (flights and advertising for all competitors) by Schultz and Hanssens (1976).

Managerial models of competition are those that handle competition in a way that enhances the likelihood that the models will be used in decision making. The practical-theoretical tradeoff between endogenous competition/management judgment and fully endogenous models is one that deserves further research. For that matter, only no-competition models are ruled out by the theory of optimal marketing decisions. The broad research issue, then, is how best to estimate competitive reaction.

MARKETING DECISION SYSTEMS

A marketing decision system requires, in addition to a marketing decision model, a formal method of processing both input and output from the model. It would thus include the estimation of model parameters and the evaluation of environmental change. In its ideal form, a marketing decision system would be self-adjusting or adaptive so that changes in the environment are reflected by changes in the model and parameter estimates are continuously updated. Although there are no fully developed empirical marketing decision systems reported in the literature or known to us from corporate applications, several authors have discussed the concept.

Montgomery and Urban (1969) conceive of a marketing information system made up of a data bank, a statistical methods bank, a model bank, and a display unit which interfaces with the manager and with the environment. In their scheme, data from (about) the environment is stored in the data bank, processed by the statistical bank, evaluated in the model bank, and then decisions are made directly by the model or indirectly by the manager based on model output. Montgomery and Urban note that direct decisions by models are possible given "repetitive decisions characterized by an accepted formal analysis procedure and the existence of accurate, measurable input data" but will probably be "rare." Even in these cases, they add, new or exceptional situations must be handled by the manager. The notion of an empirical marketing decision system fits into this scheme quite well; it is characterized by econometric measurement of environmental data on sales response, formal solution of a decision model for optimal marketing mix decisions, and direct utilization of the model by managers in making decisions.

Kotler (1971), in discussing marketing information systems, suggests that "future management gains in decision making effectiveness will depend on the development of 'man-computer' systems of decision making." The systems to which Kotler refers include not only marketing mix decisions, but also new product decisions, advertising media selection decisions, sales territory design decisions, and others—in short, all recurring marketing decisions. Thus, the question arises: How general is the approach to making decisions on the basis of empirical models outlined in this book?

The answer is that, as long as a response function is involved, the principles and procedures presented in this book can be completely generalized to marketing decision making. A response function may be defined in terms of sales or market share response or in terms of some *intermediate*-level response. Thus, in the above examples, the relevant responses can be *sales* for new product decisions, *exposures* for media selection decisions, *coverage* for sales territory design decisions, etc. In each case the response function has the form

$$\text{Response variable} = f(\text{Decision variable(s)})$$

and thus the estimation of this relationship is fundamental to making optimal marketing decisions.

Intermediate-level responses can also be considered at different levels of consumer choice aggregation. At the level of individual behavior, for example, we may be interested in the response of attitudes to advertising or preferences to perceived product quality or even the response of preferences to attitudes. In all of these cases, the methods of econometrics are appropriate to estimate the relationships. Similarly, family behavior, group behavior and other "behavioral" areas of marketing research can be analyzed from the perspective of econometric models. In fact, we argue in the final chapter that, as buyer behavior theories become better specified, they will *necessarily* take the form of econometric models if they are to be tested.

The relationship holds that marketing decision systems depend on marketing decision models which depend on sales response functions or, as we have just shown, on response functions in general. In Chap. 11, we consider factors related to the implementation of such models and systems into human organizations.

FOOTNOTES

[1] See, for example, Kotler and Schultz (1970) or Guetzkow, Kotler and Schultz (1972); also, Schultz (1974).

[2] This section is based on material in Schultz (1973) and Schultz and Dodson (1974a, 1974b).

[3] These are shown in dynamic form because this is the form in which they have been applied.

Part Four. Policy and Research Implications

Chapter 10

INDUSTRY ADVERTISING EFFECTS

The importance of measuring industry advertising effects should be apparent from the discussion of optimal marketing decisions; estimates of total market demand are necessary in market share response models and implicit in sales response formulations of empirical decision models. Beyond this managerial interest, the economic question of advertising's impact on total industry demand is highly interesting. In this chapter,[1] we first look at studies of industry advertising and sales and then discuss theoretical and empirical aspects of the measurement of industry advertising effects. The fact that we focus on advertising to the exclusion of other marketing decision variables is simply a matter of the state of the art.

PREVIOUS STUDIES OF
INDUSTRY ADVERTISING AND SALES

A number of studies of industry advertising-sales relationships are reported in Table 10.1 together with comments on the type of model (method of estimation), data, evidence, and other factors. Ordinary least squares (OLS) has been used exclusively in studies purposely designed to investigate industry sales-advertising relationships, with no consideration of identification problems or aggregation problems.

Other studies, dealing primarily with the competitive effect of advertising (i.e., relationships between sales and advertising for a set of brands within a certain industry), have only touched on the potential effect of branded advertising on industry sales. Simultaneous-equation systems have been employed to incorporate two-way causations and interactions between brands, but not with industry advertising effects as the target of research. Here, in most cases, the estimation of cross-elasticities has been used as a basis for admittedly tentative conclusions about the effect of advertising on primary demand. It is not clear, however, that this is an appropriate basis for making statements about the industry sales-advertising relationship.

Table 10.1

Studies of Industry Advertising and Sales

Year	Researcher(s)	Type of Model	Data	Evidence	Comment
1933	Schoenberg	OLS	Yearly data	Advertising significant (<.10) using total newspaper advertising by the 4 leading cigarette manufacturers	
1961	Meissner	OLS	Yearly data	Inconclusive	
1961	Nerlove & Waugh	OLS	Yearly data	Both long- and short-run advertising significant (<.05)	
1969	Ball & Agarwala	OLS	Quarterly data	Generic (i.e., primary) advertising had significant effect on consumption	If all advertising (generic and branded) is included in a single variable, there is a substantial decline in fit
1969	Bass & Parsons	Simultaneous equation brand and remainder	Bimonthly data	Advertising does "appear to stimulate primary demand" (p. 123)	Basis: advertising of remainder influences sales of brand under study
1972	Beckwith	OLS	Monthly data	Advertising not significantly related to primary demand in OLS test	Simultaneous-equation check showed OLS estimates to be unbiased
1970-71	Samuels	Simultaneous equation brand and remainder	Four-weekly data	Analysis completed for 5 different brands in 3 different markets; cross-elasticity positive in 4	Use of monetary outlays

Year	Author	Model	Data	Findings	Remarks
				cases* which "suggests that any industry-advertising stimulates the primary demand as a whole" (p. 204) *one significant (<10)	
1971	Peles	OLS	Monthly data	Advertising significant for autos but not for beer or cigarettes	
1971	Schultz	OLS	Quarterly data	Advertising effect positive and significant (<10)	
1972b	Lambin	OLS	Quarterly data	Advertising has negligible effect on overall primary demand	In Belgium, Denmark: small, positive, significant; in Italy: small, negative, significant
1972	Clarke	Simultaneous equation for 7 categories (groups of brands)	Bimonthly data	Only 1 of 7 categories (a new-brand category) "did indeed increase industry demand, . . . the question remains whether or not advertising contributed a measurable effect to this increase . . ." (p. 141)	This study is an important antecedent of this chapter
1974	Wildt	OLS	Bimonthly data	Network television advertising expenditures have positive but not significant effect upon industry unit sales	
1972	Schmalensee	OLS	Yearly data	Unable to conclude that industry advertising had any effect on industry demand	Promotional variables (local advertising activity) do appreciably affect industry unit sales

The studies listed in Table 10.1 have a number of important limitations with respect to dealing with the issue of industry advertising effects. These include:

1. All of the studies using aggregate industry data are single-equation formulations (OLS estimation) which ignore the aggregation problem and neglect the problem of identifying advertising budget rules and sales response equations. Simultaneous-equation models are suggested by the potential existence of such two-way causal relations.

2. The studies based on data for individual brands were not primarily designed to test industry advertising effects and so the conclusions must be regarded as tentative.

3. No study considers the nature of industry sales-advertising relationships by isolating primary sales and primary demand effects and by concurrently examining the structure of competition.

In light of these deficiencies, we propose to study industry advertising effects *directly* (insofar as this is possible) recognizing the *simultaneity* of advertising and sales and working within an overall *theory* of selective and primary advertising.

A THEORY OF INDUSTRY ADVERTISING EFFECTS

The distinction between primary and selective advertising is apparently a straightforward one. Primary advertising is defined as *the effort expended by the collective firms in an industry either as an ad hoc attempt or systematically through a trade association for the express purpose of increasing primary demand by means of mass communication.* Selective advertising is defined as *the effort expended by individual companies to influence sales for a brand or for the firm by means of mass communication.* But selective advertising may also affect industry demand. We are thus concerned with the identification and measurement of the effects of selective advertising on firm *and* industry (or market) demand.

Consider an example illustrating these points. We think that a campaign to "drink frozen orange juice" influences (if it has any effect) the total market sales of frozen orange juice and that each individual brand shares in this change to an extent which depends upon the amount of relative selective advertising, viz., campaigns of the sort, "drink Brand A frozen orange juice." The distinction seems to be in the influence of the advertising *across* brands.

The orange juice example shows a clear difference in at least the intent of the advertising. Because it is a realistic example, we can recall that both orange juice associations and competing brands advertise with these two purposes (primary and selective advertising) in mind. But consider another example, say the advertising for a brand of cola soft drink. The campaign, "buy Brand X cola," may be intended to increase the sales of Brand X at the expense of the sales of its competitors, but it could also increase Brand X's sales without decreasing any competitor's sales. If the competitors' sales are not decreased, then they either (also) increase or remain unchanged. If part of the "buy Brand X cola" campaign really produces a change in primary demand, then all brands should benefit in some way because the impact must be similar to the impact from a campaign saying, "buy cola." However, if competing brands' sales are not affected, then we can say that the advertising can increase the brand's sales but that it does not produce a "primary demand effect."

This idea can be clarified if we consider, with no loss of generality, an industry made up of just two brands: Brand 1 and Brand 2. When the effect of a brand's advertising is to increase its own sales without affecting competitive sales, we call this the *primary sales effect* of selective advertising. When the effect of a brand's advertising is to increase its own sales and that of its competitors, we call this the *primary demand effect* of selective advertising. In addition, the situation where the effect of a brand's advertising is to increase its own sales and to decrease sales of its competitors can be referred to as *competitive advertising.*

MEASURING INDUSTRY ADVERTISING EFFECTS

To measure industry advertising effects, a procedure is needed that allows the various types of advertising effects to be separated. There are three *pure* cases of advertising effect: primary demand effect, primary sales effect, and competitive advertising. These pure cases can be confounded in any real empirical situation, however, and the result is a number of mixed cases of advertising effect. If our purpose is to isolate the primary demand effect of advertising, it is necessary first to discriminate among the cases and then to estimate the advertising effect. Such a procedure would lead to unambiguous statements about the nature of industry advertising.

If the purpose of an empirical study is to investigate competitive advertising, the possible presence of industry advertising effects should not be ignored. What seems to be needed is a method that permits the various effects to be studied simultaneously within a common analytical framework.

Theoretical Cases of Advertising Effect

We consider now a more precise definition of the theoretical cases of advertising effect, both pure and mixed. The format is to develop the cases in terms of partial derivatives of equations in an econometric model of a real market. We treat the case of a duopoly which can be generalized into an n-competitor market by considering $n - 1$ firms to be the remainder.[2] The form of the system from which the derivatives come can be specified later.
First define

$$
\begin{aligned}
Q &= \text{total industry sales} \\
Q_1 &= \text{firm 1's sales} \\
Q_2 &= \text{firm 2's sales} \\
A &= \text{total industry selective advertising} \\
A_1 &= \text{firm 1's advertising} \\
A_2 &= \text{firm 2's advertising} \\
m_1 &= \text{firm 1's market share} \\
m_2 &= \text{firm 2's market share}
\end{aligned}
$$

and thus

$$
\begin{aligned}
Q &= Q_1 + Q_2 \\
A &= A_1 + A_2 \\
m_1 &= Q_1/Q \\
m_2 &= Q_2/Q
\end{aligned}
$$

and assume

$$
\frac{\partial Q_1}{\partial A_1} > 0, \quad \frac{\partial Q_2}{\partial A_2} > 0.
$$

The cases of advertising effect follow:[3,4]

Pure cases

Case I. Primary demand effect only

$$\frac{\partial Q_1}{\partial A_1} > 0 \qquad \frac{\partial m_1}{\partial A_1} = 0 \qquad \frac{\partial Q}{\partial A_1} > 0$$

$$\frac{\partial Q_2}{\partial A_1} > 0 \qquad \frac{\partial m_2}{\partial A_1} = 0$$

Case II. Primary sales effect only

$$\frac{\partial Q_1}{\partial A_1} > 0 \qquad \frac{\partial m_1}{\partial A_1} > 0 \qquad \frac{\partial Q}{\partial A_1} > 0$$

$$\frac{\partial Q_2}{\partial A_1} = 0 \qquad \frac{\partial m_2}{\partial A_1} < 0$$

Case III. Competitive advertising

$$\frac{\partial Q_1}{\partial A_1} > 0 \qquad \frac{\partial m_1}{\partial A_1} > 0 \qquad \frac{\partial Q}{\partial A_1} = 0$$

$$\frac{\partial Q_2}{\partial A_1} < 0 \qquad \frac{\partial m_2}{\partial A_1} < 0$$

Mixed cases.   Besides the pure cases, several mixed cases, where various forces are in operation at the same time, may hold. To aid marketing management in identifying the type of advertising effect in operation, the following three mixed cases are considered.

Case IV. Primary demand and primary sales effect. This combination of effects will occur if the selective advertising for Brand 1 positively affects the sales of Brand 1 and Brand 2, but has a stronger effect for Brand 1. The result is that the market share of Brand 2 will decrease as a result of an increase in selective advertising for Brand 1, but sales of Brand 2 will increase.

$$\frac{\partial Q_1}{\partial A_1} > 0 \qquad \frac{\partial m_1}{\partial A_1} > 0 \qquad \frac{\partial Q}{\partial A_1} > 0$$

$$\frac{\partial Q_2}{\partial A_1} > 0 \qquad \frac{\partial m_2}{\partial A_1} < 0$$

Case V. Primary demand effect and competitive advertising. This mix of forces has the curious effect of both increasing and decreasing sales of Brand 2, that is, the primary demand effect serves to increase sales of both brands, but the competitive effect takes sales away from Brand 2. Depending on the relative strength of these forces, sales for Brand 2 will increase, remain unchanged, or decrease, although its market share will necessarily decline.

$$\frac{\partial Q_1}{\partial A_1} > 0 \qquad \frac{\partial m_1}{\partial A_1} > 0 \qquad \frac{\partial Q}{\partial A_1} > 0$$

$$\frac{\partial Q_2}{\partial A_1} \; ? \qquad \frac{\partial m_2}{\partial A_1} < 0$$

Case V cannot be distinguished from Case IV if $\partial Q_2 / \partial A_1 > 0$, nor is it different from Case II if $\partial Q_2 / \partial A_1 = 0$.

Case VI. Primary sales effect and competitive advertising. Finally, consider a case with jointly operating primary sales effect and competitive advertising. Here, sales of Brand 2 can only decrease, but the decrease is not as great as the decrease in its market share.

$$\frac{\partial Q_1}{\partial A_1} > 0 \qquad \frac{\partial m_1}{\partial A_1} > 0 \qquad \frac{\partial Q}{\partial A_1} > 0$$

$$\frac{\partial Q_2}{\partial A} < 0 \qquad \frac{\partial m_2}{\partial A_1} < 0$$

It is now clear that the mixed forces represented in Case V prevent complete discrimination between the six cases. Case V cannot be distinguished from either Case II, Case IV, or Case VI, depending upon the sign associated with $\partial Q_2/\partial A_1$. In fact, Case V represents two contradictory forces. It is unlikely that advertising for Brand 1 is such that sales of Brand 2 will be both positively and negatively affected; hence, for practical purposes, Case V can be disregarded.

Three Possible Models

Three possible models that come closest to representing industry advertising effects in the sense that we have defined them are a naive model, the model of Clarke (1973), and the model of Bass and Parsons (1969). We already have excluded further consideration of the aggregate model (i.e., $\partial Q/\partial A$) except for the measurement of the influence of primary advertising.

Naive model. This model assumes that the effects can be distinguished and measured by $\partial Q/\partial A_1$. To our knowledge this model has never been used.

Clarke model. This model states that the elasticity of advertising on primary demand (Q) can be determined from the advertising elasticities on sales (Q_1) and market share (m_1). In particular, letting η indicate the elasticity: $\eta_{ms} - \eta_s - \eta_{pd}$.[5]

Bass and Parsons model. This model asserts that an industry advertising effect is evidenced by examining $\partial Q_2/\partial A_1$, a parameter of a system of simultaneous equations.

These models, taken separately, provide necessary but not sufficient conditions to distinguish among the theoretical cases of adversing effect. The specific limitations of each model are given in Schultz and Wittink (1974). In addition to being limited in showing the *existence* of various cases, the models are limited as a means of *measurement*. Only Clarke's model in Case I or possibly Case III is a measure of the appropriate effect. Bass and Parsons' model does not measure in this sense. Clarke's model can measure in Case II if the ambiguity is removed. It should be noted that none of these models was designed to do exactly what we propose.

A Discrimination Model

We now present a model that combines features of the other three models to discriminate among the pure cases of industry advertising effects. The model includes conditions that are both necessary and sufficient to remove ambiguity.

The model requires η_s, η_{ms}, $\partial Q_2 / \partial A_1$, and $\partial Q / \partial A_1$.

1. Case I is uniquely identified when the following conditions hold:

$$\eta_s > 0, \quad \eta_{ms} = 0.$$

2. Case II is uniquely identified when the following conditions hold:

$$\eta_s > 0, \quad \eta_{ms} > 0, \quad \eta_s > \eta_{ms}, \quad \frac{\partial Q_2}{\partial A_1} = 0.$$

3. Case III is uniquely identified when the following conditions hold:

$$\eta_s > 0, \quad \eta_{ms} > 0, \quad \eta_s = \eta_{ms}, \quad \frac{\partial Q}{\partial A_1} = 0.$$

An essential characteristic of the proposed model is that it leads to a *measure* of the identified effect. It turns out that Clarke's equation, $\eta_{pd} = \eta_s - \eta_{ms}$, can now be employed because it has been expanded in concept (to include primary sales effects) and shown to be unambiguous when other conditions are imposed. Letting E_1, E_2, and E_3 represent the measure of a primary demand effect, primary sales effect, and competitive advertising effect, respectively, then

$$E_1 = \eta_s$$

$$E_2 = \eta_s - \eta_{ms}$$

$$E_3 = \eta_s = \eta_{ms}$$

Furthermore, the mixed cases are identified as follows:

4. Case IV is uniquely identified when the following conditions hold:

$$\eta_s > 0, \quad \eta_{ms} > 0, \quad \eta_s > \eta_{ms}, \quad \frac{\partial Q_2}{\partial A_1} > 0.$$

5. Case V is disregarded as implausible.

6. Case VI is uniquely identified when the following conditions hold:

$$\eta_s > 0, \quad \eta_{ms} > 0, \quad \eta_s > \eta_{ms}, \quad \frac{\partial Q_2}{\partial A_1} < 0.$$

The mixed cases are by definition such that exact determination of the effect of selective advertising is impossible. However, besides being able to provide marketing management with the information that (1) one of the three pure cases is operating or (2) some mixed case is in operation, the procedure can show the existence of a primary sales effect along with either a primary demand effect or competitive advertising. The model will provide management with information to determine whether the effect of advertising is consistent with the intent of advertising.

The operationalization of this model in an empirical setting requires a procedure for estimating η_s, η_{ms}, $\partial Q_2/\partial A_1$, and $\partial Q/\partial A_1$. The quality of the estimates is important because one use of such models is in making policy decisions. Only estimates of the parameters can be obtained, of course. The procedures used should be such that at least consistent estimates are obtained to minimize classification and measurement errors.

Estimation

Use of the discrimination model requires a procedure for estimating the necessary parameters. This procedure should at least yield consistent estimates so that classification and measurement errors will be minimized. A major complication is the probable existence of a simultaneous relationship between advertising and sales. Because this chapter is focused on the theoretical conditions rather than on an empirical demonstration, we only suggest the origin of these estimates.

An estimate of η_s and the sign of $\partial Q_2/\partial A_1$ can be obtained from a model such as

$$Q_{1,t} = f(A_{1,t}, Q_{1,t-1}, A_{2,t}, Q_{2,t}, \ldots) \tag{10.1}$$

$$A_{1,t} = f(Q_{1,t}, A_{1,t-1}, Q_{2,t-1}, A_{2,t-1}, \ldots) \tag{10.2}$$

$$Q_{2,t} = f(A_{2,t}, Q_{2,t-1}, A_{1,t}, Q_{1,t}, \ldots) \qquad (10.3)$$

$$A_{2,t} = f(Q_{2,t}, A_{2,t-1}, Q_{1,t-1}, A_{1,t-1}, \ldots), \qquad (10.4)$$

where $Q_{i,t}$, $A_{i,t}$ are as defined previously for $i = 1, 2$. In this model, η_s can be obtained from a double-log form of Eq. (10.1) and the sign of $\partial Q_2/\partial A_1$ from Eq. (10.3). Equations (10.2) and (10.4) are not used directly in the estimation scheme, but may be necessary to circumvent the problem of inconsistency where two-way causation appears. Thus, the appropriate estimation technique depends upon the form of the model.

An estimate of η_{ms} can be obtained indirectly from models such as those of Clarke (1973), Beckwith (1972), or Schultz (1971), where market share depends upon advertising share (among, perhaps, other things), or directly from a double-log form of the market share equation.

Finally, an estimate of $\partial Q/\partial A_1$ can be obtained from a model where industry sales is a function of each firm's advertising. Given the set of estimated parameters, η_s, η_{ms}, $\partial Q_2/\partial A_1$, and $\partial Q/\partial A_1$, the discrimination model can be used to show the existence of an industry advertising effect and a measure of its quantitative impact for any one firm or brand. Each of the estimating models presents certain problems (as we have discussed herein), but together they provide the means for operationalizing the theory presented in this chapter.

FOOTNOTES

[1] This chapter is based on Schultz and Wittink (1974) and Schultz and Wittink (1976).

[2] This procedure for making the model "manageable" has been used in a number of studies, notably Bass and Parsons (1969). The simplification is similar to, although not as severe as, the assumptions inherent in market share formulations of the normalized attraction kind [Bell, Keeney and Little (1975)]. The validity of this form of aggregation can be tested.

[3] We exclude the case of independent markets, i.e.:

$$\frac{\partial Q_1}{\partial A_1} > 0 \qquad \frac{\partial m_1}{\partial A_1} = 0$$

$$\frac{\partial Q_2}{\partial A_1} = 0 \qquad \frac{\partial m_2}{\partial A_1} = 0.$$

This case can arise when *a priori* knowledge of the "market" is weak, as for example, when speaking of paper products or breakfast foods. The set of competitors may not be self-evident.

[4] We consider A_1's effect only; other brands operating in the same industry can be considered in turn.

[5] Following Clarke (1972):

$$\frac{\partial m_1}{\partial A_1} = \frac{\partial}{\partial A_1}\left[\frac{Q_1}{Q}\right] = \frac{1}{Q^2}\left[Q\frac{\partial Q_1}{\partial A_1} - Q_1\frac{\partial Q}{\partial A_1}\right] = \frac{1}{Q}\left[\frac{\partial Q_1}{\partial A_1}\right] - \frac{Q_1}{Q^2}\left[\frac{\partial Q}{\partial A_1}\right].$$

Multiplying by A_1/m_1 we obtain

$$\frac{\partial m_1}{\partial A_1}\left[\frac{A_1}{m_1}\right] = \frac{\partial Q_1}{\partial A_1}\left[\frac{A_1}{Q_1}\right] - \frac{\partial Q}{\partial A_1}\left[\frac{A_1}{Q}\right]$$

or

$$\eta_{ms} = \eta_s - \eta_{pd}.$$

Chapter 11

IMPLEMENTING EMPIRICAL
DECISION MODELS

In many areas of management, including marketing, the development of normative models for making decisions has clearly outdistanced the development of positive descriptions of decision behavior. A large number of optimizing techniques have recently been developed which offer promise in helping marketing management to solve complex and difficult problems. The usefulness of these techniques is, however, highly dependent on how close a "fit" they provide to actual marketing situations. Since these marketing situations include both market and organizational factors, the "validity" of management science models should be assessed in terms of their fit with market behavior (i.e., how well the model represents a real market) and also their fit with organizational behavior (i.e., how compatible they are with the organization using them). When both fits are good, the model is presumably "workable" and the firm can use the model with some assurance that it leads to better decisions. If the model provides a poor fit to either the market or the organization, then the outcome is uncertain at best.

The concept of *market validity* is related to the *technical validity* of marketing decision models and this, in turn, to *organizational validity*. This chapter[1] discusses these validities within the context of general model building and shows how they are related to the probability of success of normative models. The chapter also discusses methods for empirical research and implications of the theory and research. The major focus of the chapter is on the implementation of management science models: We argue that implementation considerations should be part of the model-building process and that implementation can be managed.

MODEL BUILDING PARADIGMS

Marketing decision models have been traditionally developed by researchers or management scientists working independently of

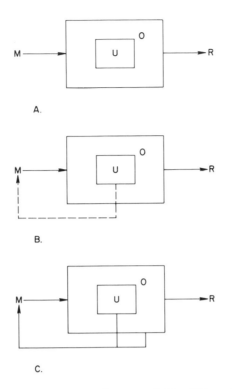

Fig. 11.1. Model building paradigms. (a) Traditional model building (TMB); (b) Evolutionary model building (EMB); (c) Behavioral model building (BMB). *Legend* M = model builder; U = model user(s); O = organization: R = response; – – – – – = informal feedback;————= formal feedback.

model users and user organizations. The result has been that few models are actually implemented and used. Urban and Karash (1971) have urged that this *traditional model building* be replaced by *evolutionary model building*. In the latter, some interaction between the model builder and user takes place and this supposedly increases the usefulness of the model. *Behavioral model building* is an extension of both the traditional and evolutionary concepts in that it provides for significant monitoring of individual and organizational behavior as the model is being developed. This behavioral knowledge can aid in both model building and implementation.

Traditional Model Building

Three major model building paradigms are shown in Fig. 11.1. Traditional model building (TMB) implies that the model is created independently from the user (or user group) and the organization. The user and organization are confronted with the model and this leads to some response. Most of the early marketing decision models were built under this paradigm. Some interaction between model builder and user undoubtedly takes place under TMB, but it is largely for the benefit of the model builder himself. He understands his assignment better, which is not to say that he understands his user better or that his user better understands the model.

Evolutionary Model Building

In evolutionary model building (EMB), the model builder interacts with his user in an informal way, at least informal to the extent that the model builder is primarily concerned with the learning process of his user rather than with the user's behavior or organizational behavior. The premise is a good one: If the user better understands the model, by working with successively more complex versions of it, he will be more inclined to use it. The evolution of Urban's own SPRINTER model is a case-example of this approach. The approach is discussed in a broader context of normative model building by Little (1970). EMB increases the chance of developing a "successful" model.

Behavioral Model Building

The difference between behavioral model building (BMB) and EMB is one of degree and kind. First, the degree of interaction between the model builder and user is greater. In BMB, the model builder wants the user to learn not only about the model, but also about the process of building it. The feedback becomes a formal information flow. Second, the model builder studies the behavioral characteristics of his user and of the organization. This allows him to adjust the structure of the model so that it better represents the organization, and to plan for the implementation of the model. The feedback can change the development of the model. Thus, the behavioral approach is an evolution of EMB.

A Case-Example

To illustrate the differences among these model building paradigms, consider a normative model for determining sales calls. The purpose of the model is to aid salesmen in planning their calls on customers. It includes a representation of the market (some sales response function) and, at least implicitly, a representation of the organization (including the users). Several prototypes of this kind of model are now available [Kotler (1971), 380-403].

Under TMB, the sales call planning model is developed by a management scientist for a (generalized) salesman and delivered to the sales organization. Since the model addresses an important and practical problem, it has some chance of success. Its success depends upon how well the user thinks it represents the market (Is this the way the market works?) and how well it represents the organization (Is this the way we make decisions?). If company sales policy or an individual salesman's attitudes conflict sharply with the structure or output of the model, the model's chance of success is significantly reduced. A number of other individual, group, and organizational factors may preclude the successful application of the model, including the salesman's knowledge of it.

EMB would attempt to increase the chance of success by helping salesmen to learn about the model in stages. As they move from simple to more complex models, the salesmen would be expected to begin to appreciate the potential of the model. Of course, even under EMB, the model's market and organizational validity are moot questions.

Under BMB the management scientist would use inputs from both the organization and the user in developing the model. He would ask himself questions such as: Is the model threatening to the user? Does it call for a dramatic change in the way decisions are made in the organization? Is it compatible with the organizational structure? The use of behavioral inputs in the model building process is intended to produce a model with high organizational validity: compatibility with the user organization.

THEORY OF BEHAVIORAL MODEL BUILDING

The theory of behavioral model building rests on three basic concepts. The first concept is that of a successful model and what determines the probability of success of a model. The second concept is that of technical validity and the third, that of organizational validity. Each of these ideas is developed in turn.

Successful Models

A successful model is one which adequately represents the phenomenon being modeled and is used for the purpose for which it was designed. Since we are mostly concerned with decision models, a successful decision model is one which is used to *make* effective decisions. Any other use of the model makes it unsuccessful. A decision model can be helpful in a number of ways, but unless it has a direct and unambiguous influence on the decision making process it is a failure. This definition probably makes most extant models failures, but this unhappy state motivates our discussion of behavioral model building.

The response in Fig. 11.1 is, according to our definition, either a success (S) or a failure (F). The two factors determining the probability of success are technical validity and organizational validity, the former referring to the capability of the model in solving the problem and the latter to the compatibility of the model with the organization. Both of these factors are themselves multidimensional. In the simples terms,

$$P(S) = f(TV, OV),$$

where

$P(S)$ = the probability of success, $0 \leqslant P(S) \leqslant 1$ (11.1)
TV = technical validity
OV = organizational validity.

We expect that a model which has greater technical and organizational validity will have a larger probability of success. Since perfect technical validity does not imply perfect organizational validity or vice versa, the two concepts must be examined separately, although they are not necessarily independent.

Technical Validity

The technical validity of a marketing decision model refers to its capability of providing some solution, usually an optimal one, to the stated problem. This notion of technical validity has considerable intuitive appeal for, as management scientists, we strive to develop models which can solve some problem in an optimal manner; in so doing, we like to think that, on a technical level at least, we have produced a model which *can* solve the problem if it is used. In other words, for any given definition of a problem, there is some possible technical solution to it, and, the better the technical solution, the more capable the model is in its role of a decision-making device.

One important aspect of technical validity for marketing models is market validity. The market validity of a marketing decision model is its "fit" to the market in terms of structure and behavior. The concept has to do with how well a model *represents* a market. It should not be confused with "goodness of fit," especially common measures of goodness of fit. Market validity is broader and more general. The concept refers not only to the *closeness* with which the model approximates the real market but also with the *correctness* of this representation. Every decision model contains some mechanism for relating marketing decisions to market actions. This mechanism is (at least implicitly) a theory of market behavior and it is the validity of the theory that we are seeking to test.

Although a decision model could work even if the market specification was incorrect, this situation would be one of spurious correlation between the model's output and the real world—in any event a rather dubious basis for either understanding the market or making decisions, especially in dynamic and competitive markets. Thus, it seems wise to attempt to maximize market validity subject to cost-benefit problems and problems of measurement. The main task of this book has been to show how this can be done.

Technical validity is usually measured by the degree to which the model optimizes and the degree to which the model represents the decision situation. Measures of representativeness range from simple face validity and Turing tests to more complex measures of goodness

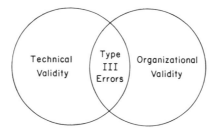

Fig. 11.2. Technical and organizational validity.

of fit and methods for testing theories. Measures of optimization exist in the sense that a *model* can be solved optimally or not. This restricted view, however, does not consider whether or not the problem is solved optimally. Since solving the problem means that (1) the problem has been correctly identified and (2) the solution is implemented, these two additional factors must be taken into account in determining the success of a model.

If a model solves the wrong problem, then this involves both the technical and the organizational validity of the model. On the technical side, this has been called a Type III error and it means that the optimization is spurious since the problem has been incorrectly defined. The *process* of making an error of this kind, though, is a behavioral one. The management scientist has misread the situation or, perhaps, has been misled about it. In any event, the result is an error in model formulation stemming from behavioral as much as technical factors. This overlap in the two concepts is illustrated in Fig. 11.2. The final type of error that we consider might be termed a Type IV error, that is, the "error" of developing a model that solves the right problem but which is not used. Much of our argument revolves around the fact that models can be technically valid but still not used. We posit that the answer lies in a consideration of organizational validity.

Organizational Validity

While the market is the external environment of the marketing model, the human organization is its internal environment. A model with perfect market validity would still have a finite probability of failure (perhaps large) if it failed to account for human behavioral factors. The organizational validity of a marketing decision model is its fit to the organization in terms of structure and behavior. The concept has to do with how compatible the model is with the organization. The parallel with market validity, however, is not perfect. Whereas the firm has no control over market structure and little over market behavior, the firm can control its organizational behavior and help to shape the attitudes of its employees. In other words, if a model doesn't represent the market, the market can't be changed to represent the model, although an organization can be changed if the model requires it.[2] Thus, organizational validity can be achieved through model building and/or implementation.

To illuminate this concept, let us return to the sales-call planning model. The behavioral model building approach would require attention to both the model's market and organizational validity before and during the model building process. The model builder would measure market validity through traditional instruments or tests. Armed with new instruments for measuring organizational validity, he would seek to develop his model in such a way that its probability of success was significantly enhanced. This would probably require the model builder to study the user's attitudes toward models and innovations and his background for using the model, the user group and its dynamics, and the factors of organizational behavior bearing on the use of the model. The concept of organizational validity can address some simple but important questions, such as: Will the salesmen use a computer model? Who will use it? Depending upon their attitudes and backgrounds, how can they be introduced to the call model? Will the organization permit them to make independent decisions with the model? How will their group dynamics affect acceptance of the model? All of these questions and others can be answered through an explicit focus on human organizational factors.

Consider a more tangible example of organizational validity. In a model developed by one of the authors [Schultz (1971)], a method was offered for airlines to make scheduling and advertising decisions. The normative model was based on a positive description of market behavior. The market validity of the model was judged to be high, but this did not ensure its future success as a decision making tool. The model requires, for example, a close coordination between marketing management and the advertising and scheduling departments of airlines. If this coordination does not exist or cannot be made to exist (because of organizational inflexibility), the chance of the model being successful is lessened.[3] In this example, the behavioral model building approach could have changed the structure of the decision model and would almost certainly have changed the structure of the organization interfacing with the model.

Before organizational validity can be shown to be an important factor in building and implementing management science models, a program of research must be undertaken which (1) identifies critical organizational factors and (2) develops measures of critical factors (instruments). In the following section, a number of methods are discussed which can lead to measures of the fit between models and human organizations.

RESEARCH ON ORGANIZATIONAL VALIDITY

Although the problem of implementing management science models is critical to their success, it has only recently gained the attention of management researchers and practioners. Churchman, Ackoff, and Arnoff (1957) argued for such research by observing that no well-formulated methodology for implementation was available and yet the implementation problem was one of the most significant ones facing management scientists. During the next decade, programs of research were carried out at Berkeley, Northwestern, and other centers. Progress in understanding the problem has been slow, however, and recent literature reviews [cf. Schultz and Slevin (1975)] show few studies devoted specifically to implementation with many of these being highly speculative. Our conclusion is that there is still no well-formulated methodology for implementation.

The following discussion proposes a way in which such a methodology could be developed within the framework of behavioral model building. We specifically deal with the concept of organizational validity, i.e., the fit between the model and the organization. Since organizational validity is multidimensional, the concept of "fit" consists of a variety of factors such as attitudes of users, group dynamics of the informal organization, and communications and authority structures of the formal organization. These factors seem to fall within three levels of aggregation: individual, small group, and organizational. For this reason, we propose an approach to implementation research that measures fits at each level and combines them in an overall measure of organizational validity.

A Measure of Organizational Validity

A quantitative measure of the fit between a model and an organization is the degree of organizational change required to implement the model. This degree of change could be measured by the distance between the initial and final states of each variable. One possible representation of this distance could be

$$\text{Change} = [(X_1 - X_0)^2 + (Y_1 - Y_0)^2 + (Z_1 - Z_0)^2]^{1/2}, \qquad (11.2)$$

where

$$
\begin{aligned}
X_1 &= \text{required state of individual variables} \\
X_0 &= \text{actual state of individual variables} \\
Y_1 &= \text{required state of small group variables} \\
Y_0 &= \text{actual state of small group variables} \\
Z_1 &= \text{required state of organizational variables} \\
Z_0 &= \text{actual state of organizational variables.}
\end{aligned}
$$

The total change required is a function of the changes needed at individual, small group, and organizational levels. By measuring these variables it may be possible to determine the total amount of change required *before* the implementation is begun. The model builder can use this diagnostic information in deciding on the appropriate mix of two alternative courses of action: (1) change the model to improve its organizational validity and (2) change the behavioral variables to improve this fit. The appropriate implementation steps will be a function of the costs and benefits of each strategy.

Individual, Small Group, and Organizational Factors

One of the first requirements for the successful implementation of a model is acceptance on the part of the user, i.e., the *individual*. The individuals affected by the model must have a favorable, open attitude in order to be motivated to accept the model. Although several well-developed methodologies have been offered by behavioral scientists for attitude scaling [Fishbein (1967); Guilford (1954); Torgerson (1958)] few have been applied to the problem of implementation. Some authors have measured attitudes in doing implementation research [Dyckman (1967); Ladd (1965); Vertinsky (1972)], however, most of these efforts have been directed at measuring a small component of user attitudes. Manley (1971) constructed a multiplicative attitude model using the paired comparison technique of Metfessel (1947) and the semantic differential technique as developed by Osgood and others (1957). To this date, though, a research effort designed to measure a broad spectrum of user attitudes in a general, replicative fashion has not been presented and yet it seems to be a necessary step in implementation research. An instrument that could be used by a number of OR practitioners in a variety of settings would be valuable in generating a body of research data on this topic. Efforts to develop such an instrument are reported by Schultz and Slevin [(1975), Chap. 7]. Lucas (1976) shows that individual attitudes are related to the implementation of computer-based models. New research along these lines can be expected.

The importance of *small group* variables on the implementation of change has been known since the classic Coch and French study (1948). Since that time a large body of evidence about small group behavior has been accumulated [see for example Cartwright and Zander (1968); Hopkins (1964); Roby (1968)]. Variables such as cohesion, group norms, pressures to conformity and group composition have been known to be important for some time. It is difficult to select from this large array which variables and which research findings are most appropriate to implementation. One fact does seem to stand out clearly: The implementation of a management science decision model may often change the communication pattern of the small group. For example, if one member of the group is the primary model user, he may become a communication focus in the group. For this reason the communication net experiments initiated by Bavelas and continued by Leavitt, Shaw, and others appear particularly important [Bavelas (1950); Leavitt (1951) Shaw (1971)]. A measurement instrument that determines the required changes in communication structure would give insight into the scope of the implementation problem.

While the small group area is very important to the practitioner (most managers recognize the tremendous power of the small group to accept or reject innovation), it is also the most difficult for the researcher. First, it may be difficult to identify the real "informal" groups without spending considerable time in the organization. Second, so many variables are important that it is difficult to select a starting point for measurement. For these reasons, small group variables would be considered in the later phases of an implementation research program.

In searching for a methodology that might be used to measure the fit between a model and the *organization*, we would like it to possess two properties. First, it should be general, focusing on the systemic properties of organizations and applicable to a wide variety of organizational types. Second, it should focus on variables that are important and will predict the probable success of the model. We would like to be able to focus on structural variables that can be changed both in the organization and in the model. Instruments that measure organizational climate, trust, etc. may be of little value since we may not know how the model affects these variables even after we have measured them. Fortunately, a methodology for measuring organizational structure exists and has been reasonably well-tested.

Lawrence and Lorsch (1967) have developed and tested instruments for measuring two systemic properties of organizations: differentiation and integration. Differentiation is defined as the difference in cognitive and emotional orientation among managers in different functional departments. Differentiation is measured on four dimensions: orientation toward goals, time orientation, interpersonal orientation, and formality of structure. Highly differentiated organizational subunits would have managers that are quite different while organizational subunits that are slightly differentiated would have managers that are similar in these four attributes.

On the other hand, every system that is highly differentiated must have some degree of integration in order to have the unity of purpose necessary to accomplish its objectives. Integration is defined as the quality of the state of collaboration that exists among departments that are required to achieve unity of effort by the demands of the environment. Integration is necessary to resolve subunit conflicts and to provide the necessary coordination. It is measured by soliciting management opinion on the amount of coordination that exists between various departments.

The Lawrence and Lorsch concepts of differentiation and integration appear well-suited to organizational validity research.

They have developed instruments that are standardized and can be used in a variety of settings. They have spearheaded a program of research that has resulted in the measurement of these attributes in a variety of organizational settings, from highly diversified companies [Allen (1970)] to individual plants [Walker and Lorsch (1968)]. A primary finding has been that the organization-environment match is a crucial one in determining the effectiveness of the organization. In a dynamic environment, for example, high levels of both differentiation and integration are needed. This has significant implications for the study of organizational validity. If the model requires a change in integration or differentiation for an organization that is well-matched to its environment, the model must be changed. If the model requires a change in integration and differentiation that would result in a better match between the organization and its environment, then the model builder must concentrate on ways to change the organization. Lawrence and Lorsch (1969) have used their instruments in organization development work to point out the need for and ways to accomplish needed change. Hence the measurement of integration and differentiation might not only lead to problem diagnosis, but also help in problem solution.

A number of research questions might be asked concerning these concepts. Are models more easily implemented in highly differentiated organizations? What is the role of integration in model implementation? Can models be easily changed so they have varying effects on differentiation and integration? Once some research data are accumulated, it may be possible to measure the integration and differentiation of an organization and then to comment on the likelihood of success of a particular model.

DIMENSIONS OF MODELS

A number of interesting but difficult research questions are raised by the theory of behavioral model building. One of the most important is how can hypotheses regarding the nature of models and organizations be developed that lead to empirically verifiable tests of organizational validity. A promising approach seems to be an investigation of the dimensions of models which lead to behavioral considerations of implementation.

Analyzing Dimensions

The number of marketing decision models developed in recent years has grown dramatically, although the use of decision models has been less than spectacular. Models have appeared that deal with advertising budgeting decisions, media selection decisions, sales-call planning decisions, distribution size and location decisions, and many others. What are some of the dimensions of these models that have behavioral implications?

Table 11.1 lists a number of dimensions of marketing decision models together with their logical ranges. A multidimensional analysis of the characteristics of models should be as complete as possible. But since our objective here is more modest—to identify leading behavioral hypotheses—we will concentrate on the two major dimensions of use of data and use of computers. This focus seems to be quite consistent with the features of many decision models discussed in this book.

Figure 11.3 is a simple two-dimensional diagram which shows the data-computer space of a marketing decision model. The use of data in models ranges from those which require only subjective inputs of marketing executives to those which require only empirical inputs of actual market data. Models which fall in between combine subjective and empirical data in some appropriate fashion. The use of computers in models ranges from those which require the computer for data processing and/or analysis without the direction interaction

Table 11.1

Some Dimensions of Marketing Decision Models

Dimension	Range
Number of variables	Univariate-multivariate
Use of data	Subjective-empirical
Use of computer	Noninteractive-interactive
Handling of uncertainty	Stochastic-deterministic
Method of solution	Algorithmic-heuristic
Character of system	Steady state-transient
Relationships between variables	Linear-nonlinear
System boundary	Open-closed
Variation over time	Static-dynamic

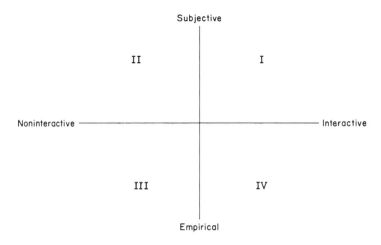

Fig. 11.3. Behavioral factors in two dimensions.

of the user to those which require the user to interact with the computer via conversational-type programs. Of course, some models may not use the computer at all, but we have not considered this case.

Behavioral Hypotheses

Consider again our two-dimensional scheme. The following hypotheses are made with respect to organizational change necessary for successful implementation of marketing decision models.

Hl. $(X_1 - X_0)$ *increases* as models become more interactive.

It seems reasonable to assume that traditional marketing decision making involves the analysis of historical data that are assembled in some report format. The use of an interactive model is going to require that the decision maker relegate some of this analysis to the computer *while* he is in the process of making a decision. The use of the interactive console and the change in decision making style is going to require substantial learning and substantial attitude change on the part of the individual decision maker.

H2. $(X_1 - X_0)$ *decreases* as models become more empirical.

An *a priori* argument can be made either for or against this hypothesis. On the one hand, one could argue that the decision maker is accustomed to analyzing empirical data and that having the computer perform part of this function represents only a small change from the status quo. On the other hand, one could maintain that a model using the decision maker's subjective inputs is less threatening because it still requires his judgment as *input* and therefore less attitude change is needed.

H3. $(Y_1 - Y_0)$ *increases* as models become more interactive.

H4. $(Y_1 - Y_0)$ *increases* as models become more empirical.

There are no good *a priori* arguments either in favor of or against these hypotheses. The degree of change needed in the group in each case will depend on the details of the situation and the interaction between the group and the model. Empirical research is needed to gain more insight into the effect of model dimensions on group change.

H5. $(Z_1 - Z_0)$ *increases* as models become more interactive.

The use of interactive models requires that certain members of the organization become specialists in their use. This requires an increase in organizational differentiation (differences in cognitive and emotional orientation among managers in different functional departments). At the same time, the interactive specialist must coordinate his activities with other members of the organization. This requires an increase in integration (quality of the state of collaboration that exists among departments). Both of these increases (differentiation and integration) will require an increase in organizational change needed $(Z_1 - Z_0)$.

H6. $(Z_1 - Z_0)$ *increases* as models become more empirical.

If a subjective model is used, the role of the decision maker using the model changes little in the organization. Previously he made subjective decisions; now he makes computer-aided subjective decisions. However, if an empirical computer model is used, it requires a new reliance on empirical computer output. This requires that individuals who previously made decisions themselves rely more heavily on empirical computer output. This may result in changes in the differentiation and integration of the organization and hence an increase in $(Z_1 - Z_0)$.

Similar behavioral hypotheses could be made for the other dimensions of marketing decision models given in Table 11.1. How they actually affect implementation is, of course, a research question. Schultz, Slevin and Keith (1975) studied hypotheses similar to H1 and H2 in an experiment using scenarios to reflect levels of use of computer (noninteractive, interactive) and use of data (subjective, empirical). They found that these factors were not significantly related to intended acceptance of the marketing model. Although the problems associated with conducting a field experiment are great, this would seem to be the ideal vehicle for testing such hypotheses. A laboratory experiment with real models (as opposed to scenarios) would at least provide a more sensitive replication environment. It should be clear that additional research is necessary on the behavioral dimensions of marketing models.

Costs of Organizational Change

In all cases, the final determination of whether an organization is changed to fit a model should depend on whether the *benefits* from the model outweigh the *costs* of the change. The quantitative measure of change presented in this chapter is felt to be representative of the *total organizational energy* required to implement the model. The formal accounting system of the organization may not reflect the total costs of the change required; nevertheless, the organization will use up resources in terms of human energy proportionate to the change required.

Some models, although requiring substantial change, may be implemented quickly because their benefits are substantial. The methodology proposed here for measuring the change will help the model builder to think in terms of the total energy of the organizational system required to implement the models. Changes in the model may reduce the amount of energy required, or prior knowledge of the energy required may enable the implementation process to go more smoothly.

EXAMPLES OF MARKETING DECISION MODELS

A number of marketing decision models reported in the literature are classified in data-computer space in Fig. 11.4. The

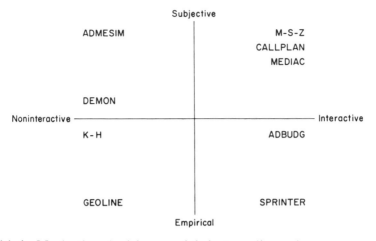

Fig. 11.4. Marketing decision models in two dimensions.

following models are included: Little and Lodish's MEDIAC (1969), Montgomery, Silk and Zaragoza's multiple product sales force allocation model (M-S-Z) (1971), Lodish's CALLPLAN (1971), Gensch's ADMESIM (1969), Charnes and others' DEMON (1969), Kuehn and Hamburger's warehouse location model (K-H) (1963), Hess' GEOLINE (1971), Little's ADBUDG (1966), and Urban's SPRINTER (1970).[4] The questions to be asked are: What degree of change is required to implement them? What is the cost of such change?

Reported Results on Implementation

Most published reports of marketing decision models omit substantive discussions of implementation problems and prospects. It is thus difficult to inquire about the degree of organizational change effected or its cost without interviewing the model builders and user organizations. If a model is reported to be successfully implemented in one or more organizations, it is still not possible to conclude that organizational change was small or large or to infer its cost because of the (usually) unknown dollar benefits of the model. Clearly, new research is necessary to sort out these complex behavioral considerations of implementation. A special issue of *Management Science*, edited by David B. Montgomery, however, focused on new marketing models and included some welcome comments on implementation. For example, consider two models reported there that fall within our quadrant I: the M-S-Z model and CALLPLAN.

Montgomery, Silk, and Zaragoza developed a model to allocate selling effort across products and over time for situations where several products are marketed by the same sales force. The model falls in quadrant I because it is interactive and the data input is subjective. On the basis of our hypotheses regarding the implementation of such a model we would expect substantial individual and moderate organizational change (H1, H2, H5).

Although they may not have been thinking in individual, small group, and organizational behavior terms, the researchers did note some of the actual and required state variables. It was noted that product managers (the users) initially had "little exposure to modeling concepts and no experience at all with interactive systems." Yet it was required that they be involved in the development of the model to gain understanding of it and to appreciate its potential. To induce behavioral change, the researchers attempted to change attitudes (the users were given a chance to use an existing interactive model), group interactions (product managers and executives were brought together in discussion groups), and perhaps organizational structure (although this was not reported). Once implemented, the indicated profit improvement in the first year of use exceeded development costs by more than three times. Assuming that the development costs included the costs of organizational change, this seems to be a case where the benefits of the model make the change economically worthwhile.

Lodish developed a model (CALLPLAN) for salesmen or sales management to allocate sales call time more efficiently. It is an interactive model and relies on subjective estimates of response parameters, thus falling in quadrant I. Our behavioral hypotheses would be the same for CALLPLAN as M-S-Z. Lodish reports fourteen preliminary applications of the model in various product areas, but some had questionable benefits because (we suppose) of either poor fits to the market or organizational environments of the firm. Lodish did collect some behavioral data by interviewing salesmen and other users. He concludes that the subjective and interactive features of the model contributed to its success, that a good deal of learning took place, that better communication was fostered between the salesman and his manager, and that the model served as a motivating device. Like the example above, this seems to indicate that organizational change took place with some cost but that benefits often exceeded cost. A rigorous test of these ideas seems to be important and overdue.[5]

Empirical Marketing Decision Models

The models that are the primary subject of this book fall at the extreme point of the empirical dimension in Fig. 11.3. We have seen in Chap. 9 how the handling of competition can be highly subjective or highly empirical. The handling of estimates of total industry demand can also be measured on this dimension. Thus, these ideas on organizational validity, at all behavioral levels, seem to be quite relevant to the ultimate test of empirical decision models, i.e., whether or not they are *used*.

ATTITUDES AND IMPLEMENTATION

If we take models to be a type of product, then an implementation decision process can be regarded as substantially similar in nature to a consumer decision process. Although there are some general theoretical models of consumer behavior that perform a synthesizing function, much useful research is analytical in character. One of the more interesting developments has been the focus of research on attitude models that, while not comprehensive, are in some sense central to the process of choice. Considerable research has centered on multi-attribute attitude models for different products with different characteristics. In the implementation process the product is always the same—a decision model—although it can have different characteristics. If dimensions of implementation attitudes can be found that are reasonably general, then work can proceed on more inclusive models of implementation choice.

Schultz and Slevin [(1975), Chap. 7] studied the adoption of a sales forecasting model by managers of a large corporation in order to define dimensions of implementation attitudes. Their focus on individuals and models rather than, say, organizations and projects seems especially appropriate to empirical marketing decision models since many are designed to be used by more than one person, e.g., by several brand managers, or salesmen, or sales managers. They first constructed an attitude instrument and then piloted and field-tested the questionnaire. A factor analysis of the structure of the responses showed the following dimensions:

PERFORMANCE–Effect of Model on Manager's Job Performance

INTERPERSONAL–Interpersonal Relations

CHANGES–Changes Resulting from the Model

GOALS–Goal Achievement and Congruence

SUPPORT/RESISTANCE–Support for the Model/Lack of Resistance

CLIENT/RESEARCHER–Client-Researcher Interface

URGENCY–Urgency for Results

These factors were then correlated with such dependent variables as probability of use of the model and evaluation of worth of the model. Their results indicate that for intended use two factors are most important: *PERFORMANCE* and *URGENCY* ($r = .60$ and $r = .59$, respectively). These are *personal* factors and suggest that the appeal of a model to a manager may be greatest in terms of "what can the model do for him." *SUPPORT* and *GOALS* are also important ($r = .30$ and $r = .26$, respectively). These factors seem to be *organizational* and suggest that they augment personal benefits in the manager's mind. *CLIENT/RESEARCHER* is not significant, but the application may be a special case; the model in the study was designed at the corporate staff level without much (if any) interaction with most ultimate users. For this reason, the client-researcher relationship may be interpreted as irrelevant by the manager who is being asked to use the model. This factor is significant, however, when the respondent assesses the accuracy and worth of the model. *INTERPERSONAL* and *CHANGES* are not significantly related to probability of use.

The parallel with consumer behavior research implies that the attitudinal dimensions shown to be related to intended behavior in the Schultz and Slevin study can serve as input to other kinds of studies. For example, the seven factors could be considered to be the "attributes" of a decision model and a study could be done to possibly improve predictive ability by incorporating them in a multi-attribute attitude model where they are linearly weighted and combined for individuals. This approach allows the inclusion of more direct attributes such as model complexity and user understanding with the basic dimensions, as in the work of Lucas (1976). Another possible study would be to relate attitudes to actual behavior. Because the use of a model is so related to an individual's job, there is reason to believe that intended behavior correlates more closely with actual behavior in the implementation setting than in a consumer choice situation. To our knowledge, however, there is no empirical evidence on this question.

For a marketing manager interested in utilizing a decision model to improve his decision-making effectiveness, these findings suggest how the implementation process could be managed. Each attitude dimension can be considered to be a policy variable that could be controlled to influence implementation success. For example, if similar results are established in future studies (and recent research suggests that the dimensions are generalizable), then the following conclusions emerge. First, it may be most useful to emphasize the *personal benefits* of the model or innovation. By stressing how its use will help the manager *himself*, the likelihood of successful implementation may be increased. Second, by giving *general (top management) support* and by indicating *goal congruence* between organizational tasks and the model, the implementers may facilitate model use. Third, where the potential user is involved with the researcher, or should be involved, *the relationship between the client and the researcher* is important to implementation success. Finally, *change* and *interpersonal relations* do not seem to be very critical and may be factors to be de-emphasized in managing implementation.

The implementation problem is an important one in marketing because it is through successful implementation that needed organizational change occurs. In this chapter we have considered the objects of implementation to be decision models designed to improve marketing decision making. The main point is that with empirical marketing decision models, as well as with models in general, the factors determining individual use seem to be both behavioral and technical.

FOOTNOTES

[1] This chapter is based on material in Schultz and Slevin (1972) and Schultz and Slevin [(1975), Chapter 3].

[2] In the long run a firm's actions could affect both market structure and behavior, but this is clearly not a practical way to judge market validity.

[3] In this study little prior coordination did exist and there has been little organizational change to date.

[4] Other models could be considered as well, e.g., Urban's (1975) PERCEPTOR, a model combining empirical and subjective data; Aaker's (1975) ADMOD, primarily empirical with some subjective inputs; and Little's (1975) BRANDAID, an on-line, subjective input model.

[5] Another perspective on the use of marketing decision models is in Larréché (1974).

Chapter 12

SALES RESPONSE
AND BUYER BEHAVIOR

We have made the argument that econometric modeling is a general procedure for representing theories of marketing behavior and hence for testing models of (sales) response. In this chapter we discuss the relationship between sales response and buyer behavior. It will be shown that the methods and models presented in this book are equally applicable to the study of individual or household behavior, even though they place strong demands on the conceptual precision and quantitative representation of "behavioral" theories. We first discuss several aggregate response studies that include intervening behavioral variables as well as marketing decision inputs and sales response outputs. Then we discuss the future of econometric research on marketing behavior.

MODELING INTERMEDIATE PROCESSES

The econometric approach can be used to describe intermediate processes occurring between a marketing input and a sales response. While the results thus far have not been encouraging, this level of detail will eventually provide for a better understanding of the marketing process. Most of the research to date has focused on the communication process.

Lavidge and Steiner (1961) suggested that measurement of advertising effectiveness cannot focus on immediate sales response alone, but must also consider the intermediate process. They viewed this process as knowledge, liking, preference, and conviction to purchase. One refinement to this theory allows a consumer to skip one or more steps while maintaining the overall one-way flow.

Palda (1966) attempted to evaluate this hierarchy-of-effects hypothesis. He examined the relationship of advertising intensity and awareness to market shares by trying a variety of linear multiple regression equations. These equations represented a number of functional forms of the equation—simple linear, semilogarithmic, and logarithmic—and contained variables lagged for different time intervals.

Palda found the presence of a strong concurrent relationship between awareness and market share. However, higher levels of advertising activity failed to strengthen the awareness-purchase relationship. Furthermore, regressions using lagged awareness failed to fit as well as those of the concurrent form. Thus, Palda was able to show that higher awareness coexists with higher purchasing rate, but unable to confirm that awareness tends to precede or even contribute to the rate of purchase. Palda's study was limited by lack of data on attitudes which is an important modifier variable in the hierarchy of effects theory. Furthermore, determination of the appropriate lead-lag relationships was handicapped because data were available for only three time periods.

More recently, Assael and Day (1968) found for the products they studied (analgesics, deodorants, and instant coffee) that attitudes, awareness, and usage predicted subsequent market share. Their analysis was based on a multiple regression equation of time series data for 13 brands. They reported briefly on a separate regression equation that related market share, awareness, and usage to attitude.

Assael and Day concluded that intervening variables in the purchasing process are important factors in explaining variance in aggregate behavior. The importance of a particular intervening variable varies by product class and by brand. Support was found for the proposition that changes in attitude are more closely related to subsequent behavior change than are changes in awareness. Assael and Day's findings also suggest that attitudes predict market share better than market share predicts attitudes. This result led to their tentative conclusion that attitude change precedes rather than follows a behavior change.

A major methodological weakness in this study is that the equations representing the effects of attitudes on behavior change and the effects of behavior change on attitudes were estimated separately. The identification problem is ignored. A correct understanding of these effects requires the use of a system of equations. The managerial implications of their results also were limited because the interrelationships between advertising and awareness, attitudes, usage, and market share were not studied.

Aaker and Day (1971) overcame some of the deficiencies of past research through some exploratory work involving a system of equations. The dependent variables were awareness, attitude, and market share. The predetermined variables included advertising as well as lagged dependent variables. The results indicated that the influence of advertising flowed from awareness directly to behavior bypassing attitude. In addition, strong support emerged for the conclusion that attitude change precedes behavior.

Methodological deficiencies mar the Aaker and Day study. They uncritically adopted Wold's (1954) notion that a "good" model should represent causal chains *and therefore be recursive*. However, the modern principle of causality imposes no constraints on the detailed form of scientific models and theories. Basmann (1963) provides more detailed insight into this issue. Our own opinion is that *interdependent* simultaneous equation models are more appropriate in most marketing situations unless there is strong *a priori* evidence of asymmetry. Moreover, Aaker and Day did not test the key assumption of the recursive model—the assumption that the contemporaneous covariance matrix is diagonal. Hence the appropriateness of ordinary least squares estimation can not be assured.

A general model was postulated in which the "benefit" that it avoided *a priori* specification of structure was claimed. However, this means that any finding is accepted. Moreover, this led to their extreme rationalization of the results. In any event, precise interpretation of the results was handicapped by the presence of significant multicollinearity. Finally, the values of R^2 for individual equations were said to be "certainly respectable". The concept of a "respectable" R^2 is ambiguous and words such as certainly, obviously, and transparently are often indicators of the weakness of one's argument.

One reason why the nature of the attitude-behavior relationships remains unresolved is the inadequacy of the measures of the concepts. Measure validation is a necessary precursor to testing. Otherwise, unsatisfactory test results could be the result of the quality of the theory or the quality of the measures or both. This ambiguity occurred in an empirical test of the Howard-Sheth model conducted by Farley and Ring (1970). Parsons (1971) has proposed a research design for testing the hierarchy of effects theory.

Earlier sales response models were shown to adequately differentiate between the effects of various media. Knowledge of the intermediate process will allow for a better approximation. Media are believed to work in different ways; at each step in the intermediate process, one medium might be superior to another. Econometric methods can test this hypothesis.

There is no theoretical reason why econometric models could not be used to specify response functions which would lead to intramedia optimization, although, pragmatically, the outlook is pessimistic. The data needs of such a model would be substantial and no single firm could likely afford the costs.

Econometric models permit determination of which copy appeals and campaign approaches have been successful *ex post*. This is the ability to see, after the event, what should be done. While insights are provided, the ability to predict the impact of future new appeals has not been materially improved. A system for pretesting themes within the context of an econometric model needs to be developed. Some type of a controlled field experiment seems to be required. Again, this is an issue for future discussion and research.

Aggregate intervening-variable models are likely to be useful for decision making. As a practical matter, decision making requires that market segments greater than size one be used. However, this aggregation does not permit inferences about individual behavior. It is to the contribution of econometrics to the understanding of individual behavior that we now turn.

ECONOMETRIC STUDIES OF BUYER BEHAVIOR

Farley and Ring Study

The best known econometric study of buyer behavior is Farley and Ring's (1970) "test" of a version of Howard and Sheth's (1969) theory of buyer behavior. The work has raised interest because (1) it suggested how behavioral theories can be put into a form amenable to testing; (2) it generated controversy over just what kind of test it was; (3) it illustrates the relationship between model building and model testing.

Farley and Ring formulated an operational version of Howard

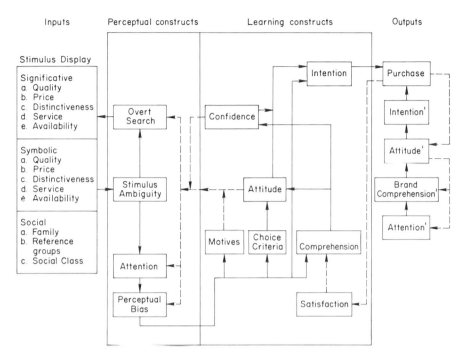

Fig. 12.1. The Howard-Sheth model of buyer behavior. Source: Howard and Sheth (1969, p. 30).

and Sheth's conceptual model of buyer behavior. The conceptual model is diagrammed in Fig. 12.1 while a revised version of the operational model is diagrammed in Fig. 12.2.[1] The original 1970 operational model (not shown) met the order condition for identification. However, Lutz and Resek (1972) pointed out that the model did not satisfy the rank conditions for identification. Thus, Farley and Ring (1972) revised the operational model slightly.

The congruence between the conceptual and operational model can be evaluated, in part, by comparing the two diagrams. Farley and Ring appear to have added two links between variables: the feedback from stimulus ambiguity to perceptual bias and causal connection between motive and intention. They seem to have reversed the direction of causality between attention and stimulus ambiguity. Most importantly, the feedbacks from attitude and confidence to overt search, perceptual bias, and attention have been omitted.

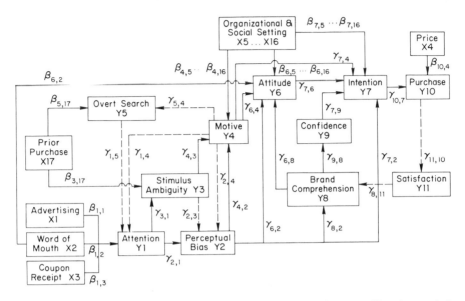

Fig. 12.2. Operational version (revised) of the Howard-Sheth model where the Organizational and Social Setting variables are:

Company at meal, X5	Spouse's age, X11
Homemaking skill, X6	Spouse's education, X12
Leadership, X7	Spouse's hours/week employed, X13
Household size, X8	Household income, X14
City 10,000-100,000, X9	Time/week spent in kitchen, X15
City over 100,000, X10	Size of meal eaten, X16

Source: Adapted from Farley and Ring (1970, 1972).
Direct causal relation:————; feedback effects: − − − − − .

Dominguez (1974) argues that the absence of feedback is contrary to the relationship between the learning and perceptual systems that forms the foundation for the consumer dynamics of the conceptual model, i.e., problem solving. Dominguez also calls attention to the fact that the operational model is static whereas the conceptual model is not.[2] This is a problem of inadequate data and not an inherent limitation of econometric model building.

Farley and Ring recognize in constructing an operational version of the Howard-Sheth model that many variables involved substantial definitional and measurement problems. Conventional market research questions currently available do not give good measures of some of the variables which are key elements of the Howard-Sheth

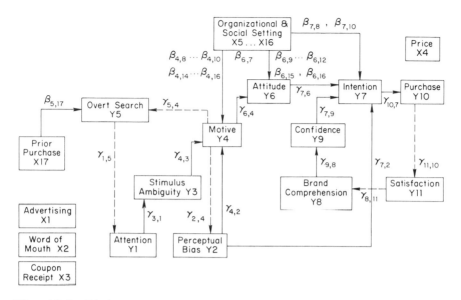

Fig. 12.3. Linkages confirmed by Farley and Ring. Direct causal relation:————; feedback effects: – – – – –.

model. Indeed, Dominguez (1974), Lutz and Resek (1972), and others have commented on deficiences in the operational definitions of various variables employed by Farley and Ring.

Farley and Ring had data on the purchase behavior of 693 individual households who were members of a consumer panel. The product was a new convenience breakfast food being test marketed in Portland, Oregon. At the end of four months, the brand achieved a retail distribution of only about 50%.

Everything considered, Farley and Ring found that the empirical evidence tended to support the Howard-Sheth model. If the test statistics applicable to a single-equation model are conjectured to hold for a multiple-equation model,[3] then two-thirds (14 out of 21) of the linkages among the endogenous variables could not be rejected at the 0.10 level of significance using two-stage least-squares estimation. The coefficients of the endogenous variables were postulated *a priori* to be positive. Two of the "significant" relationships were negative. The "significant" linkages are shown in Fig. 12.3.

The Howard-Sheth theory makes no statement about which variables should be included in the set of social and organizational variables. Among other things, this ambiguity contributed to identification problems which Farley and Ring did not recognize. In addition, if the presence or absence of these variables is unspecified, then the sign of the coefficients associated with each of these variables must also be unspecified. Again this is a situation in which any finding must be accepted. More discouragingly, none of the market variables (advertising, word of mouth, coupon receipt, or price) appeared to influence consumer behavior.

The order condition for identifiability states that for an equation in a model consisting of L linear equations to be identified, the equation must exclude at least $L - 1$ of *the variables contained in that model* (i.e., their coefficients are zero).[4] A variable is contained in a model *a priori* if in at least one structural equation its coefficient is *assumed* to be nonzero. However, the values of the population parameters are unknown. Consequently, the hypothesis that individual coefficients are equal to zero should be *tested*. If this hypothesis can not be rejected for the coefficient of a given variable in at least one structural equation, then this particular variable is irrelevant and should not be counted in the identifiability test on any equation. Thus, a structural equation which seems to satisfy the order condition *a priori* may not, in fact, satisfy this condition after the irrelevant variables have been removed. This situation occurred in Farley and Ring (1970).

While we are interested in whether parameters assumed as nonzero are, in fact, nonzero, we may also like to know if some of the parameters specified as zero are, in fact, zero. This seems to be the crux of Hunt and Pappas's (1972) muddled comment on Farley and Ring's test.[5] If the order condition indicates overidentifiability, the *identifiability test statistic* (discussed in Chap. 5) can be used to judge if, in light of the data, it is a correct specification to exclude more variables from an equation than is necessary for exact identification.

Dominguez Study

Dominguez (1971) extended the work of Farley and Ring by constructing a dynamic model of the process of consumer choice. This model is shown in Fig. 12.4. The model involves a synthesis of the theories of Engel, Kollat, and Blackwell (1973), Howard and Sheth (1969), Nicosia (1966), and others. One consequence is that his *a priori* model can not be compared with any one conceptual model.

Dominguez collected the data necessary to estimate the parameters of his model by means of an experimental game. The nature of the experimental game is discussed by Dominguez and Burger (1971). As with an experimental situation, atypical behavior may have been produced. Thus, the results should be interpreted with caution. Moreover, Russ (1974) notes a specification-measurement incongruence. While the model shown in Fig. 12.4 specifies that attitude be measured between exposure to word-of-mouth communication and brand choice, attitude was actually measured before exposure to word-of-mouth or after-use experience.

Dominguez was able to confirm only 9 of the 21 linkages shown in Fig. 12.4. Moreover, one-third of these (3 out of 9) were of the wrong sign. His main substantive conclusion was that postchoice factors rather than prechoice communication have the most direct effects on attitude and choice behavior.

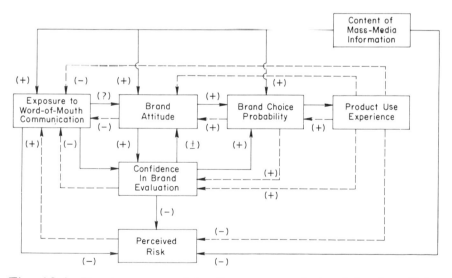

Fig. 12.4. Dominguez model of consumer choice behavior. (Price effects were left out. Also the effects of some lagged variables have been merged with the effects of current values of those variables.) Feedback effects from experience:– – – – –; other relations:——➤
Source: Luis V. Dominguez (1974, p.31).

Comment

The research stream on econometric modeling of individual behavior is still near its source. Work thus far must be classified as exploratory. Yet discussion of testing these models is not premature. In the absence of *a priori* information about the structural coefficients, estimation of a general model provides no test of the *a priori* model since any finding is accepted. Moreover, many different models may be consistent with a given set of observations. This is a problem of observational equivalence. Thus we first want to consider only those alternative models which can be derived from competing theories. Next, so that we might discriminate among these alternative models, we want to identify those situations in which the models yield different predictions. The concept of predictive testing is appropriate for all studies.[6]

Russ (1974) raises an interesting issue. He argues that our models of buyer behavior still treat the buyer as a "black box." On the whole, these models do not represent how information enters the awareness of the buyer, how attitudes are formed, how alternatives are evaluated. That is, they do not model process. Russ reaches the opinion that econometric models can not contribute to the understanding of buyer information processing. Despite his pessimism, we think that if for whatever reason the focus of a study is on individual or household behavior, theories will necessarily take the form of econometric models, but that this will require a good deal of work on both conceptual and measurement problems. The simultaneous attitude-belief model of Beckwith and Lehmann (1975) is one step in this direction.

ECONOMETRICS AND MARKETING SCIENCE

We have seen how econometric models of marketing systems lead to empirical decision models relevant to marketing decision making. We have also seen how econometric modeling is a general procedure for developing and testing theories of marketing response. Thus, far from being a fad of multivariate analysis, econometric research in marketing is an enduring methodology appropriate to both marketing theory and to marketing practice.

In our opinion, by applying the same standard by which other sciences are defined, there are today two possible fundamental aspects to marketing behavior. The first is the idea of sales response and the second is the notion of brand choice, and these are related by aggregation. A sales response function relates an aggregate pattern of human choice to the variation of controllable (marketing) factors. Although the idea of a response function is not new to human behavior, the nature of the variables and response is unique. Only in areas such as public opinion or voting behavior do similar mechanisms occur, and these may be a subset of a broadened definition of marketing. Economics, of course, deals with demand at individual and aggregate (market) levels, but traditional economic theory deals with only the price variable and so, in a sense, demand is a special case of sales response. Since sales response functions are the central feature of marketing systems and of marketing decision models, this book is directly related to this interpretation of a marketing science.

The phenomenon of brand choice is the second possible basis for defining a marketing science. Brand choice describes a situation of recurring human choice among a (usually large) set of alternatives (product or brands). Although human choice is a proper occupation of behavioral scientists, the special nature of recurring choice among many alternatives seems to make this process unique. If this is also a fundamental aspect of marketing behavior, it is because of the focus on choice and not on consumer behavior per se. In our view, all of the studies of consumer behavior except those seeking to directly describe and explain brand choice are more appropriately considered as applied behavioral science. Concepts such as preferences and attitudes, for example, are not unique to marketing. If fundamental findings are made about these constructs, they are contributions to psychology and not to marketing science. Using the criterion of elementary behavior, only brand choice seems to survive at the individual level.

As we have noted, sales response and brand choice are related through aggregation, although the relationship is yet unclear. Our dichotomy of marketing science, then, may be simply a state-of-the-art conception. In this book, for example, we discussed consumer behavior and executive behavior through the unifying concept of marketing systems. The idea of a marketing system (as it is used in the text) is also a candidate for defining marketing science, but the elementary processes are clearly sales response and brand choice. Executive behavior is relevant to the understanding of this process because it determines the pattern of marketing factors (stimuli), but executive decision making itself is not part of marketing science.

If we consider that a marketing science can be built from (1) the definition of elementary units of marketing behavior, (2) the empirical knowledge of fundamental relationships, and (3) the theoretical explanation of marketing phenomena, then it should be apparent that econometric applications are virtually assured. We would no more expect econometric modeling to lose its relevance for marketing research than we would expect empirical econometrics to disappear from economic study. The fact is that economic generalizations, the empirical knowledge of the field, have been and will continue to be established by just this method.

The method we have been dealing with is, in the final analysis, simply a method for measuring relationships. Whether these relationships come from experimental or nonexperimental data makes no difference; the methods are exactly the same. Both marketing as a profession and marketing as a science are concerned with the relationships among marketing variables. Hence, neither can be unconcerned with econometric research.

FOOTNOTES

[1] The model deviates from Theil's notation in that it is written as $\Gamma Y + BX = E$.

[2] In another study by the Columbia group [Farley, Howard, and Lehmann (1974)], data in an Argentine test market were collected at three points in time. However, their simultaneous equation model was still static. Separate estimates of the parameters of the model were obtained for each time period. In another report on this study, they did report on the cross-lagged correlations among variables [Lehmann, O'Brien, Farley, and Howard (1974)].

[3] As we have noted previously in Chap. 5, and as Lutz and Resek (1972) have reminded marketing researchers, the statistical properties of most multiple equation systems are not known.

[4] Identification is discussed in detail in Chap. 3.

[5] Hunt and Pappas confuse matters by introducing an atheoretical model, HAPPISIMM. More importantly, they claim to provide an example of their "crucial test." However, in this illustration, the key equation in their Model II is *unidentified*!

[6] Also see the discussion in Lehmann, Farley, and Howard (1971).

[7] Dominguez in a personal communication has indicated the strengths and weaknesses of the econometric approach relative to the information processing approach. Look for a publication on this important subject from him.

REFERENCES

Aaker, David A. "The New-Trier Stochastic Model of Brand Choice," *Management Science*, **17** (April 1971), 435-450.

_____. "Toward a Normative Model of Promotional Decision Making," *Management Science*, **19** (February 1973), 593-603.

_____. "ADMOD: An Advertising Decision Model," *Journal of Marketing Research*, **12** (February 1975), 37-45.

_____, and George S. Day. "A Recursive Model of Communication Processes," in David A. Aaker, ed., *Multivariate Analysis in Marketing: Theory and Application*. Belmont, California: Wadsworth, 1971, 101-114.

Allen, Stephen A., III. "Corporate-Divisional Relationship in Highly Diversified Firms," in Jay W. Lorsch and Paul R. Lawrence, eds., *Studies in Organizational Design*. Homewood, Ill.: Richard D. Irwin, 1970, 16-35.

Amstutz, Arnold. *Computer Simulation of Competitive Market Response*. Cambridge, Mass.: M.I.T. Press, 1967.

Assael, Henry, and George S. Day. "Attitude and Awareness as Predictors of Market Share," *Journal of Advertising Research*, **8** (December 1968), 3-10.

Balderston, F. E., and A. C. Hoggatt. *Simulation of Market Processes*. Berkeley, Calif.: Institute of Business and Economic Research, University of California, 1962.

Ball, R. J., and R. Agarwala. "An Econometric Analysis of the Effects of Generic Advertising on the Demand for Tea in the U.K.," *British Journal of Marketing*, **4** (Winter 1969), 202-217.

Banks, Seymour. "Some Correlates of Coffee and Cleanser Brand Shares," *Journal of Advertising Research*, **1** (June 1961), 22-28.

Barry, Christopher B., and Albert R. Wildt. "Model Selection and Marketing Decisions: A Bayesian Approach," working paper, College of Business Administration, University of Florida, May 1975.

Basmann, Robert L. "The Causal Interpretation of Non-Triangular Systems of Economic Relationships," *Econometrica*, **31** (July 1963), 439-448.

_____. "Remarks Concerning the Application of Exact Finite Sample Distribution Functions of GCL Estimators in Econometric Statistical Inference," *Journal of the American Statistical Association*, **58** (December 1963), 943-976.

————. "On Predictive Testing a Simultaneous Equation Model: The Retail Market for Food in the U.S." Institute Paper No. 78, Krannert Graduate School of Industrial Administration, Purdue University, 1964.

————. "On the Application of Identifiability Test Statistic in Predictive Testing of Explanatory Economic Models," *The Indian Economic Journal,* **13** (1965), 387-423.

————. "A Note on the Statistical Testability of 'Explicit Causal Chains' Against the Class of 'Interdependent' Models," *The Journal of The American Statistical Association,* **60** (December 1965), 1080-1093.

————. "Hypothesis Formulation in Quantitative Economics: A Contribution to Demand Analysis," in James P. Quirk and Arvid M. Zarley (eds.). *Papers in Quantitative Economics.* Lawrence, Kansas: University Press of Kansas, 1968, 143-198.

Bass, Frank M. "A Dynamic Model of Market Share and Sales Behavior," *Proceedings.* Winter Conference, American Marketing Association, 1963, 263-276.

————. "A Simultaneous Equation Regression Study of Advertising and Sales of Cigarettes," *Journal of Marketing Research,* **6** (August 1969), 291-300.

————. "Application of Regression Models in Marketing: Testing Versus Forecasting," Institute Paper No. 265, Krannert Graduate School of Industrial Administration, Purdue University, December 1969.

————. "Testing vs. Estimation in Simultaneous-Equation Regression Models," *Journal of Marketing Research,* **8** (August 1971), 388-389.

————. "The Theory of Stochastic Preference and Brand Switching" *Journal of Marketing Research,* **11** (February 1974), 1-20.

————, and Darral G. Clarke. "Testing Distributed Lag Models of Advertising Effect," *Journal of Marketing Research,* **9** (August 1972), 298-308.

————, Abel Jeuland and Gordon P. Wright. "Equilibrium Stochastic Choice and Market Penetration Theories: Derivations and Comparisons," *Management Science* (1976), in press.

————, and Leonard J. Parsons. "A Simultaneous Equation Regression Analysis of Sales and Advertising," *Applied Economics* **1** (May 1969), 103-124.

————. "Regression Methods with Simultaneous Equations," in Robert Ferber, ed., *Handbook of Marketing Research.* New York: McGraw-Hill, 1974, 2.427-2.441.

————, and Dick R. Wittink. "Pooling Issues and Methods in Regression Analysis with Examples in Marketing Research, *Journal of Marketing Research,* **12** (November 1975), 414-425.

Baumol, William J. *Economic Theory and Operations Analysis* (2nd Edition). Englewood Cliffs, N.J.: Prentice-Hall, 1965.

Bavelas, Alex. "Communication Patterns in Task-Oriented Groups," *Journal of the Acoustical Society of America,* **22** (1950), 725-730.

Beckwith, Neil E. "Multivariate Analysis of Sales Responses of Competing Brands to Advertising," *Journal of Marketing Research,* **9** (May 1972), 168-176.

―――――. "Analysis of the Responses of Competing Brands to Advertising Using Seasonal Models," *Combined Proceedings.* Spring and Fall Conferences, American Marketing Association, 1972, 505-510.

―――――. "Concerning the Logical Consistency of Multivariate Market Share Models," *Journal of Marketing Research,* **10** (August 1973), 341-344.

―――――. "Comparison of Coefficients for Monthly and Annual Models of Cumulative Advertising Effects," working paper, Columbia University, no date.

―――――. "Regression Estimation of the Time-Varying Effectiveness of Advertising, With a Test of Equal Coefficients in Several Regressions," working paper, Columbia University, no date.

―――――, and Donald R. Lehmann. "The Importance of Halo Effects in Multi-Attribute Models," *Journal of Marketing Research,* **12** (August 1975), 265-275.

Bell, David E., Ralph E. Keeney and John D. C. Little. "A Market Share Theorem," *Journal of Marketing Research,* **12** (May 1975), 136-141.

Belsley, David A. "On the Determination of Systematic Parameter Variation in the Linear Regression Model," *Annals of Economic and Social Measurement,* **2** (October 1973), 487-494.

Berg, Sanford V., ed. "Time-Varying Parameters," *Annals of Economic and Social Measurement,* **2** (October 1973).

Bernhardt, Irwin, and Kenneth D. MacKenzie. "Some Problems in Using Diffusion Models for New Products," *Management Science,* **19** (October 1972), 187-200.

Blalock, Hubert M., Jr. *Causal Inferences in Nonexperimental Research.* Chapel Hill, N.C.: University of North Carolina Press, 1964.

Bond, Richard O., and David B. Montgomery. "**MULCAN MOD I,**" Technical Report, Marketing Science Institute, September 1970.

Broadbent, S.R., and S. Segnit. "Response Functions in Media Planning," in *Ten Years of Advertising Media Research.* London: The Thomson Organization, 1972.

Brunner, Karl. "Review of *Econometric Models of Cyclical Behavior,*" *Journal of Economic Literature,* **11** (September 1973), 926-933.

Bultez, Alain V., and Philippe A. Naert. "Consistent Sum-Constrained Models," *Journal of the American Statistical Association,* **70** (September 1975), 529-535.

Buzzell, Robert D. "Predicting Short-Term Changes in Market Share as a Function of Advertising Strategy," *Journal of Marketing Research,* 1 (August 1964), 27-31.

Campbell, Donald T. "From Description to Experimentation: Interpreting Trends as Quasi-Experiments," in C. W. Harris, ed., *Problems in Measuring Change.* Madison, Wisc.: University of Wisconsin Press, 1962, 212-242.

Carman, James M. "Consumer Panels," in Robert Ferber, ed., *Handbook of Marketing Research.* New York: McGraw-Hill, 1974, 2.200-2.216.

Cartwright, Dorwin, and Alvin Zander. *Group Dynamics: Research and Theory.* New York: Harper & Row, 1968.

Charnes, A., J.K. Devoe and D.B. Learner. "**DEMON**: Decision Mapping Via Optimum Go-No Networks—A Model for Marketing New Products," *Management Science,* 12 (July 1960), 865-887.

Chow, Gregory. "Tests of Equality Between Sets of Coefficients in Two Linear Regressions," *Econometrica,* 28 (July 1960), 591-605.

Chou, Ya-lun. *Statistical Analysis.* New York: Holt, Rinehart and Winston, 1969.

Christ, Carl. *Econometric Models and Methods.* New York: John Wiley and Sons, 1966.

Churchman, C. West, Russell L. Ackoff and E. Leonard Arnoff. *Introduction to Operations Research.* New York: John Wiley, 1957.

Clarke, Darral G. "An Empirical Investigation of Advertising Competition," unpublished doctoral dissertation, Purdue University, 1972.

————. "Sales-Advertising Cross-Elasticities and Advertising Competition" *Journal of Marketing Research,* 10 (August 1973), 250-261.

————. "Econometric Measurement of the Duration of the Advertising Effect on Sales," Working Paper No. 75-106, Marketing Science Institute, April 1975.

————, and John M. McCann. "Measuring the Cumulative Effects of Advertising: A Reappraisal," *Combined Proceedings.* Spring and Fall Conferences, American Marketing Association, 1973, 135-139.

Coch, L., and J.R.P. French. "Overcoming Resistance to Change," *Human Relations,* (1948), 512-532.

Cooley, Thomas F., and Edward C. Prescott, "Varying Parameter Regression: A Theory and Some Applications," *Annals of Economic and Social Measurement,* 2 (October 1973), 463-473.

Cowling, Keith. "Optimality in Firms' Advertising Policies: An Empirical Analysis," Paper No. 20, Centre for Industrial Economic and Business Research, University of Warwick, July 1972.

Cunnyngham, Jon. "Econometric Model Construction and Predictive Testing," in Karl Brunner, ed., *Problems and Issues in Current Econometric Practice*. Columbus, Ohio: The Ohio State University Press, 1972, 238-261.

D'Agostino, Ralph B. "An Omnibus Test of Normality for Moderate and Large Size Samples," *Biometrika*, **58**, 2(1971), 341-348.

Dalrymple, Douglas J., and George H. Haines, Jr. "A Study of the Predictive Ability of Market Period Demand-Supply Relations for a Firm Selling Fashion Products," *Applied Economics*, **1** (January 1970), 277-285.

Dewey, Donald. *The Theory of Imperfect Competition: A Radical Reconstruction*. New York: Columbia University Press, 1969.

Dhrymes, Phoebus J. *Distributed Lags: Problems of Estimation and Formulation*. San Francisco: Holden-Day, 1971.

_____, et al. "Criteria For Evaluation of Econometric Models," *Journal of Economic and Social Measurement*, **1** (July 1972), 291-324.

Dominguez, Luis V. "An Experimental Analysis of the Process of Buyer Behavior," unpublished doctoral dissertation, Northwestern University, 1971.

_____. "Determining the Nature of the Process of Household Decision Making: An Experimental Gaming Approach," *Combined Proceedings*. Spring and Fall Conferences, American Marketing Association, 1972, 349-354.

_____. "Experimentation, Market Performance, and Econometric Model Building: Toward a Unified Approach," *Combined Proceedings*. Spring and Fall Conferences, American Marketing Association, 1973, 360-366.

_____. "Econometric Analysis of Consumer Information Processing: Emerging Conclusions and Conceptual and Methodological Considerations," in G. David Hughes and Michael L. Ray, eds., *Buyer/Consumer Information Processing*. Chapel Hill: The University of North Carolina Press, 1974, 24-50.

_____, and Philip C. Burger. "An Empirical Test of the Process of Buyer Behavior," *Combined Proceedings*. Spring and Fall Conferences, American Marketing Association, 1971, 391-396.

_____, and Albert L. Page. "A Note on a Simultaneous-Equation Regression Study of Advertising and Sales of Cigarettes," *Journal of Marketing Research*, **8** (August 1971), 386-389.

Dorfman, Robert, and Peter O. Steiner. "Optimal Advertising and Optimal Quality," *American Economic Review*, **44** (December 1954), 826-836.

Doyle, Peter. "Economic Aspects of Advertising: A Survey," *Economic Journal*, (1968), 570-599.

Dyckman, Thomas R. "Management Implementation of Scientific Research: An Attitudinal Study," *Management Science*, **13** (June 1967), 612-620.

Durbin, J. "Testing for Serial Correlation in Least Squares Regression When

Some of the Regressors Are Lagged Variables," *Econometrica*, **38** (May 1970), 410-421.

Ebbeler, Donald H. "On the Maximum $\bar{R}^2$ Choice Criterion," Claremont Economic Paper Number 113, The Claremont Colleges, August 1974.

Ehrenberg, A. S. C. *Repeat-Buying: Theory and Applications*. Amsterdam: North-Holland Publishing Company, 1972.

Elliot, J. W. "A Comparison of Models of Marketing Investment," *Quarterly Review of Economics and Business*, **11** (Spring 1971), 53-70.

Engel, James F., David T. Kollat and Roger D. Blackwell. *Consumer Behavior* (2nd Edition). New York: Holt, Rinehart and Winston, 1973.

Farley, John U., and Melvin J. Hinich. "A Test for a Shifting Slope Coefficient in a Linear Model," *Journal of the American Statistical Association*, **65** (September 1970), 1320-1329.

————, John A. Howard, and Donald R. Lehmann. "Evaluating Test Market Results: Buyer Behavior Analysis in Argentina," *Journal of Business Administration*, **5** (Spring 1974), 69-88.

————, and H. J. Leavitt. "A Model of the Distribution of Branded Products in Jamaica," *Journal of Marketing Research*, **5** (November 1968), 362-369.

————, and L. Winston Ring. "An Empirical Test of the Howard-Sheth Model of Buyer Behavior," *Journal of Marketing Research*, **7** (November 1970), 427-438.

————. "On L and R and HAPPISIMM," *Journal of Marketing Research*, **9** (August 1972), 349-353.

Farrar, Donald E., and Robert R. Glauber. "Multicollinearity in Regression Analysis: The Problem Revisted," *The Review of Economics and Statistics*, **49** (February 1967), 92-107.

Fishbein, M., ed. *Readings in Attitude Theory and Measurement*. New York: John Wiley, 1967.

Fisher, Franklin M. *The Identification Problem*. New York: McGraw-Hill, 1966.

————. "Tests of Equality Between Sets of Coefficients in Two Linear Regressions: An Expository Note," *Econometrica*, **38** (March 1970), 361-366.

Fisher, Walter D. *Clustering and Aggregation in Economics*. Baltimore: The John Hopkins Press, 1969.

Frank, Ronald E., and William F. Massy. "Effects of Short-Term Promotional Strategy in Selected Market Segments," in Patrick J. Robinson, ed., *Promotional Decisions Using Mathematical Models*. Boston: Allyn and Bacon, 1967, 147-199.

————. *An Econometric Approach to a Marketing Decision Model*. Cambridge, Massachusetts: The MIT Press, 1971.

Friedman, Lawrence. "Game-Theory Models in the Allocation of Advertising Expenditures," *Operations Research,* **6** (September-October 1958), 699-709.

Gaver, Kenneth M., and Martin S. Geisel. "Discriminating Among Alternative Models: Bayesian and Non-Bayesian Methods," In Paul Zarembka, ed., *Frontiers in Econometrics.* New York: Academic Press, 1974, 13-48.

Gensch, Dennis H. "A Computer Simulation Model for Selecting Advertising Schedules," *Journal of Marketing Research,* **6** (May 1969), 203-214.

Godfrey, L. G., and D. S. Poskitt. "Testing the Restrictions of the Almon Lag Technique," *Journal of the American Statistical Association,* **70** (March 1975), 105-108.

Goldberg, Samuel. *Introduction to Difference Equations* (Science Edition).New York: John Wiley, 1961.

Goldberger, Arthur S. *Econometric Theory.* New York: John Wiley, 1964.

————. "Unobservable Variables in Econometrics," in Paul Zarembka, ed., *Frontiers in Econometrics.* New York: Academic Press, 1974, 193-213.

Goldfeld, Stephen M., and Richard E. Quandt. "Some Tests for Homoscedasticity," *Journal of the American Statistical Association,* **60** (June 1965), 539-547.

————. *Nonlinear Methods in Econometrics.* Amsterdam: North Holland Publishing Company, 1972.

Gould, John P. "Diffusion Processes and Optimal Advertising Policy," in E. Phelps et al., *Micro Economic Foundation of Unemployment and Inflation Theory.* New York: W. W. Norton, 1970, 338-368.

Green, H. A. J. *Aggregation in Economic Analysis.* Princeton, N.J.: Princeton University Press, 1964.

Green, Paul E., and Vithala R. Rao. *Applied Multidimensional Scaling: A Comparison of Approaches and Algorithms.* New York: Holt, Rinehart and Winston, 1972.

————, and Donald S. Tull. *Research for Marketing Decisions* (3rd Edition). Englewood Cliffs, N.J.: Prentice-Hall, 1975.

Griliches, Zvi. "Distributed Lags: A Survey," *Econometrica,* **35** (January 1967), 16-49.

————. "Errors in Variables and Other Unobservables," *Econometrica,* **42** (November 1974), 971-998.

Guetzkow, Harold, Philip Kotler and Randall L. Schultz, eds. *Simulation in Social and Administrative Science.* Englewood Cliffs, N.J.: Prentice-Hall, 1972.

Guilford, J. P. *Psychometric Methods.* New York: McGraw-Hill, 1954.

Gujarati, Damodar. "Use of Dummy Variables in Testing for Equality Between

Sets of Coefficients in Linear Regression: A Generalization," *American Statistician,* **24** (December 1970), 18-22.

Haines, George H. "A Theory of Market Behavior After Innovation," *Management Science,* **10** (July 1964), 634-658.

―――. *Consumer Behavior: Learning Models of Purchasing.* New York: The Free Press, 1969.

Hanson, Norwood Russell. *Patterns of Discovery: An Inquiry into the Conceptual Foundations of Science.* Cambridge: The University Press, 1961.

Herniter, Jerome D. "A Probabilistic Market Model of Purchase Timing and Brand Selection," *Management Science,* **18** (December 1971), 102-113.

―――. "An Entropy Model of Brand Purchase Behavior," *Journal of Marketing Research,* **10** (November 1973), 361-375.

―――, and Victor Cook. "A Multidimensional Stochastic Model of Consumer Purchase Behavior," Report No. 7024, Center for Mathematical Studies in Business and Economics, University of Chicago, June 1970.

Hoerl, Arthur E., and Robert W. Kennard. "Ridge Regression: Biased Estimation for Nonorthogonal Problems," *Technometrics,* **12** (February 1970), 55-67.

―――. "Ridge Regression: Applications to Nonorthogonal Problems," *Technometrics,* **12** (February 1970) 69-82.

Hood, Wm. C., and Tjalling C. Koopmans, eds. *Studies in Econometric Method.* New York: John Wiley, 1953.

Hopkins, Terrence K. *The Exercise of Influence in Small Groups.* Totowa, N.J.: Redminster Press, 1964.

Horsky, Dan. "A Theoretical and Empirical Analysis of the Optimal Advertising Strategy," unpublished doctoral dissertation, Purdue University, 1974.

Horst, Paul. *Psychological Measurement and Prediction.* Belmont, Calif.: Wadsworth, 1966.

Houston, Franklin S., and Doyle L. Weiss. "An Analysis of Competitive Market Behavior," *Journal of Marketing Research,* **11** (May 1974), 151-155.

―――. "Cumulative Advertising Effects: The Role of Serial Correlation," *Decision Science,* **6** July 1975), 471-481.

―――, ―――, and Lawrence W. Westermeyer. "Integrative Marketing Analysis: A Comparison of Econometric Methods and Multidimensional Scaling Techniques," paper presented at the Southern Marketing Association Meeting, November 1974.

Howard, John A. *Marketing: Executive and Buyer Behavior.* New York: Columbia University Press, 1963.

―――, and William M. Morgenroth, "Information Processing Model of Executive Decision," *Management Science,* **14** (March 1968), 416-428.

_____, and Jagdish N. Sheth. *The Theory of Buyer Behavior.* New York: John Wiley, 1969.

Hulbert, James, John U. Farley and John A. Howard. "Information Processing and Decision Making in Marketing Organizations," *Journal of Marketing Research,* **9** (February 1972), 75-77.

_____, and Donald R. Lehmann. "Assessing the Importance of the Sources of Error in Structured Survey Data," in John U. Farley and John A. Howard, eds., *Control of "Error" in Market Research Data.* Lexington, Massachusetts: Lexington Books, 1975, 81-107.

Hunt, Shelby D., and James L. Pappas. "A Crucial Test for the Howard-Sheth Model of Buyer Behavior," *Journal of Marketing Research,* **9** (August 1972), 346-348.

Imhof, J. P. "Computing the Distribution of Quadratic Forms in Normal Variables," *Biometrika,* **48** (1961), 419-426.

Jastram, Roy W. "A Treatment of Distributed Lags in the Theory of Advertising Expenditure," *Journal of Marketing,* **20** (July 1955), 36-46.

Johansson, Johny K. "A Generalized Logistic Function with an Application to the Effect of Advertising," *Journal of the American Statistical Association,* **68** (December 1973), 824-827.

_____. "Price-Quantity Relationships Varying Across Brands and Over Time," paper presented at the ORSA/TIMS National Meeting, San Juan, Puerto Rico, October 1974.

_____. "A User's Introduction to Econometric Techniques for Analyzing Panel Data," *Combined Proceedings.* Spring and Fall Conferences, American Marketing Association, 1975, 112-116.

_____. "Estimating the Effects of Advertising Using Polynomial Distributed Lags," working paper, Graduate School of Business Administration, University of Washington, no date.

Johnston, J. *Econometric Methods* (2nd Edition). New York: McGraw-Hill, 1972.

Jorgenson, Dale W. "Rational Distributed Lag Functions," *Econometrica,* **32** (January 1966), 135-149.

Kadiyala, Koteswara Rao. "Efficient Estimation of Partially Identified Systems of Equations," Institute Paper No. 506, Krannert Graduate School of Industrial Administration, Purdue University, March 1975.

Kassarjian, Harold H., and Thomas S. Robertson, eds. *Perspectives in Consumer Behavior* (Revised). Glenview, Illinois: Scott, Foresman, 1973.

Kemeny, John G. *A Philosopher Looks at Science.* New York: Van Nostrand Reinhold, 1959.

Kendall, Maurice, and Alan Stuart. *The Advanced Theory of Statistics: Volume 2* (3rd Edition). New York: Hafner, 1973.

Koerts, J., and A. P. J. Abrahamse. *On the Theory and Application of the General Linear Model*. Rotterdam: Rotterdam University Press, 1969.

Kohn, Meir G., and Yakir Plessner. "An Applicable Model of Optimal Marketing Policy," *Operations Research,* **21** (March-April 1973), 401-412.

Kotler, Philip. "A Design for the Firm's Marketing Nerve Center," *Business Horizons,* **9** (Fall 1966), 63-74.

————. *Marketing Decision Making: A Model Building Approach*. New York: Holt, Rinehart and Winston, 1971.

————. *Marketing for Nonprofit Organizations*. Englewood Cliffs, N.J.: Prentice-Hall, 1975.

————, and Sidney J. Levy. "Broadening the Concept of Marketing," *Journal of Marketing,* **33** (January 1969), 10-15.

————, and Randall L. Schultz. "Marketing Simulations: Review and Prospects," *Journal of Business,* **43** (July 1970), 237-295.

————. "Marketing System Simulation" in Harold Guetzkow, Philip Kotler and Randall L. Schultz, eds., *Simulation in Social and Administrative Science*. Englewood Cliffs, N.J.: Prentice-Hall, 1972, 481-549.

————, and Gerald Zaltman. "Social Marketing: An Approach to Planned Social Change," *Journal of Marketing,* **35** (July 1971), 3-12.

Koyck, L. M. *Distributed Lags and Investment Analysis*. Amsterdam: North-Holland Publishing Company, 1954.

Kuehn, Alfred A., and Michael J. Hamburger. "A Heuristic Program for Locating Warehouses," *Management Science,* **9** (July 1963), 643-666.

————, Timothy W. McGuire and Doyle L. Weiss. "Measuring the Effectiveness of Advertising," *Proceedings.* Fall Conference, American Marketing Association, 1966, 185-194.

————, and Albert C. Rohloff. "Fitting Models to Aggregate Data," *Journal of Advertising Research,* **7** (March 1967), 43-47.

————, and Doyle L. Weiss. "Marketing Analysis Training Exercise," *Behavioral Science,* **10** (January 1965), 51-67.

Kumar, T. Krishna. "Multicollinearity in Regression Analysis," *Review of Economics and Statistics,* **57** (August 1975), 365-336.

Ladd, D, E. "Report on a Group's Reaction to 'The Researcher and the Manager: A Dialectic of Implementation'," *Management Science,* **12** (October 1965), 24-25.

Lambin, Jean-Jacques. "Measuring the Profitability of Advertising: An Empirical Study," *Journal of Industrial Economics,* **17** (April 1969), 86-103.

————. "Optimal Allocation of Competitive Marketing Efforts: An Empirical Study, *Journal of Business,* **43** (October 1970), 468-484.

————. "Advertising and Competitive Behavior: A Case Study," *Applied Economics,* **2** (January 1971), 231-251.

————. "A Computer On-Line Marketing Mix Model" *Journal of Marketing Research,* 9 (May 1972), 119-126.

————. "Is Gasoline Advertising Justified?" *Journal of Business,* 45 (October 1972), 585-619.

. "Advertising, Competition, and Market Conduct in Oligopoly Over Time," Paper No. 17-0773, Center of Socio-Economic Studies in Advertising and Marketing, Catholic University of Louvain, 1975.

————, Philippe A. Naert, and Alain Bultez, "Optimal Marketing Behavior in Oligopoly," *European Economic Review,* 6 (1975), 105-128.

Laroche, Michael. "Is the Durbin-Watson Test a Useful Tool for Marketing Researchers?" *Combined Proceedings.* Spring and Fall Conferences, American Marketing Association, 1975, 137-140.

Larréché, Jean-Claude. "Managers and Models: A Search for a Better Match," unpublished doctoral dissertation, Stanford University, 1974.

Lavidge, Robert J., and Gary A. Steiner. "A Model for Predictive Measurement of Advertising Effectiveness," *Journal of Marketing,* 25 (October 1961), 59-62.

Lawrence, Paul R., and Jay W. Lorsch. *Organization and Environment.* Boston: Division of Research, Graduate School of Business Administration, Harvard University, 1967.

————. *Developing Organizations: Diagnosis and Action.* Reading, Mass.: Addison-Wesley, 1969.

Leavitt, H. J. "Some Effects of Certain Communication Patterns on Group Performance," *Journal of Abnormal and Social Psychology,* 46 (1951), 38-50.

————. Terrence V. O'Brien, John U. Farley, and John A. Howard, "Some Empirical Contributions to Buyer Behavior Theory," *Consumer Research* 1 (December 1974), 43-55.

Lehmann, Donald R., John U. Farley and John A. Howard. "Testing of Buyer Behavior Models," *Proceedings.* Association for Consumer Research, 1971, 232-242.

Little, John D. C. "A Model of Adaptive Control of Promotional Spending," *Operations Research,* 14 (November-December 1966), 1075-1097.

————. "Model and Managers: The Concept of a Decision Calculus," *Management Science,* 16 (April 1970), 466-485.

————. "BRANDAID: A Marketing Mix Model, Part 1: Structure," *Operations Research,* 23 (July-August 1975), 628-655.

————. "BRANDAID: A Marketing Mix Model, Part 2: Implementation, Calibration, and Case Study," *Operations Research,* 23 (July-August 1975), 656-673.

————, and Leonard M. Lodish. "A Media Planning Calculus," *Operations Research,* **17** (January-February 1969), 1-35.

Little, T. E., and Randall L. Schultz. "A Managerial Model of Competitive Behavior," paper presented at the Joint National Meeting, ORSA and TIMS, Chicago, April 1975.

Lodish, Leonard M. "CALLPLAN: An Interactive Salesman's Call Planning System," *Management Science,* **18** (December 1971), 25-40.

Lucas, Henry C., Jr. *The Implementation of Computer-Based Models.* New York: National Association of Accountants, 1976.

Lutz, Richard J., and Robert W. Resek. "More on Testing the Howard-Sheth Model of Buyer Behavior," *Journal of Marketing Research,* **9** (August 1972), 344-345.

MacLachlan, Douglas L. "A Model of Intermediate Market Response," *Journal of Marketing Research,* **9** (November 1972), 378-384.

Maddala, G. S. "Generalized Least Squares with an Estimated Variance Covariance Matrix" *Econometrica,* **39** (January 1971), 23-33.

————. "The Use of Variance Components Models in Pooling Cross Section and Time Series Data," *Econometrica,* **39** (March 1971), 341-382.

————. "Ridge Estimators for Distributed Lag Models," Working Paper No. 69, National Bureau of Economic Research, October 1974.

Manley, John H. "A Measure of the Probability of Success for OR/MS Projects Due to Client Behavior," unpublished doctoral dissertation, University of Pittsburgh, 1971.

Mann, Don H. "Optimal Advertising Stock Models Incorporating Modal-Delayed Distributed Lags," unpublished doctoral dissertation, University of California, Los Angeles, 1973.

————. "Optimal Theoretic Advertising Stock Models: A Generalization Incorporating the Effects of Delayed Response from Promotional Expenditure," *Management Science,* **21** (March 1975), 823-832.

Margenau, Henry. *The Nature of Physical Reality.* New York: McGraw-Hill, 1950.

Martin, Warren S. "The Effect of Scaling on the Correlation Coefficient: A Test of Validity," *Journal of Marketing Research,* **10** (August 1973), 316-318.

Massy, William F. "Forecasting the Demand for New Convenience Products," *Journal of Marketing Research,* **6** (November 1969), 405-412.

————, David B. Montgomery, and Donald G. Morrison. *Stochastic Models of Buyer Behavior.* Cambridge, Mass.: M.I.T. Press, 1970.

McCann, John M. "Comparison of Methods of Pooling Time-Series and Cross-Section Data," *Combined Proceedings.* Spring and Fall Conferences, American Marketing Association, 1974, 167-171.

_____. "Market Segment Response to the Marketing Decision Variables," *Journal of Marketing Research,* **11** (November 1974), 399-412.

McGee, Victor E., and Willard T. Carleton. "Piecewise Regression," *Journal of the American Statistical Association,* **65**(September 1970), 1109-1124.

McGuinness, A.J. "Advertising, Price, and Commodity Demand," Paper No. 57, Center for Industrial Economic and Business Research, University of Warwick, December 1974.

McGuire, Timothy. "Measuring and Testing Advertising Effectiveness with Split-Cable TV Panel Data," *Proceedings.* Business and Economic Statistics Section, American Statistical Association, 1972, 376-381.

_____, John U. Farley, Robert E. Lucas and L. Winston Ring. "Estimation and Inference for Linear Models in Which Subsets of the Dependent Variable are Constrained," *Journal of the American Statistical Society,* **63** (December 1968), 1201-1213.

_____, and Doyle L. Weiss. "Logically Consistent Market Share Models–II," working paper, Graduate School of Industrial Administration, Carnegie-Mellon University, June 1975.

_____, _____, and Franklin S. Houston. "The Multinomial Logit as a Logically Consistent Market Share Model," working paper, University of British Columbia, May 1975.

Meissner, F. "Sales and Advertising of Lettuce," *Journal of Advertising Research,* **1** (March 1961), 1-10.

Melrose, Kendrick B. "An Empirical Study on Optimizing Advertising Policy," *Journal of Business,* **42** (July 1969), 282-292.

Metfessel, M. "A Proposal for Quantitative Reporting of Comparative Judgements," *Journal of Psychology,* **24** (1947), 229-235.

Mickwitz, Gosta. *Marketing and Competition.* Helsingfors, Finland: Central-tryckeriet, 1959.

Montgomery, David B., ed. "Marketing Management Models," *Management Science,* **18** (December 1971), Part II.

_____, and Donald G. Morrison. "A Note on Adjusting R^2," *Journal of Finance,* **28** (February 1973), 1009-1013.

_____, and Alvin J. Silk. "Estimating Dynamic Effects of Market Communications Expenditures," *Management Science,* **18** (June 1972), 485-501.

_____, _____, and Carlos E. Zaragoza, "A Multiple-Product Sales Force Allocation Model," *Management Science,* **18** (December 1971), 3-24.

_____, and Glen L. Urban. *Management Science in Marketing.* Englewood Cliffs, N.J.: Prentice-Hall, 1969.

Moriarity, Mark. "Cross-Sectional, Time-Series Issues in the Analysis of Marketing Decision Variables," *Journal of Marketing Research,* **12** (May 1975), 142-150.

Morris, William T. "On the Art of Modeling," in Ralph Stogdill, ed., *The Process of Model-Building in the Behavioral Sciences.* Columbus, Ohio: The Ohio State University Press, 1970, 76-93.

Morrison, Donald G. "Regressions With Discrete Dependent Variables: The Effect on R^2," *Journal of Marketing Research,* 9 (August 1972), 338-340.

————. "Reliability of Tests: A Technique Using the 'Regression to the Mean' Fallacy," *Journal of Marketing Research,* 10 (February 1973), 91-93.

————, and Donald J. Gluck. "Spurious Correlations That Result From 'Awareness vs. Usage' Type Regressions," *Journal of Marketing Research,* 7 (August 1970), 318-324.

Naert, Philippe A., and Alain Bultez. "Logically Consistent Market Share Models," *Journal of Marketing Research,* 10 (August 1973), 334-340.

Nakanishi, Masao. "Advertising and Promotion Effects on Consumer Response to New Products," *Journal of Marketing Research,* 10 (August 1973), 242-249.

————, and Lee G. Cooper. "Parameter Estimation for a Multiplicative Competitive Interaction Model—Least Squares Approach," *Journal of Marketing Research,* 11 (August 1974), 303-311.

Nerlove, Marc. "Further Evidence on the Estimation of Dynamic Economic Relations from a Time Series of Cross Sections," *Econometrica,* 39 (March 1971), 359-382.

————, and Kenneth Arrow. "Optimal Advertising Under Dynamic Conditions," *Economica,* 29 (May 1962), 129-142.

————, and F.V. Waugh. "Advertising Without Supply Control: Some Implications of a Study of the Advertising of Oranges," *Journal of Farm Sciences,* 43 (October 1961), 813-837.

Nicosia, Francesco M. *Consumer Decision Processes: Marketing and Advertising Implications.* Englewood Cliffs, N.J.: Prentice-Hall, 1966.

————, and Barr Rosenberg. "Substantive Modeling in Consumer Attitude Research: Some Practical Uses," in Russell I. Haley, ed., *Attitude Research in Transition.* Chicago: American Marketing Association, 1972, 213-247.

O'Hagan, John, and Brendan McCabe. "Tests for the Severity of Multicollinearity in Regression Analysis: A Comment," *Review of Economics and Statistics,* 57 (August 1975), 368-370.

Osgood, E.E., G.J. Suci and P.H. Tannenbaum. *The Measurement of Meaning.* Urbana, Ill.: University of Illinois Press, 1957.

Palda, Kristian S. "The Evaluation of Regression Results," *Proceedings.* Winter Conference, American Marketing Association, 1963, 279-290.

————. *The Measurement of Cumulative Advertising Effects.* Englewood Cliffs, N.J.: Prentice-Hall, 1964.

_____. "The Hypothesis of a Hierarchy of Effects: A Partial Evaluation," *Journal of Marketing Research,* 3 (February 1966), 13-24.

_____. "Contributions of Econometrics to Marketing Analysis—with Special Reference to Engel Curves," *Proceedings.* Fall Conference, American Marketing Association, 1966, 123-135.

_____, and Larry M. Blair. "A Moving Cross-Section Analysis of Demand for Toothpaste," *Journal of Marketing Research,* 7 (November 1970), 439-449.

Parks, Richard W. "Efficient Estimation of a System of Regression Equations When the Disturbances are Both Serially and Contemporaneously Correlated," *Journal of the American Statistical Association,* 62 (June 1967), 500-509.

Parsons, Leonard J. "Predictive Testing: A Simultaneous Equations Model of Sales and Advertising," unpublished doctoral dissertation, Purdue University, 1968.

_____. "The Hierarchy of Effects Controversy: A Research Design," First Place Award, American Marketing Association's Research Design Contest, 1971.

_____. "An Econometric Analysis of Advertising, Retail Availability, and Sales of a New Brand," *Management Science,* 20 (February 1974), 938-947.

_____. "The Product Life Cycle and Time-Varying Advertising Elasticities," *Journal of Marketing Research,* 12 (November 1975), 476-480.

_____. "A Rachet Model of Advertising Carryover Effects," *Journal of Marketing Research,* 13 (February 1976), 49-55.

_____, and Frank M. Bass. "Optimal Advertising Expenditure Implications of a Simultaneous-Equation Regression Analysis," *Operations Research,* 19 (May-June 1971), 822-831.

_____, and Walter A. Henry. "Testing Equivalence of Observed and Generated Time Series Data by Spectral Methods," *Journal of Marketing Research,* 9 (November 1972), 391-395.

_____, and Randall L. Schultz. "The Impact of Advertising on the Aggregate Consumption Function: I. Preliminary Results," paper presented at the European Meeting, Econometric Society, Oslo, Norway, August 1973.

Peles, Yoram. "Economics of Scale in Advertising Beer and Cigarettes," *Journal of Business,* 44 (January 1971), 32-37.

_____. "Rates of Amortization of Advertising Expenditures,'. *Journal of Political Economy,* 79 (September-October 1971), 1032-1058.

Poirier, Dale J. "Piecewise Regression Using Cubic Splines," *Journal of the American Statistical Association,* 68 (September 1973), 515-524.

Popper, Karl R. *The Logic of Scientific Discovery.* New York: Basic Books, 1961.

Preston, Lee E., and Norman R. Collins. *Studies in a Simulated Market*. Berkeley, Calif.: Institute of Business and Economic Research, University of California, 1966.

Quandt, Richard E. "Estimating Advertising Effectiveness: Some Pitfalls in Econometric Methods," *Journal of Marketing Research*, 1 (May 1964), 51-60.

Ramsey, James B. "Tests for Specification Errors in Classical Least-Squares Regression Analysis," *Journal of the Royal Statistical Society, Series B,* 21 (1969), 350-371.

_____. "Classical Model Selection Through Specification Error Tests," in Paul Zarembka, ed., *Frontiers in Econometrics*. New York: Academic Press, 1974, 13-48.

Rao, Ambar G. *Quantitative Theories in Advertising*. New York: John Wiley, 1970.

_____, and Peter B. Miller. "Advertising/Sales Response Functions," *Journal of Advertising Research,* 15 (April 1975), 7-15.

Rao, Vithala R. "Alternative Econometric Models of Sales-Advertising Relationships," *Journal of Marketing Research*, 9 (May 1972), 177-181.

Rasmussen, A. "The Determination of Advertising Expenditure," *Journal of Marketing,* 16 (April 1952), 439-446.

Rich, Kenneth L. "An Adaptive Optimization Model for Setting Advertising Budgets," working paper, Marketing Science Institute, February 1971.

Robertson, Thomas S. *Consumer Behavior*. Glenview, Ill.: Scott, Foresman, 1970.

Roby, Thornton B. *Small Group Performance*. Chicago: Rand McNally, 1968.

Rosenberg, Barr. "A Survey of Stochastic Parameter Regression," *Annals of Economic and Social Measurement,* 2 (October 1973), 381-397.

_____. "The Analysis of a Cross-Section of Time Series by Stochastically Convergent Parameter Regression," *Annals of Economic and Social Measurement,* 2 (October 1973), 399-428.

Rosenbleuth, Arturo, and Norbert Weiner. "The Role of Models in Science," *Philosophy of Science*, 12 (October 1945), 316-321.

Russ, Frederick A. "On Econometric Analysis of Consumer Information Processing: A Discussion of the Dominguez Paper," in G. David Hughes, ed., *Buyer/Consumer Information Processing*, Chapel Hill: The University of North Carolina Press, 1974, 51-58.

Salmon, Wesley C. *The Foundations of Scientific Inference*. Pittsburgh: University of Pittsburgh Press, 1967.

Samuels, J.M. "The Effect of Advertising on Sales and Brand Shares," *European Journal of Marketing,* 4 (Winter 1970/71), 187-207.

Sasieni, Maurice W. "What Can We Measure in Marketing," *Journal of Advertising Research,* **4** (June 1964), 8-11.

_____. "Optimal Advertising Expenditure," *Management Science* **18** (December 1971, Part II), 64-72.

Sasser, W. Earl, Jr., and John M. Vernon, "Marketing Simulation Models: The Problem of Specification Error," working paper, Marketing Science Institute, March 1970.

Sawyer, Alan G. "The Effects of Repetition of Refutational and Supportive Advertising Appeals," *Journal of Marketing Research,* **10** (February 1973), 23-33.

Schoenberg, E.H. "The Demand Curve for Cigarettes," *Journal of Business,* **6** (January 1933), 15-35.

Schmalensee, Richard. *The Economics of Advertising.* Amsterdam: North-Holland Publishing Company, 1972.

Schmidt, Peter. "Calculating the Power of the Minimum Standard Error Choice Criterion," *International Economic Review,* **14** (February 1973), 253-255.

Schultz, Randall L. "The Development of a Marketing Planning Model Through Simultaneous-Equation Multiple Regression Analysis: An Airline Study," unpublished doctoral dissertation, Northwestern University, 1970.

_____. "Market Measurement and Planning With a Simultaneous-Equation Model," *Journal of Marketing Research,* **8** (May 1971), 153-164.

_____. "Methods for Handling Competition in Dynamic Market Models," *European Journal of Marketing,* **7** (Spring 1973), 18-27.

_____. "The Use of Simulation for Decision Making," *Behavioral Science,* **19** (September 1974), 344-350.

_____, and Joe A. Dodson, Jr. "An Empirical-Simulation Approach to Competition," paper presented at the Annual Meeting, Western Economic Association, Las Vegas, Nevada, June 1974.

_____. "A Normative Model for Marketing Planning," *Simulation and Games,* **5** (December 1974), 363-382.

_____, and Dominique M. Hanssens. "AIRPLAN IV: A Simulation of Competitive Behavior With Systems of Simultaneous Equations," working paper, Purdue University, January 1976.

_____, and T.E. Little. "Competitive Interaction in a Regulated Market," paper presented at the Joint National Meeting, ORSA and TIMS, Chicago, April 1975.

_____, and Dennis P. Slevin. "Behavioral Considerations in the Implementation of Marketing Decision Models," *Combined Proceedings.* Spring and Fall Conferences, American Marketing Association, 1972, 494-498.

_____, _____, eds. *Implementing Operations Research/Management Science.* New York: American Elsevier, 1975.

————, ————, and Nancy K. Keith. "Model Characteristics and Implementation: An Experimental Study" paper presented at the Joint National Meeting, ORSA and TIMS, Las Vegas, Nevada, November 1975.

————, and Edward M. Sullivan. "Developments in Simulation in Social and Administrative Science," in Harold Guetzkow, Philip Kotler and Randall L. Schultz, eds., *Simulation in Social and Administrative Science*. Englewood Cliffs, N.J.: Prentice-Hall, 1972, 3-47.

————, and Dick R. Wittink. "The Measurement of Industry Advertising Effects," Institute Paper No. 445, Krannert Graduate School of Industrial Administration, Purdue University, March 1974.

————. "The Measurement of Industry Advertising Effects," *Journal of Marketing Research,* 13 (February 1976), 71-75.

Semlow, Walter J. "How Many Salesmen Do You Need?" *Harvard Business Review,* 37 (May-June 1959), 126-132.

Sethi, Suresh P. "Optimal Control of the Vidale-Wolfe Advertising Model," *Operations-Research,* 21 (July-August 1973), 998-1013.

Sexton, Donald E. "Estimating Marketing Policy Effects on Sales of a Frequently Purchased Product," *Journal of Marketing Research,* 7 (August 1970), 338-347.

————. "A Microeconomic Model of the Effects of Advertising," *Journal of Business,* 45 (January 1972), 29-41.

————. "A Cluster Analytic Approach to Market Response Functions," *Journal of Marketing Research,* 11 (February 1974), 109-114.

Shakun, Melvin F. "Advertising Expenditures in Coupled Markets—A Game-Theory Approach," *Management Science,* 11 (February 1965), 42-47.

Shapiro, S.S., and M.B. Wilk. "An Analysis of Variance Test for Normality," *Biometrika,* 52 (1965), 591-611.

Shaw, Marvin E. *Group Dynamics: The Psychology of Small Group Behavior.* New York: McGraw-Hill, 1971.

Sheth, Jagdish N., ed. *Models of Buyer Behavior: Conceptual, Quantitative and Empirical.* New York: Harper & Row, 1974.

Simon, Herbert A. "Causal Ordering and Identifiability," in Wm.C. Hood and Tjalling C. Koopmans, eds., *Studies in Econometric Method.* New York: John Wiley, 1953, 49-74.

————. "On Judging the Plausibility of Theories," in B. Van Rootselaar and S. F. Staal, eds., *Logic, Methodology, and Philosophy of Science III.* Amsterdam: North-Holland Publishing Company, 1968.

Simon, Julian L. "A Simple Model for Determining Advertising Appropriations," *Journal of Marketing Research,* 2 (August 1965), 285-292.

————. "The Effect of Advertising on Liquor Brand Sales," *Journal of Marketing Research,* **6** (August 1969), 301-313.

Sims, Christopher A. "Distributed Lags," in Michael E. Intriligator and David A. Kendrick, eds., *Frontiers in Quantitative Economics, Volume II.* New York: American Elsevier, 1974, 289-332.

Staelin, Richard, and Russell S. Winer. "An Unobservable Variables Model for Determining the Effects of Advertising on Consumer Purchases," working paper, Graduate School of Industrial Administration, Carnegie-Mellon University, 1975.

Stigler, George J. "The Economics of Information," *The Journal of Political Economy,* **69** (June 1961), 213-225.

Stobaugh, Robert B. and Phillip L. Townsend. "Price Forecasting and Strategic Planning: The Case of Petro-chemical," *Journal of Marketing Research,* **12** (February 1975), 19-29.

Swamy, P.A.V.B. *Statistical Inference in Random Coefficient Regression Models.* New York: Springer-Verlag, 1971.

————. "Linear Models with Random Coefficients," in Paul Zarembka, ed., *Frontiers in Econometrics.* New York: Academic Press, 1974, 143-168.

Tapiero, Charles S. "On-Line and Adaptive Optimum Advertising Control by a Diffusion Approximation," *Operations Research,* **23** (September-October 1975), 890-907.

Telser, Lester G. "The Demand for Branded Goods as Estimated From Consumer Panel Data," *The Review of Economics and Statistics,* **44** (August 1962), 300-324.

————. "Advertising and Cigarettes," *Journal of Political Economy,* **70** (October 1962), 471-499.

————. *Competition, Collusion and Game Theory.* Chicago: Aldine-Atherton, 1972.

Theil, Henri. *Linear Aggregation of Economic Relations.* Amsterdam: North-Holland Publishing Company, 1954.

————. "Specification Errors and the Estimation of Economic Relationships," *Review of the International Statistical Institute,* **25** (1957), 41-51.

————. "A Multinomial Extension of the Linear Logit Model," *International Economic Review,* **10** (October 1969), 251-259.

————. *Principles of Econometrics.* New York: John Wiley, 1971.

Torgerson, W. *Theory and Methods of Scaling.* New York: John Wiley, 1958.

Tull, Donald S. "A Re-Examination of the Causes of the Decline in Sales of Sapolio," *Journal of Business,* **28** (April 1955), 128-137.

Turner, Ronald E., and Charles P. Neuman. "Dynamic Advertising Strategy: A Managerial Approach," *Journal of Business Administration* (Spring 1976), in press,

_____, and John C. Wiginton. "Advertising Expenditure Trajectories: An Empirical Study for Filter Cigarettes 1953-1965," Working Paper No. 75-17, School of Business, Queen's University, June 1975.

Urban, Glen L. "A Mathematical Modeling Approach to Product Line Decisions," *Journal of Marketing Research*, 6 (February 1969), 40-47.

_____. "Sprinter Mod III: A Model for the Analysis of New Frequently Purchased Consumer Products," *Operations Research,* 18 (September-October 1970), 805-854.

_____. "PERCEPTOR: A Model for Product Positioning," *Management Science*, 21 (April 1975), 858-871.

_____, and Richard Karash. "Evolutionary Model Building," *Journal of Marketing Research,* 8 (February 1971), 62-66.

Van Wormer, Theodore A., and Doyle L. Weiss, "Fitting Parameters to Complex Models by Direct Search," *Journal of Marketing Research,* 7 (November 1970), 503-512.

Vertinsky, Ilan. "OR/MS Implementation in Valle, Columbia, S.A.: A Profile of a Developing Region," *Management Science,* 18 (February 1972), 314-327.

Vidale, M.L., and H.B. Wolfe. "An Operations-Research Study of Sales Response to Advertising," *Operations Research,* 5 (June 1957), 370-381.

Wagner, Harvey M. *Principles of Operations Research.* Englewood Cliffs, N.J.: Prentice-Hall, 1969.

Walker, Arthur H., and Jay W. Lorsch. "Organizational Choice: Product versus Function," *Harvard Business Review* (November-December 1968), 129-138.

Wallace, T.D. "Weaker Criteria and Tests for Linear Restrictions in Regression," *Econometrica,* 40 (July 1972), 689-698.

Walters, A.A. *An Introduction to Econometrics.* New York: W.W. Norton, 1970.

Ward, Scott, and Thomas S. Robertson, eds. *Consumer Behavior: Theoretical Sources.* Englewwod Cliffs, N.J.: Prentice-Hall, 1973.

Weinberg, Charles B., and Henry C. Lucas, Jr. "Semlow's Results Are Based on a Spurious Relationship," unpublished manuscript, 1974.

Weiss, Doyle L. "The Determinants of Market Share," *Journal of Marketing Research,* 5 (August 1968), 290-295.

_____. "An Analysis of the Demand Structure for Branded Consumer Products," *Applied Economics,* 1(January 1969), 37-49.

_____, and Franklin S. Houston. "Measuring the Effects of Brand Loyalty," *Journal of Business Administration,* 6 (Fall 1974), 33-44.

_____, _____, and Pierre Windal. "The Periodic Pain of Lydia E. Pinkham—Revisited," working paper, School of Commerce, University of British Columbia, July 1975.

Wildt, Albert R. "Multifirm Analysis of Competitive Decision Variables," *Journal of Marketing Research,* **11** (February 1974), 50-62.

_____. "Seasonality, Specification and Decision Making: Implications for the Estimation of Sales Response Functions," *Combined Proceedings.* Spring and Fall Conferences, American Marketing Association, 1975, 3-9.

Winer, Russell S. "Estimation and Implications of Sales-Advertising Relationships with Time-Varying Parameters," working paper, Graduate School of Industrial Administration, Carnegie-Mellon University, June 1975.

Wittink, Dick R. "Partial Pooling: A Heuristic," Institute Paper No. 419, Krannert Graduate School of Industrial Administration, Purdue University, July 1973.

_____. "Systematic and Random Variation in the Relationship Between Marketing Variables," unpublished doctoral dissertation, Purdue University, 1975.

Wold, Herman. "Causality and Econometrics," *Econometrica,* **22** (April 1954), 162-177.

Wright, Peter L. "Research Orientations for Analyzing Consumer Judgement Processes," *Proceedings.* Annual Conference, Association for Consumer Research, 1973, 268-279.

Yon, Bernard, and Timothy D. Mount. "The Response of Sales to Advertising: Estimation of a Polynomial Lag Structure," A.E. Res. 75-4, Department of Agricultural Economics, Cornell University, April 1975.

Zaltman, Gerald, Christian R.A. Pinson, and Reinhard Angelmar. *Metatheory and Consumer Research.* New York: Holt, Rinehart and Winston, 1973.

Zellner, Arnold. "On the Aggregation Problem: A New Approach to a Troublesome Problem," in K.A. Fox et al., eds., *Economic Models, Estimation and Risk Programming.* Berlin: Springer-Verlag, 1969, 365-374.

_____. "An Efficient Method of Estimating Seemingly Unrelated Regressions and Tests for Aggregation Bias," *Journal of the American Statistical Association,* **57** (June 1962), 348-368.

AUTHOR INDEX

SUBJECT INDEX